Metric Conversion Table

	1/64	1/32	1/25	1/16	1/8	1/4	3/8	2/5	1/2	5/8	3/4	7/8	1	2	3	4	5	6	7	8	9	10	11	12	36	39.4
Inches (in.)	1/64	1/32	1/25	1/16	1/8	1/4	3/8	2/5	1/2	5/8	3/4	7/8	1	2	3	4	5	6	7	8	9	10	11	12	36	39.4
Feet (ft.)																								1	3	3¼†
Yards (yd.)																									1	1¹/₁₀†
Millimeters* (mm)	0.40	0.79	1	1.59	3.18	6.35	9.53	10	12.7	15.9	19.1	22.2	25.4	50.8	76.2	101.6	127	152	178	203	229	254	279	305	914	1000
Centimeters* (cm)							0.95	1	1.27	1.59	1.91	2.22	2.54	5.08	7.62	10.16	12.7	15.2	17.8	20.3	22.9	25.4	27.9	30.5	91.4	100
Meters* (m)																								.30	.91	1.00

To find the metric equivalent of quantities not in this table, add together the appropriate entries. For example, to convert 2⅝ inches to centimeters, add the figure given for the centimeter equivalent of 2 inches, 5.08, and the equivalent of ⅝ inch, 1.59, to obtain 6.67 centimeters.

*Metric values are rounded off.
†Approximate fractions.

Conversion Factors

To change:	Into:	Multiply by:
Inches	Millimeters	25.4
Inches	Centimeters	2.54
Feet	Meters	0.305
Yards	Meters	0.914
Miles	Kilometers	1.609
Square inches	Square centimeters	6.45
Square feet	Square meters	0.093
Square yards	Square meters	0.836
Cubic inches	Cubic centimeters	16.4
Cubic feet	Cubic meters	0.0283
Cubic yards	Cubic meters	0.765
Pints (U.S.)	Liters	0.473 (Imp. 0.568)
Quarts (U.S.)	Liters	0.946 (Imp. 1.136)
Gallons (U.S.)	Liters	3.785 (Imp. 4.546)
Ounces	Grams	28.4
Pounds	Kilograms	0.454
Tons	Metric tons	0.907

To change:	Into:	Multiply by:
Millimeters	Inches	0.039
Centimeters	Inches	0.394
Meters	Feet	3.28
Meters	Yards	1.09
Kilometers	Miles	0.621
Square centimeters	Square inches	0.155
Square meters	Square feet	10.8
Square meters	Square yards	1.2
Cubic centimeters	Cubic inches	0.061
Cubic meters	Cubic feet	35.3
Cubic meters	Cubic yards	1.31
Liters	Pints (U.S.)	2.114 (Imp. 1.76)
Liters	Quarts (U.S.)	1.057 (Imp. 0.88)
Liters	Gallons (U.S.)	0.264 (Imp. 0.22)
Grams	Ounces	0.035
Kilograms	Pounds	2.2
Metric tons	Tons	1.1

THE FAMILY
Handyman ®

Updating Your Home

Updating Your Home

Easy Ways to Make Your Home Look and Work Better

THE READER'S DIGEST ASSOCIATION, INC.

Pleasantville, New York/Montreal

A READER'S DIGEST BOOK

Produced by Roundtable Press, Inc.
Directors: Susan E. Meyer, Marsha Melnick
Executive Editor: Amy T. Jonak
Project Editor: David R. Hall
Editor: Tom Neven
Assistant Editor: Abigail A. Anderson
Design: Sisco & Evans, New York
Editorial Production: Steven Rosen

For The Family Handyman
Editor in Chief: Gary Havens
Special Projects Editor: Ken Collier
TFH Books Editor: Spike Carlsen

Library of Congress Cataloging in Publication Data
The family handyman updating your home: easy ways to make your home
    look and work better.
         p.   cm.
    Includes index.
    ISBN 0-89577-851-3
    1. Dwellings—Remodeling—Amateurs' manuals.   I. Reader's Digest
    Association. II. Family handyman.
TH4816.F353   1996
643'.7—dc20   95-44751

Reader's Digest and the Pegasus logo are registered trademarks of
The Reader's Digest Association, Inc.
The Family Handyman is a registered trademark of RD Publications, Inc.
Printed in the United States of America.

A Note from the Editor

The projects in this book are all candidates for *The Family Handyman* Hit Parade, a compendium of America's top forty home improvement projects. There are no blockbusters here, no roof raisers, just lots of good solid projects that can make your home a whole lot better looking and better living.

I can say this because, in addition to being the editor of TFH, I've been a homeowner for more than twenty years. Moreover, I was a very late bloomer when it came to learning do-it-yourself skills, a real klutz with a hammer and saw. Years ago I attempted—and botched—some of the very projects in these pages.

That changed when I quit a nice clean office job and entered into a carpentry apprenticeship program. Why I decided on this career change with a wife and two youngsters to support isn't relevant here, but change I did.

And I learned. Framing . . . drywall . . . front doors . . . garage doors . . . ventilating fans—I was put through it all. Frankly, I think I got pretty good: no more botched projects.

But I've never forgotten that I was once a klutz, without the simple skills it takes to mount a kitchen pot rack. Now I take it as my mission here at *The Family Handyman* to explain things so that a guy or gal who feels completely helpless at the start, as I once did, can complete a project and take pride in a job well done.

That's why as editor I insist on clear, step-by-step photos, detailed drawings, and understandable instructions. They're not for my benefit—I know how to do it—but for the benefit of the helpless klutz I once was.

And that's also why the projects here will not only make your home look better but will make you feel better, too.

Gary Havens

Editor in Chief, *The Family Handyman*

Updating Your Home

Enhance Home Systems

Protect Against the Elements

Introduction

As you sit in your favorite chair, you think how sweet it is: this is a pretty comfortable home. But then your mind wanders; you look around and start to wonder how the room would look if you hung a ceiling fan over there, or added some plantation-style shutters to frame the windows. And you realize it's time for new wallpaper in the master bedroom, or paneling in the basement. You can easily visualize that a spanking-new entry door would enhance your home's curb appeal—but then you'd want to repair the crumbling sidewalk leading to it. The more you think about it, the more you realize that almost every area of the house could do with a little updating. Here now is just the book for you.

Here are more than thirty timely projects and many smart suggestions to update your house. All these projects require only a moderate amount of time to complete. The majority can be done over a weekend, the rest finished over stages as you find the time.

As you work with basic plumbing and wiring or framing carpentry, wallpapering or painting, your confidence and skills will increase with every project. But never get cocky: always keep safety foremost, regardless of the project you are doing. Wear appropriate clothing and eye and ear protection when working with power tools, hammering, or demolishing walls or sidewalks. Observe the specific safety precautions supplied with each project. Follow the manufacturer's directions whenever you are operating power tools, making sure that electrical cords and plugs are not frayed or broken. Some of the projects here can produce quite a mess, but try to keep your work area as clean and free of debris as possible. And always try to keep your tools clean and well maintained, according to the suggestions here, so they will work better and last longer.

No matter which of these projects you undertake to update your home, you'll find them cost effective as well as affordable in time and effort. And the results will do much to enhance your home's livability and value.

create a new look

Make a Grand Entrance
Give your drab front entrance a face-lift with a beautiful but affordable new front door.

Add a Great-Looking Screen Door
An elegant wood screen door provides an easy way to dress up your front entryway.

Smart Suggestions for Perfect Paneling
These ideas take you beyond basic installation, to a perfectly professional-looking paneling job.

Smart Suggestions for Papering Walls
Wallpapering can be tricky. Make the job easier and get better results with these suggestions.

Make a Grand Entrance

Here's a surefire way to update the front of a house that has begun looking dated. An improved entrance is an ideal way to make a distinctive, dramatic statement about your home.

Sizing Up the Project

This project requires you to cut into the wall around the existing door and then frame a new rough opening for a prehung door. It also involves installing a new header over the opening to support the weight above it. The door must be set in its new opening and maneuvered to fit until it is flush and plumb. For all these reasons, this job is beyond the scope of a beginning do-it-yourselfer. To tackle it successfully, you should have some basic carpentry experience, particularly with framing a wall. The project also calls for some exacting measuring and finish carpentry.

Front Door Basics

Most front doors come prehung in a frame with an attached aluminum sill at the bottom and factory-installed weatherstripping.

Home centers and lumberyards often carry prehung entry doors. Shop around at these outlets and at retailers who specialize in doors and windows (look in the Yellow Pages under "Windows" and "Doors").

Prehung doors cost anywhere from a few hundred dollars for the simplest to several thousand for the most elaborate. They are available in wood, steel, and fiberglass, with windows, panels, and sidelights as options.

Planning Considerations

Not every house's entranceway has the extra space required to accommodate a larger door or a door with sidelights, like the one shown on the facing page. To determine what size door your house will be able to handle, measure the space available on both the inside and outside walls, making note of potential obstructions like plumbing lines or ductwork. These are not likely to be near the front door, but it's better to be safe and check. Don't worry about electrical lines, which can easily be rerouted.

Keep the following considerations in mind when planning your project.

▶ If you choose to install a larger door, the wider framed opening will require a stronger overhead top beam, called a header. You will need the services of a building inspector or structural engineer to determine the correct size header to install.

▶ Determine whether the house's floor joists run perpendicular to or parallel to the door opening. A building inspector will have to advise you on framing requirements if the joists are parallel to the door.

▶ If the house's exterior is made of brick or stucco and you want to add a larger door, hire a professional to redo the masonry or cut and blend in the stucco to fit the unit.

Ordering the Door

Before ordering your new door, decide which side of the door you want the hinges to be on. Draw a sketch indicating which way you want the door to swing.

▶ The door frame, or jamb, should be as wide as the wall is thick, including the outside sheathing and the inner wall surface (see the Prehung Door Installation Plan on page 14).

▶ Some doors come with predrilled holes for a lockset. Ask if your dealer will drill the lockset holes for you. If so, buy the lockset before the door so the dealer can use the set's template to drill the holes accurately.

If you have chosen to install sidelights, you might want to consider buying a double-cylinder lock, which requires a key on the inside as well as outside, to prevent someone from breaking the glass and reaching through to open the door from inside. But first check with your local authorities to make sure this style of lock is allowed in your community, because leaving the house in an emergency is more difficult if a key is not immediately at hand.

▶ Most prehung door units come with 2-inch wide exterior trim as part of the set. If you choose to use different trim, as we did for the

A new front door presents a fresh face to visitors and is the perfect way to update an older looking house.

unit installed on these pages, which uses wider trim, order it along with the door. Exterior trim is usually more than an inch thick, cut from what is called 5/4 lumber.

Storm Doors

Even an attractive storm door may obscure the handsome door you've installed, and a new, thermal-insulated entry door should not require one. But a storm door that combines screens with windows protects a door from rain and snow, and it lets in breezes while keeping out insects. It holds pets and children inside while you're answering the door as well as offering some measure of security by allowing you to talk to strangers through the screen.

If you do decide to add a storm door, find a design that mirrors the new door's style. Otherwise, choose one with a full-length window.

Prehung Door Installation Plan

Tools You Need

Wrecking bar

Drywall saw

Ladder

Stud finder

Hammer

Circular saw

Utility knife

Level

Hacksaw

Caulking gun

Reciprocating saw (optional)

Materials

Prehung door unit

Plywood shims

Shims

2x4 framing lumber

2x10 lumber for header

Exterior caulk

16d galvanized casing nails

2-1/2 in. galvanized screws

26-gauge galvanized steel flashing

No. 15 roofing felt

Fiberglass insulation

Expandable foam insulation

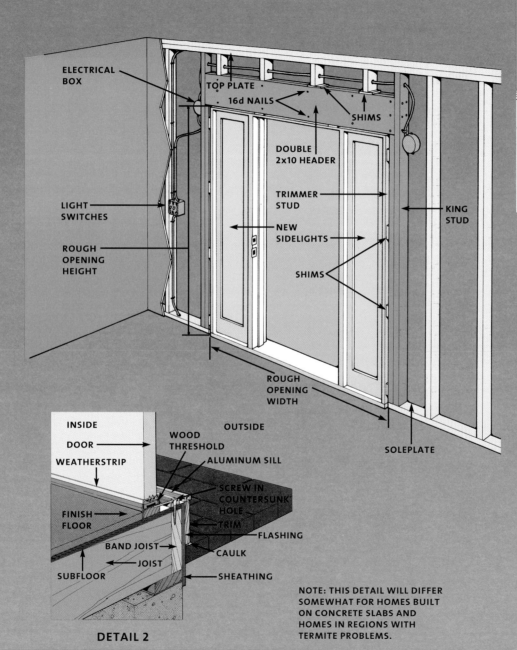

ELECTRICAL BOX

TOP PLATE

16d NAILS

SHIMS

DOUBLE 2x10 HEADER

TRIMMER STUD

LIGHT SWITCHES

NEW SIDELIGHTS

ROUGH OPENING HEIGHT

SHIMS

KING STUD

ROUGH OPENING WIDTH

SOLEPLATE

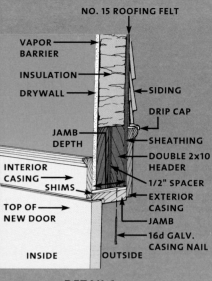

NO. 15 ROOFING FELT

VAPOR BARRIER

INSULATION

DRYWALL

SIDING

DRIP CAP

JAMB DEPTH

SHEATHING

INTERIOR CASING

DOUBLE 2x10 HEADER

SHIMS

1/2" SPACER

TOP OF NEW DOOR

EXTERIOR CASING

JAMB

16d GALV. CASING NAIL

INSIDE

OUTSIDE

DETAIL 1

INSIDE

OUTSIDE

DOOR

WOOD THRESHOLD

WEATHERSTRIP

ALUMINUM SILL

SCREW IN COUNTERSUNK HOLE

FINISH FLOOR

TRIM

FLASHING

BAND JOIST

CAULK

JOIST

SUBFLOOR

SHEATHING

DETAIL 2

NOTE: THIS DETAIL WILL DIFFER SOMEWHAT FOR HOMES BUILT ON CONCRETE SLABS AND HOMES IN REGIONS WITH TERMITE PROBLEMS.

Frame the Opening

Careful measuring is absolutely essential when cutting into the existing wall and reframing the enlarged opening.

▷ The size of the rough opening required will be provided by the door manufacturer. Mark the dimensions of the rough opening on the inside wall, then cut and strip the drywall or plaster, the baseboards, and the door casings within the marks.

▷ Remove the plaster or drywall all the way to the first stud on each side of the new rough opening and at least 12 inches above the opening to allow enough room for installing the new header (Photo 1).

Building a Temporary Brace

▷ Locate and mark the floor and ceiling joists within the cut-out area, using a stud finder. If they run perpendicular to the wall, construct a temporary support wall of 2x4's that extends from floor to ceiling. This wall will help bear the weight above as you cut into the framing members of the front wall.

▷ Position the support wall 2 to 3 feet out from the section of wall you are about to remove (Photo 2). Use pieces of cardboard on the top to avoid marring the ceiling and to wedge the wall securely in place, making sure the studs of this brace are placed directly under the joists.

▷ If the joists run parallel to the wall, you might not need this support, depending on what your local building inspector determined earlier about how much weight the outer wall supports.

Installing a New Header

▷ Remove the door from its hinges and pry out the nails holding the old door casing and sill or cut them with a hacksaw blade or a reciprocating saw with a metal-cutting blade. Then remove the casing and sill.

▷ Frame in the new header (opposite and Photo 3), adding new king and trimmer studs. Use a level to make sure the new studs are vertical.

Electrical Safety

Turn off the electricity at the main service panel before cutting into walls. Tape a note there to prevent others from turning it on by mistake.

FRAME THE OPENING

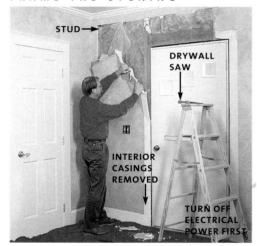

Photo 1. After shutting off the power at the electrical panel, strip the drywall or plaster from an area about 12 in. wider and higher than the new door frame.

Photo 2. Erect a temporary stud wall 2 to 3 ft. out from the door if joists run 90° to the doorway. If parallel, ask a building inspector if you need a temporary wall.

Photo 3. Install the new header beam, king studs, and trimmer studs to frame the rough opening. Use a level to make sure the studs are perfectly vertical.

Install the Door

Now that the new framing is in place, you can cut into the exterior wall to prepare for the installation of the door.

▷ On the inside of the sheathing, drill a hole through each corner. Then draw lines connecting the holes on the outside siding to mark the rough opening.

▷ Set the blade on a circular saw to cut through the house's siding and sheathing, then cut the rough opening (Photo 4). Be extremely cautious when operating a saw from a ladder. It is safer to use electrical equipment on a wood, not aluminum, ladder. Precision cutting isn't necessary at this stage, because the siding will be trimmed more accurately in a later step.

▷ Finally, cut away the soleplate of the wall with a handsaw.

Next, with the rough opening completely clear and the old subfloor exposed, measure the door and the new opening to make sure that all the measurements are correct.

▷ Make sure the subfloor is level across the new opening (Photo 5). If it is not, shim it level with strips of plywood.

▷ If the old door frame was notched into the floor joists, build up the floor there with plywood to the height of the subfloor. Then install additional plywood on the subfloor so the installed door will swing about 1/2 inch above the finish floor or carpeting. If the house was built on a concrete slab, set the sill of the door frame directly on the concrete.

Test-Fitting the Door

▷ Now slip the entire prehung door into the rough opening. The closed door itself usually keeps the frame square, but with the added

Restore Termite Protection

In regions with termite problems, be sure to restore any termite barriers that were removed while cutting and framing the door opening.

sidelights the unit might be too heavy to lift with the door in place, even for two people. In this case, first tack a temporary diagonal brace to the frame to keep it square, then remove the door to lighten the assembly.

▷ With the unit in place, double-check that the frame sits level and its sides are vertical.

▷ To indicate how far to trim back the siding, outline the position of the exterior casing on the siding (Photo 6).

Finishing the Opening

Remove the door frame so that you can complete the installation.

▷ Set the depth of the saw blade to cut through the siding—but not the sheathing—then carefully cut the siding away (Photo 7). Tack up a straight board to use as a saw guide to ensure a clean and accurate cut. If necessary, use a sharp utility knife to carve the small curves to fit the protruding molding on top.

▷ Bend and lay 26-gauge galvanized steel flashing over the subfloor and tuck No. 15 roofing felt 2 inches under the siding. This will keep water from penetrating the wall and causing rot (Photo 8).

▷ Add a metal drip cap wide enough to extend over the top casing (see the Prehung Door Installation Plan on page 14).

Setting the Door

▷ Before lifting the door unit back into place, run a bead of exterior caulk around the outer edges of the opening and across the floor under the sill to make the frame airtight.

▷ Now slip the frame into place, set a level on the sides to make sure they're perfectly vertical, and tack the frame in place with three 16d

galvanized casing nails (Photo 9). Don't drive these nails all the way in yet.

▷ Put the door back on its hinges and close it to test its fit. Adjust the door frame with shims until it's vertical (Photo 10). Then nail it in permanently, spacing the nails every 16 inches along the casings. In addition, drive a nail through the jamb at each set of shims.

▷ Because doors with sidelights can eventually bow outward at the bottom, countersink and drive 2-1/2 inch galvanized screws down through the aluminum sill into the floor (see Detail 2 on page 14) on each side of the door, sealing each with a dab of silicone caulk.

▷ Ensure an airtight seal by running a bead of expandable foam insulation deep into the gap between the door frame and the 2x4 framing. Do not completely fill this gap with foam, because the pressure from its expansion might bow the frame. Loosely fill the rest of the gap with fiberglass insulation (Photo 11).

Final Touches

Now that the door is in place, you can take down the temporary support wall.

▷ Rewire whatever electrical switches you need to, and then reinstall the wall insulation and the plastic vapor barrier.

▷ Install needed wallboard and interior trim.

▷ On the outside, nail on the trim board that fits under the sill. Then caulk the gap between the siding and the door casing along both sides with exterior caulk.

▷ Fill all nail holes with exterior-grade wood putty, then touch up any paint areas that were marred while you were working.

Photo 4. Mark the rough opening on the exterior siding and cut out the siding and sheathing with a circular saw. Trim the soleplate back with a handsaw.

Photo 5. Level the rough sill, using thin strips of plywood as shims. Adjust the height with filler strips so the door threshold sits about 1/2 in. above the finish floor.

Photo 6. Slip the door frame into place—without the door, if that makes it too heavy—center it, check it for level, and outline the profile of the exterior trim on the siding.

Photo 7. Set a circular saw blade's depth to cut the siding only, and then cut out the profile. Following the guide board temporarily tacked on keeps the cut straight.

Photo 8. Add metal flashing on the bottom, slip No. 15 roofing felt 2 in. behind the siding along the sides, and slide a metal drip cap up under the siding on top.

Photo 9. Squeeze caulk around the opening and tack the frame in place. Hang the door to make sure that it fits and that it opens and closes smoothly, then drive the nails home.

Photo 10. Shim the frame and drive a nail through the jamb at each shim. If the door has sidelights, screw the aluminum sill to the floor at each side of the door.

Photo 11. Insulate and seal around the frame with a bead of expanding foam and fiberglass insulation. Restore the vapor barrier and refinish the inside.

Add a Great-Looking Screen Door

The front entryway is the focal point of your house, and an elegant wooden screen door like the one shown here will go a long way toward dressing it up. You have a wide variety to choose from, to match any style of house from contemporary to log cabin.

The charm of a new full-length elegant wooden screen door (above) provides an inviting contrast to the old entrance (left).

Sizing Up the Project

Hanging wooden screen doors can involve some tricky measurements and cutting, because they are made slightly larger than standard door openings and must be trimmed to size. Few door openings are perfectly square, so be prepared for some trimming and fine-tuning. Otherwise, if you have basic carpentry skills and patience you can handle this project.

Before You Begin

Before buying a new screen door, determine not just the measurements of the door but also the condition of the surrounding trim.

Assessing the Condition of the Existing Door

Take a look at the old door to see how well it swings and closes, paying particular attention to where it binds, scrapes, or sags. Remove the existing screen or storm door and all the old hardware. It's also a good idea to replace any shabby looking exterior trim surrounding the door opening so that it doesn't clash with a new screen door. Use new trim pieces of the same dimensions as the old.

Measuring the Door Opening

▶ If you have an aluminum door, remove the door and the aluminum trim before measuring, so your dimensions will be accurate.

▶ Measure between the inside edges of the exterior trim moldings along each door side (Photo 1). Measuring at three points accounts for variances.

▶ Measure the height on the left and on the right sides from the threshold, or sill, to the inside edge of the top door molding.

Photo 1. Check corners of the door frame for squareness and measure for the door size. Draw a picture of the opening, including all dimensions.

Draw the Opening

A careful drawing of the existing door opening will be of great help in hanging the new door.

▶ After measuring the distance between the trim pieces, check the squareness of all four corners, using a large framing square.

▶ Draw the door opening on a piece of paper, write down the measurements, and determine any adjustments that will need to be made on the new door. For example, hold the framing square up to the hinge side, as shown in Photo 1 (left). Even a large framing square won't be long enough to span the full width of the door, so check for a gap halfway across. A 1/16-inch gap halfway across the opening would translate into a full 1/8-inch gap if the square were long enough to reach the latch side. This means you'll need to trim the hinge side 1/8 inch shorter than the latch side.

▶ The door needs clearance space along all four edges to swing freely. Subtract 3/16 inch from the width and 1/4 inch from the height of the drawing measurements. These are the cutting dimensions for the new door.

▶ If your old wooden screen door fit well, use it as a template for the new door. Do not use an aluminum door as a template, however, since the way it fits within the opening will be different from that of a wooden door.

Cut the New Door

Before beginning, remove any screen or storm glass insert and set it aside.

▶ Transfer the cutting dimensions from the drawing onto the door. Use a long straightedge clamped on the door to guide the saw (Photo 2).

▶ Cut the door to width. If you must remove more than 1/4 inch of the width, take half of the amount from each side. If you're cutting away 1/4 inch or less, remove it all from the hinge side. This allows for more frame width on the latch side to accommodate the latch hardware.

▶ Now cut the door to height, removing most of what has to be trimmed from the bottom of the door. If the opening isn't square, most of the minor trimming and adapting should be done on the horizontal cuts.

▶ Most sills, like the one shown in the Hinges and Trim Detail on the facing page, are slanted to allow water to run off. When cutting the bottom of the door, set the blade of your circular saw at a 12-degree angle, with the bottom of the blade slanted toward the inside of the door, to match the slant of the sill (see Photo 2).

Fit the New Door

Here's where all your careful measuring and cutting pay off.

▶ Set the door into the opening. Push the door tight to the hinge side and check for a consistent 1/8- to 3/16-inch gap along the latch side. Trim more if needed. Work in small increments—you can always take a little more off, but you can't put a little more back on.

▶ Push shims in along the bottom of the door and then examine how the top fits within the frame. If it doesn't fit square along the top trim piece, carefully shave the top edge to fit, using a circular saw or belt sander.

Install the Hinges

It is best to hang the door on three hinges, to help distribute its weight.

▶ Study the detail at right for the correct way to mount hinges on the door trim. The 1/16-inch gap is critical to keep the door from binding against the jamb.

▶ Reuse the old hinge mortises on the trim if possible. Check the alignment of the existing screw holes alongside the new hinges. If the holes don't line up, fill the old ones with exterior-grade wood filler, then drill new pilot holes to match the new hinges.

▶ If the old door hinges were mounted without mortises, cut mortises for the new hinges.

▶ On the exterior trim, first measure 7 inches down from the top molding to mark the top of the upper hinge.

▶ Then measure up 11 inches from the sill to mark the bottom of the lower hinge.

▶ Now center the middle hinge between the top and bottom hinges.

▶ Hold the hinges in position one at a time, leaving a 1/16-inch gap between the edge of the hinge and the jamb (Photo 3). Trace the outline of the hinge with a utility knife to mark the outline of the mortise. A utility knife makes a cleaner, sharper line than a pencil, and the cut that it makes gives the tip of the chisel a good place to bite into the wood, so you end up with a cleaner edge to the mortise.

Tools You Need

Tape measure

Framing square

Straightedge

Clamps

Sawhorses

Circular saw with 40-tooth carbide blade

Block plane

Drill and screwdriver attachment

Screwdriver

Hammer

Pry bar

3/4-in. wood chisel

Utility knife

Hole saw

Drill and drill guide

Power sander

Medium (100-grit) sandpaper

Tack cloth

Materials

Wood filler

Shims

Sandpaper

Door latch

Hydraulic closer

Door sweep

3-in. butt hinges

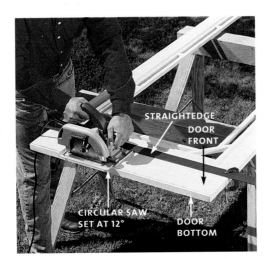

Photo 2. Trim the door to fit the opening. To make sure the door has room to close in the opening, deduct an additional 3/16 in. for width and 1/4 in. for height.

STRAIGHTEDGE

DOOR FRONT

CIRCULAR SAW SET AT 12°

DOOR BOTTOM

▶ Chisel out the mortises with a 3/4-inch wood chisel. Cut the mortises just deep enough to accept the hinge (see the Hinges and Trim Detail, below). If you accidentally take too much out, place a piece of cardboard behind the hinge leaf to shim it level with the surface.

▶ Drill pilot holes and screw the hinges to the trim. Remove the hinge pins and set aside the other halves of the hinges.

▶ Set the door in the opening with proper clearance on the hinge and latch sides, then insert shims along its bottom until it fits tight against the top molding.

▶ Mark the door 1/8 inch up from the top of each hinge mounted on the trim (Photo 4). This ensures adequate clearance along the top of the door after it is hung.

▶ Remove the door and mortise the hinges into the door edge as you did on the trim, except this time place the edge of the hinge flush with the inside face of the door. The 1/16-inch space left between the trim and the jamb allows the door to close properly.

▶ After mortising the door edges, drill pilot holes and screw the hinge halves to the door.

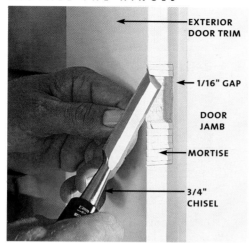

EXTERIOR DOOR TRIM

1/16" GAP

DOOR JAMB

MORTISE

3/4" CHISEL

Photo 3. Mortise the trim to accept the hinges, using a 3/4-in. wood chisel. Set the hinges 1/16 in. away from the jamb to keep the door from binding.

HINGE HALVES

SHIMS   SILL

Photo 4. Insert shims to hold the door tight against the top after mounting the trim hinges. Mark the location of the door hinge halves 1/8 in. above trim halves.

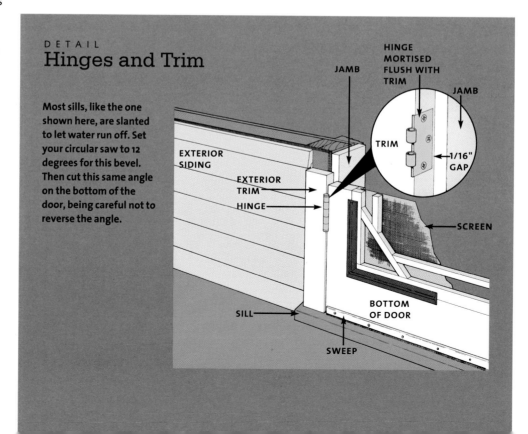

DETAIL
Hinges and Trim

Most sills, like the one shown here, are slanted to let water run off. Set your circular saw to 12 degrees for this bevel. Then cut this same angle on the bottom of the door, being careful not to reverse the angle.

JAMB

HINGE MORTISED FLUSH WITH TRIM

JAMB

TRIM

1/16" GAP

EXTERIOR SIDING

EXTERIOR TRIM

HINGE

SCREEN

SILL

BOTTOM OF DOOR

SWEEP

Mount the Door and Hardware

The fine-tuning you do next will make the difference between an adequate job and a well-fitting, craftsmanlike door that operates in a satisfying way.

Mounting the Door on the Hinges

▶ Place the door in the opening, push the halves of the hinges together, and slip in the pins. If one of the hinges doesn't line up perfectly, a light tap on it with a hammer will bring it into position.

▶ Hammer in the hinge pins and, with the door closed, examine the edges again for adequate clearance. There should be about a 1/8-inch gap on the latch edge and another 1/8 inch along the top and bottom. You may need to shave a little here and there from the latch side with a block plane (Photo 5). Close the door after each pass to check the fit.

▶ Rub chalk along the inside edge of the door frame where you suspect the door is snagging. The chalk will rub off onto the edge of the door, making it easier to see where to trim. As before, cut away only small amounts at a time, to avoid shaving off too much.

Choosing Door Hardware

You have a wide variety of latches to choose from, with many different types of finishes, including black, brass, antique brass, and brushed chrome. The door shown here uses a knob-and-lever latch with a polished brass finish (Photo 6). If you're concerned about finger marks and scratches, you might want to think about installing a latchset with a large, easily cleanable faceplate.

MOUNT THE DOOR AND HARDWARE

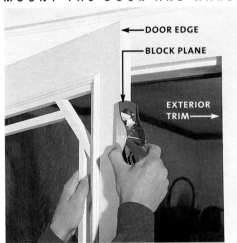

Photo 5. Fine-tune the fit with a block plane. Work in small increments—you can always take more off.

Photo 6. Install the latch so that it doesn't interfere with the latch or knob of the interior door.

Photo 7. Mount the hydraulic closer near the top of the door, following the manufacturer's directions.

Mounting Door Hardware

Latches and knobs come with their own mounting instructions, but there are a few basics that hold true in most cases.

▷ First, make sure the screen door latch does not interfere with the knob of the main door.

▷ Make the hole for the main mechanism with a hole saw or spade bit. Drill a pilot hole through the center of the mark, then bore the larger hole from each side, stopping as the small center bit of the hole saw penetrates the opposite side. This prevents the teeth of the hole saw from splintering the door as it exits the door face.

▷ Mounting a drill on a guide ensures that you will make a perpendicular hole in the edge of the door for the latch mechanism.

▷ To find out exactly where to chisel the hole for the strike box, rub lipstick on the end of the latch, close the door, and rotate the knob so the latch rubs the lipstick onto the jamb.

If you are also installing a hydraulic closer, position it about 2 inches down from the top of the door (Photo 7).

▷ Screw the metal bracket to the jamb first, then attach the hydraulic cylinder to that secured bracket.

▷ Close the door, set the rod according to the manufacturer's specifications, and attach the cylinder to the door.

Final Touches

Don't wait to apply a finish to the door. Exposing an unfinished door to moisture and weathering for even a short time can present problems down the road.

▷ Remove the door and sand it thoroughly with medium (100-grit) sandpaper, including all sharp corners. Then brush away grit and sawdust and wipe down the door with a tack cloth.

▷ If you're going to paint the door, prime it first and be sure to paint all the edges, including the top and bottom. An unfinished edge will absorb moisture from the air, which will cause the door to warp. Use a high-quality exterior oil paint in a gloss or semigloss finish so that it's easy to clean (Photo 8).

▷ If you prefer to varnish your door, use an exterior-grade varnish.

▷ After finishing, install a full-width sweep along the bottom (see the Hinges and Trim Detail on page 21), which helps seal the door along the sill to keep out the weather and bugs.

PRIME THE DOOR EDGE

Photo 8. Prime and paint both sides of the door and all four edges to prevent warping. Do this soon after installation, to avoid moisture absorption.

Weather Tip

If you live in a cold climate, consider a door that doubles as a screen door and storm door. Decorative combination models with separate screen and glass inserts are available from many distributors.

Replace Old Windows

Rain, sun, heat, and cold—not to mention thousands of openings and closings—eventually cause windows to fail. When careful maintenance can no longer keep them going, it's time to install replacements.

Sizing Up the Project

Replacing an entire window and its frame calls for intermediate do-it-yourself skills and takes about half a day's work. You will need to remove the old sashes, then cut away the existing window frame to prepare a rough opening for a new window. In addition to basic carpentry experience, this project also requires finish work, especially if you are installing new window trim. And if the replacement windows are larger or smaller than the old ones, the job becomes more complicated, particularly if the rough opening must be reframed to accommodate a bigger window.

Not all window problems call for complete window replacement. If rot hasn't weakened the window frame, and if the frame is still square, there are easier, quicker, and less expensive options available. See the three replacement options on pages 30–33.

Diagnose the Situation

Old windows can suffer from one or more problems. Wood rot attacks sashes or sills, repeated paint jobs immobilize sashes in their frames, and gaps develop that let drafts blow in during the winter. To diagnose what shape your windows are in, follow these steps.

▶ Jab a screwdriver or ice pick into the wooden sill and frame (see the Window Construction Details Diagram on page 26) to test the wood's condition. Concentrate on the lower corners. Soft spots in the frame indicate rot and mean that a complete replacement is necessary. Rotted sills, on the other hand, can often be repaired, using wood filler compounds that are formulated especially for this task.

▶ Set a large framing square on the sill with one blade extending up a side of the frame to check for square. Window frames that are out of square also need to be replaced.

If the window frames are both sound and square, but the sashes are worn out, you can update the windows simply by replacing the sashes (see page 32).

Window Considerations

Replace a window with a new one that's as close as possible in size to the old one. Choosing a larger or smaller window might change the appearance of your house, especially from the outside, and can entail extra work and expense. Shop for replacements at home centers, lumberyards, and window specialty stores. Here's a checklist to help simplify your choices.

Styles

Buy a window that's the same style as the old one, to maintain the character of the house. The type shown on these pages is a double-hung, one-over-one window. Another common type is the casement window, which swings outward like a door.

Materials

Replacement windows can be wood, wood clad in vinyl or aluminum, all vinyl, or all aluminum. Each has its own particular advantages.

▷ Wood windows maintain a traditional look and can be painted or stained. But they need to be refinished periodically to protect them against the elements.

▷ Aluminum- and vinyl-clad windows combine the attractiveness of wood as seen from inside the house with a maintenance-free exterior.

▷ All-vinyl and all-aluminum windows require no maintenance, but some people consider them less attractive on the inside than wood.

Both the aluminum- or vinyl-clad and the all-vinyl and all-aluminum windows are easier to install than all-wood windows. Examine each type and compare prices before you order.

Glass

Most windows today come with double-pane glass for energy efficiency, which means you can do away with storm windows. Other options make glass even more energy efficient (see the Types of Window Glazing Options box at right). The value of these options depends on your climate. Ask your dealer or manufacturer how long it takes for the savings in energy cost to pay back the extra cost of the feature you are considering. A seven- to ten-year payback period is usually a worthwhile investment.

Make sure replacement windows have at least a ten-year warranty against failure of the seals between the glass and the sash. Seal failure allows air and the moisture it carries to seep between the panes, causing fog to build up between them and compromise the energy efficiency of the window—to say nothing of ruining your view.

Trim

Wood windows usually arrive with narrow wood trim called brick mold nailed to their exterior trim. If this trim style doesn't match the existing trim on your house, order an exact match from the manufacturer's catalog, or tell the supplier you don't want brick mold. Exterior trim is difficult to match perfectly, so it's generally easier to buy the material you need separately and cut it to fit. Vinyl and aluminum windows do not come with exterior trim, which you will have to add later. No matter which type of window you choose, buy new interior trim or reuse the old trim by removing it carefully.

OPTIONS

Types of Window Glazing

Windows today are generally double-glazed (made of double-pane glass). Some are triple- or even quadruple-glazed to reduce heat flow significantly.

Low-E Glass

The practice of multiplying panes to increase efficiency is now augmented by the use of new low-E (for emissivity) glass that blocks the longer-wavelength infrared sunlight beams which carry heat. They also reflect back as much as 95 percent of the sun's ultraviolet rays that cause colors to fade and contribute to skin cancer.

Superwindows

Another type of pane, called simply superwindows, has three or four layers of glazing (perhaps with low-E coating) and an inert gas like argon between the layers, because it is heavier than air and makes a good insulator.

Tints

Low-E tints that can be applied to the glass in sheets are also available. This can be a good idea when your windows don't need replacement but could benefit from more insulation.

Window Construction Details

The elements of a typical double-hung window are the sash, the frame, and the sill. To calculate what size window you'll need, measure the rough opening, which is the figure manufacturers publish: the space defined by the rough sill (Sill Detail), the framing studs along the sides (Frame Detail), and the framing header (Sash Detail) at the top.

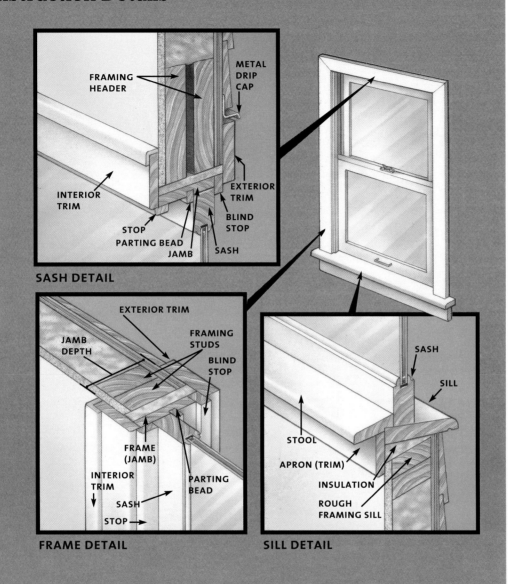

SASH DETAIL

FRAMING HEADER

METAL DRIP CAP

INTERIOR TRIM

EXTERIOR TRIM

STOP

PARTING BEAD

JAMB

BLIND STOP

SASH

FRAME DETAIL

EXTERIOR TRIM

JAMB DEPTH

FRAMING STUDS

BLIND STOP

FRAME (JAMB)

INTERIOR TRIM

PARTING BEAD

SASH

STOP

SILL DETAIL

SASH

SILL

STOOL

APRON (TRIM)

INSULATION

ROUGH FRAMING SILL

Remove the Old Window

Work carefully as you remove old windows, to avoid damaging the rough frame of the window, the interior wall, and the exterior siding. Some minor surface damage is inevitable, but most of it can be covered by the new window and new trim. Damage to the rough frame, such as cracking or splitting a framing member, for example, creates larger problems that might need professional work.

▷ Pry up the trim from around the inside of the old window. Again, work carefully if you plan to reuse it. To remove the nails, pull them out from the back side of the trim. Pulling nails from the front splinters the good face, making the patching job more difficult.

▷ Measure the height and width of the jamb. Then measure the width of the rough opening between the framing studs, and the height between the rough framing sill and the framing header (see the details at left).

Installing a new window that's larger than the rough opening means you'll have to reframe the wall, which is beyond the scope of the project shown here. Using a smaller window requires having wider exterior trim or patching the siding of the house.

▷ Now measure the depth of the window frame, called its jamb depth (see the Frame Detail, left). This measurement is the thickness of the wall excluding the exterior siding.

Prepare the Opening

Once you have removed the trim and measured the opening, begin taking out the window.

▶ Working inside, pry away the stops and pull out both of the old sashes (Photo 1).

▶ From outside, cut through the nails that hold the frame in place, using a mini-hacksaw or reciprocating saw (Photo 2). Pull the window frame out of the opening. Old double-hung windows typically have compartments on each side containing pulleys and sash weights. New double-hung windows have more compact counterweight systems. If so, remove the old compartment and install a 2x4 on each side to fill this space.

▶ Beginning at the bottom of the rough opening, tuck No. 15 asphalt-impregnated building felt 2 inches under the siding (Photo 3). Work up the sides from the bottom, overlapping the sections as you go, then push the last piece of felt into the top of the opening and down to overlap the sides. Staple all the pieces in place. With wood siding, you might have to cut through some of the siding nails to make room to push the felt into place. Stucco, vinyl, and aluminum siding can't be renailed, so just tuck the felt under as far as you can. Caulking, which will be applied later, will help make the joint weathertight.

▶ Slip a preformed metal drip cap up under the siding on top of the window opening (Photo 4). The trim will hold it in place so that you won't need to nail it.

Photo 1. From inside the house, first pry out the interior trim, then remove the stops and both of the window sashes.

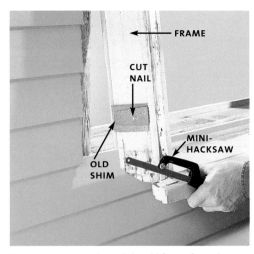

Photo 2. From outside, pull the old frame from the opening. Use a mini-hacksaw or reciprocating saw to cut nails driven in the sides or top of the frame.

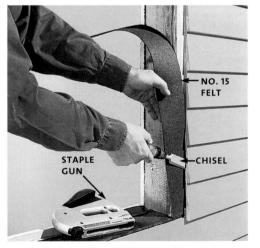

Photo 3. Slide No. 15 asphalt-impregnated building felt under the siding's edges. Begin at the bottom and go up the sides to the top, overlapping each layer.

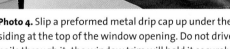

Photo 4. Slip a preformed metal drip cap up under the siding at the top of the window opening. Do not drive nails through it; the window trim will hold it securely.

Tools You Need

Carpenter's level

Caulking gun

Chisels

Framing square

Hacksaw or reciprocating saw

Hammer

Protective goggles and mask

Pry bar

Screwdrivers

Staple gun

Tape measure

Materials

Aluminum or galvanized drip cap

10d galvanized casing nails

6d and 8d finish nails

Exterior-grade caulk

No. 15 asphalt-impregnated building felt

Shims

Window trim as necessary

Mount the Window

Enlist a helper or two if you can, to make it easier to lift the new window into its opening.

▶ Set the new window into the opening, using shims if necessary to center and level it. Don't drive any nails yet.

▶ With someone steadying the window, measure from each corner of the new window to the drip cap and house siding. Then subtract 1/8 inch from each dimension to allow for sealing caulk (Photo 5). This new figure is the width of the exterior trim. Aluminum- and vinyl-clad and all-vinyl windows have nailing flanges that anchor the windows in place, so if you have one of these types of windows you can skip this step and the next one.

▶ Now remove the window and lay it down on a firm, flat surface. Fasten the exterior trim to the frame using 10d galvanized casing nails (Photo 6).

Squeeze a bead of caulk around the edge of the opening so it will be hidden behind the trim. Then reposition the window, pressing the trim evenly into the caulk (Photo 7).

▶ Tack the window in place temporarily with 10d nails, then test the sashes by lifting and lowering them a few times. If they bind and don't open and close smoothly, the frame is not square. Adjust it by using a carpenter's level to check the sill for level and the sides for plumb (Photo 8). Drive shims as necessary before nailing the window in place permanently with 10d galvanized casing nails through the exterior trim at 16-inch intervals.

Reminder

If you had to cut some of the siding nails to make room for the building felt, don't forget to replace these nails once the window is in place.

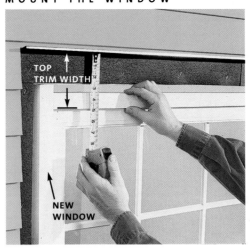

Photo 5. Test-fit the window, centering and leveling it, then measure the exterior trim sizes. Leave a 1/8-in. gap between the trim and the siding for caulk.

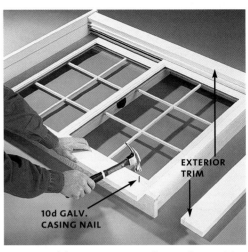

Photo 6. Nail the exterior trim to the new frame with 10d galvanized casing nails. For nonwood windows, apply the trim after the window has been installed.

Photo 7. Squeeze caulk around the opening so it will be hidden behind the trim. Slide the window into place. Temporarily tack it through the trim.

Photo 8. Use shims to level and plumb the sill. Make sure the sashes move freely. Then anchor the window with 10d galvanized nails every 16 in.

Finish the Window

All that remains now is to caulk the window seams, add the interior trim, and apply any light touch-ups that may be called for.

▷ Tuck fiberglass insulation into the gaps around the window frame (Photo 9). Alternatively, you can spray expanding foam into these gaps, but use it sparingly—it can bow the frame as it expands and interfere with the window's operation. Never use expanding foam with all-vinyl windows.

▷ Nail the interior trim to the window frame with 6d finish nails and to the wall with 8d finish nails, then paint it.

▷ Caulk and nail in a molding below the exterior sill to cover the gap. Then caulk between the house siding and the exterior trim (Photo 10).

▷ As a final step, touch up any trim that you were able to reuse.

FINISH THE WINDOW

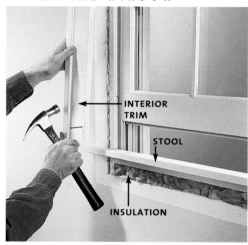

Photo 9. Tuck fiberglass insulation into the frame gaps. Wear a dust mask, long-sleeved shirt, gloves, and goggles. Then reinstall the interior trim or install new.

Photo 10. Caulk and nail a molding on the underside of the exterior sill to cover the gap. Then caulk between the siding and the trim.

TECHNIQUES

Window Finishing Tips

Fiberglass

Fiberglass insulation is an irritant for your skin, eyes, and lungs. Wear gloves, long sleeves, goggles, a hat, and a protective mask whenever you work with it. When you are finished, wash fibers off your skin with warm soapy water.

New Interior Trim

To avoid having to touch up the wall paint around the window—or having to locate and patch in skinny strips of wallpaper—select an interior trim molding that is wide enough to slightly overlap onto the existing paint or wallcovering. Before nailing the trim in place, lightly pack a strip of fiberglass insulation in the gap between the window frame and the framework of the house.

New Exterior Trim

In some cases, you can simply reapply the old interior and exterior moldings and be done. But chances are, you'll need to cover over wider, narrower, or uneven spaces so that your new window blends gracefully with its surroundings.

Use a circular saw and rip guide to cut 1x4's (1x6's for wider spaces) to the correct width to fill in the space between the exterior window frame and the existing brick or siding. The widths of the pieces may be identical or quite different from one another and from the old standard brick molding, depending on how close a match in size the old and new windows are. Position these pieces, then nail them in place using 8d galvanized nails. Apply a bead of caulk where the exterior molding meets the brick or siding.

Window Replacement Option 1

All-Vinyl Windows

All-vinyl windows cost about the same as all-wood ones. Here are some of the positive and negative factors to consider if you are thinking of installing all-vinyl windows.

Pros

▶ Easier to maintain than wood; require no painting, because the color is integral with the vinyl; do not swell.

▶ More energy efficient than wood (virtually no heat loss); better weatherstripping.

▶ Available in custom-made sizes designed to fit precisely inside the old window frame, making them easy to install.

Cons

▶ Square-edged, blocky appearance.

▶ Glass area reduced about 1 inch if custom built, up to 2 inches if purchased in stock sizes.

▶ Limited color choice; white vinyl should not be painted.

▶ Sensitive to heat; avoid dark colors in hot climates or windows with a southern exposure. In such situations, look for vinyl windows that are specially designed to withstand high temperatures.

Buying Hints

▶ Try to find at least a ten-year warranty on insulated glass.

▶ Look for the more durable vinyl that is 2mm or more thick.

▶ Vinyl windows more than 36 inches wide should have steel-reinforced frames.

▶ Check the details. Corners should be snug and weatherstripping tight.

Installation Hints

▶ All-vinyl windows must have full-width support for the sills.

▶ Avoid insulating with expanding foam, which can deform the frame.

All-Vinyl Windows

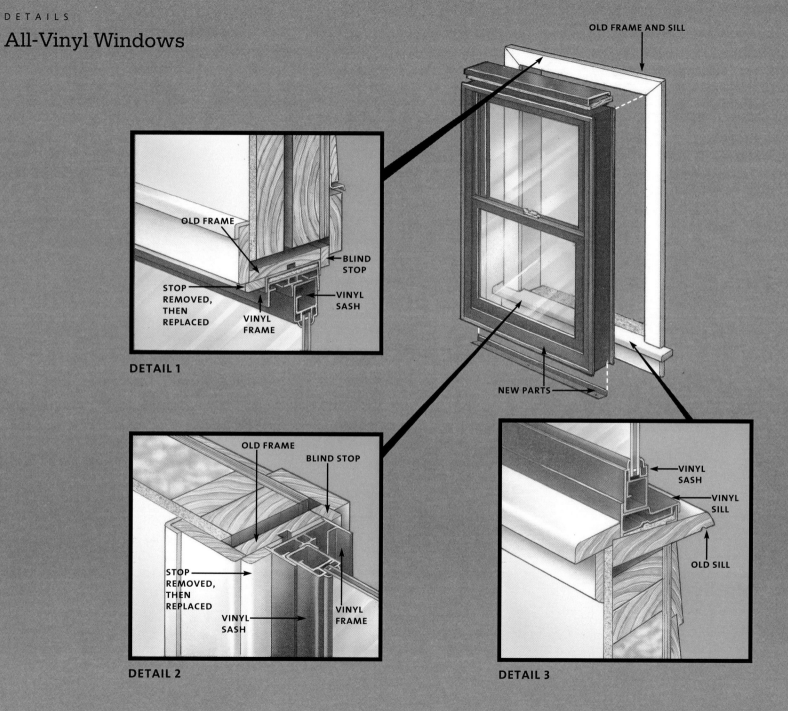

OLD FRAME AND SILL

DETAIL 1

OLD FRAME

BLIND STOP

STOP REMOVED, THEN REPLACED

VINYL FRAME

VINYL SASH

NEW PARTS

DETAIL 2

OLD FRAME

BLIND STOP

STOP REMOVED, THEN REPLACED

VINYL SASH

VINYL FRAME

DETAIL 3

VINYL SASH

VINYL SILL

OLD SILL

Window Replacement Option 2

Wood Sash Kits

Wood sash kits cost slightly less than a complete all-wood unit.

Pros

▶ Relatively easy installation.
▶ Maintain same appearance as old window.
▶ Upgrades glass to double-pane style for greater energy efficiency.

Cons

▶ Old frame must be square as well as in good condition.
▶ Windows might need some fine-tuning to make them fit if they're too tall or short.
▶ Kit windows are less airtight than a completely new unit.

Installation Hint

▶ Measure the inside of the frame side to side and top to bottom when ordering the kit.
▶ Check the lower corners of the frame and window sill for rot.

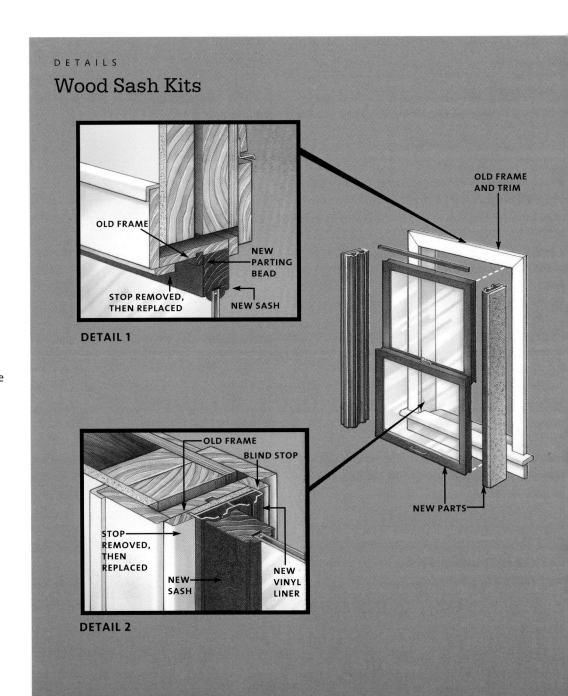

DETAILS

Wood Sash Kits

OLD FRAME

NEW PARTING BEAD

STOP REMOVED, THEN REPLACED

NEW SASH

DETAIL 1

OLD FRAME AND TRIM

OLD FRAME

BLIND STOP

STOP REMOVED, THEN REPLACED

NEW SASH

NEW VINYL LINER

NEW PARTS

DETAIL 2

Window Replacement Option 3

Reusing Old Sashes

You can improve the insulating properties of your windows by removing the sash, installing new, vinyl tracks, and reinstalling the old sash. If you decide to reuse your old window sashes, be aware that you will incur some cost to trim and reshape the edges of the old window in addition to the price of the new vinyl track and other parts. Check lumberyards and window companies for a dealer who will trim and reshape the old sash as well as sell you the new vinyl track. Check the existing window frame for rot and squareness; either problem makes this approach impossible.

Pros

▷ Inexpensive.
▷ Maintains the original appearance.
▷ Improves energy efficiency by tightening loose-fitting windows.
▷ Increases ease of operation.
▷ Easy to reinstall.

Cons

▷ Frame must be square, and both the frame and the sashes must be in good shape.
▷ No gain in energy savings available from double-pane glass; storm windows still needed.
▷ Vinyl liners may be eyesores.

Installation Hints

▷ If the sash has been heavily painted, chemically strip the paint and replace the stop.
▷ Weatherstrip the top, bottom, and center rail.

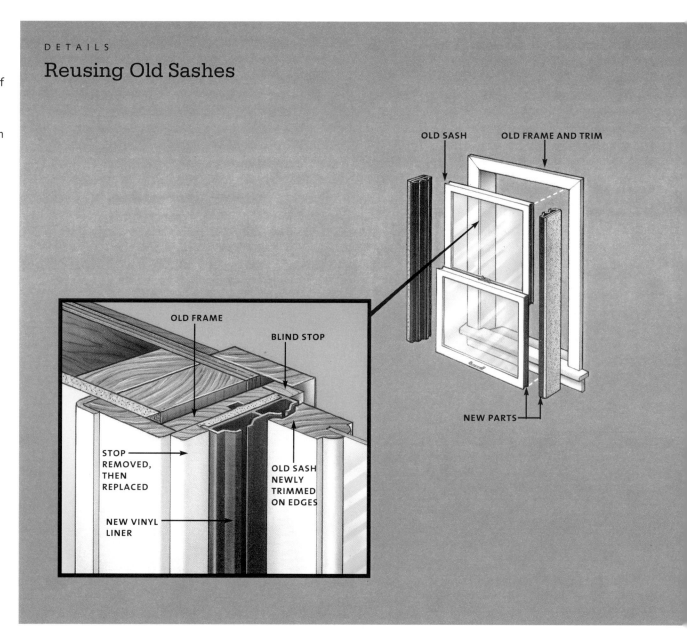

DETAILS

Reusing Old Sashes

OLD SASH

OLD FRAME AND TRIM

OLD FRAME

BLIND STOP

STOP REMOVED, THEN REPLACED

OLD SASH NEWLY TRIMMED ON EDGES

NEW VINYL LINER

NEW PARTS

Hang Interior Shutters

From bath to library, interior shutters are a time-honored window treatment. They make a strong design statement in any room, allow you to control the amount of light entering the room, and create a feeling of warmth. What's more, they come in many designs, colors, and louver widths.

Sizing Up the Project

This project involves careful measuring and precision cutting as well as installing hinges that require no mortises. Even so, with patience even a beginning do-it-yourselfer can hang interior wooden shutters.

Before You Begin

To control the amount of light entering through shutters, select ones with movable rather than fixed louvers. For the maximum amount of light, choose shutters with the widest louvers the space can accommodate. You can buy louvers as wide as 4 inches.

You can hang shutters either over the entire window or else just across the lower half. Mount them as single units, in pairs, or in groups of three or four. Standard-size shutters, available at home centers or lumberyards, come in widths from 6 to 12 inches and in heights from 20 to 48 inches. Full-length shutters or custom shutters are more often found at window specialty dealers.

Window Considerations

Interior shutters can be installed over most types of windows, including the following:

- ▶ Double-hung
- ▶ Sliding
- ▶ Awning (crank or push-up)
- ▶ Fixed windows

Because of their cranks and latches, casement windows can often cause problems with shutters. But casements with wide jambs are much less of a problem, since their hardware is recessed out of the way.

Mounting Methods

Before buying your shutters, determine the method you will need to use for hanging them—inside or outside the jamb (see the Shutter-Mounting Methods Diagram, right). Shutters installed inside the jambs have a more built-in look, although some window jambs are not wide enough to accommodate the shutter-hanging strips. Also, the larger the louvers, the more clearance is needed between shutters and window sashes, requiring some types of shutters to be installed outside the jambs. Moreover, if you find by measuring a window's two diagonals that it is more than 1/2 inch out of square, an outside-the-jamb installation is best.

Interior shutters are a tried-and-true method of enhancing the architectural look of a room and adding visual warmth to it.

Shutter-Mounting Methods

After measuring your window, determine whether the inside- or outside-mounting method best suits it. You need at least 1-1/2 in. of jamb width in front of the sash for an inside mount.

If your window opening is out of square by more than 1/2 in., use the outside-mounting technique. This method allows more flexibility, because the shutters don't have to fit the opening precisely, and you usually don't have to trim the width—you can vary the location of the hanging strips on the trim.

INSIDE-MOUNTING METHOD

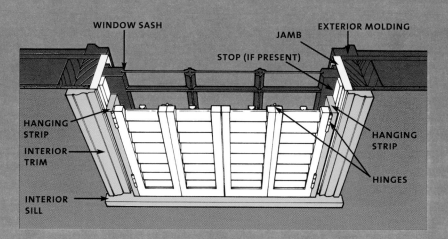

OUTSIDE-MOUNTING METHOD

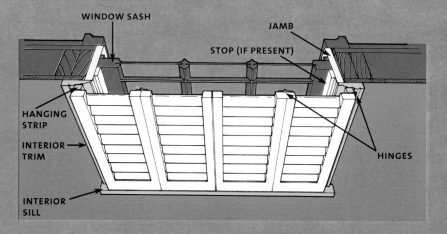

Tools You Need

Drill and self-centering drill bit, twist bits

Tape measure

Clamps

Circular saw or table saw

Straightedge

Screwdriver

Block plane

Materials

8 1-1/2 in. wood screws per shutter

1-in. wood blocks

2 or 3 1-1/2 in. no-mortise hinges per shutter

Hanging strip material

Size the Shutters

To determine the correct shutter width, measure the width and height of the window just in front of the sash (Photo 1). In the window shown here, the opening was 41-1/2 inches, which is just about right for four 10-inch wide shutter panels. Each of the hanging strips is 3/4 inch thick (see the Shutter-Mounting Methods Diagram on the previous page), so 10-inch panels had to be trimmed slightly to allow for the hinge's thickness and the gap in the middle. It usually is safe to trim 3/8 inch from each side of a shutter and a total of 1-1/4 inches from the top and bottom without affecting a shutter panel's strength.

After measuring the opening, go through the following procedures.

▶ Lay out the shutters on 1-inch blocks with the hanging strips on each side (Photo 2).

▶ Position 1-1/2 inch no-mortise hinges inside the spaces between panels.

▶ Slip quarters into the center gap as spacers.

▶ Measure the total width.

▶ Subtract the window-opening width.

▶ Divide this measurement by the number of panels. The resulting number is the amount you must cut from the width of each panel. If the figure is 1/8 inch or less, trim it from one side of each panel. If it's more than 1/8 inch, take half from each side of the panel, for a balanced appearance. Use a circular saw or block plane with great care when cutting small amounts from the sides. If you have access to a table saw, you will find the job a lot easier.

▶ Cut the panels 3/16 inch less than the opening height, which provides just enough clearance to slip a nickel into the space above and below the shutter (Photo 3).

▶ Cut the 3/4-inch x 2-3/4 inch hanging strip to fit snugly within the window opening.

SIZE THE SHUTTERS

Photo 1. Measure the window opening in front of the sash. Make sure the window is square by measuring both diagonals. If the diagonals differ by more than 1/2 in., use the outside-mounting method.

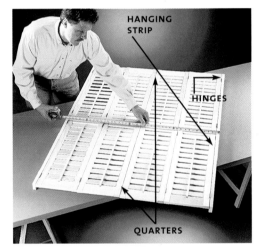

Photo 2. Lay out the panels, position the no-mortise hinges, and use quarters to gap the center. Subtract the window's width from the shutters'. Divide by the number of shutters for the amount to trim each.

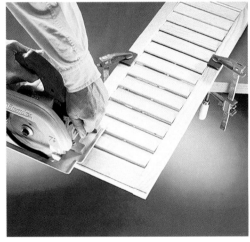

Photo 3. Cut each panel to its final length and width. Each panel's length should be 3/16 in. less than the actual height of the window opening, to provide the necessary clearance.

Mount the Shutters

Once you have chosen your shutter-mounting method and cut the shutters to size, refer to the appropriate diagram on page 35 while mounting the shutters.

Selecting the Hinges

No-mortise hinges work well on shutters, because they can be concealed on the front and back so that only the barrel of the hinge shows. If you use standard butt hinges, chisel out mortises for them in the shutters and the hanging strips, or else surface-mount them on the back side, as shown in the diagrams on page 35.

Placing the Hinges

Careful work mounting the hinges will save fussing and fudging later. Drill pilot holes for the hinge screws with a self-centering bit like a Vix bit to ensure perfect alignment (Photo 4).

▶ When mounting a set of four panels, hinge the two paired panels together on the back side (see the diagrams on page 35).

▶ For panels less than 3 feet high, use two hinges per edge; for panels 3 to 4 feet high use three hinges; and for panels more than 4 feet tall use four hinges.

▶ Place the tops and bottoms of the hinges 2-1/2 inches from the top and bottom of each panel. Space additional hinges evenly between them.

Placing the Hanging Strips

▶ To ensure proper top and bottom clearance, stand the shutter panels on nickels, then position the hanging strips next to them, flush against the work surface (Photo 5). Now attach the hinges connecting the shutter panels and the hanging strips.

▶ Drill pilot holes in the hanging strips about 1/2 inch in from the edge nearest the window sash. Space them from top to bottom as you did the hinges on the shutter panels.

▶ Finally, set the hanging strips onto the sill and screw them in place with 1-1/2 inch wood screws (Photo 6).

Fine-tuning the Fit

With the shutters closed, check the spacing along the center, the top, and the bottom.

▶ If the shutters rub on the sill or top, rub chalk on the sill where you suspect the high marks to be and then open and close the shutters to mark the points of contact. Recut the panels with a saw or sand them down a bit with a belt sander. Take off only small amounts on each pass.

▶ If the center panels touch when they are closed, mark the points of contact, using the chalk technique just explained, and shave the edges with a block plane.

Final Touches

Remove the shutters and hanging strips from the window frame, then take off the hinges. Sand all the edges with fine (120–180 grit) sandpaper and thoroughly vacuum all the dust off of the louvers.

▶ Painting shutters with a brush is tedious. The best method is to spray them with a power sprayer. If you're uncomfortable using one, try spray painting with aerosol cans, if your locality allows their sale. Expect to use at least three cans of primer and four cans of spray paint for an assembly of a size similar to that shown on the preceding pages.

▶ For staining, brush on the stain, then wipe it down with a clean, lint-free cloth. Finally, either spray or brush on a finish coat of clear varnish.

▶ After the paint or varnish is dry, remount the shutters and attach the hardware.

MOUNT THE SHUTTERS

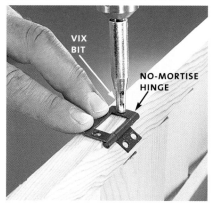

Photo 4. Drill the holes for the hinges, using a self-centering bit like the Vix bit shown here to help you align the hinge.

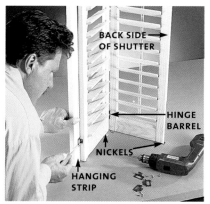

Photo 5. Hinge panels together before you mount the hanging strip. Prop the shutters on nickels for clearance and attach the strip.

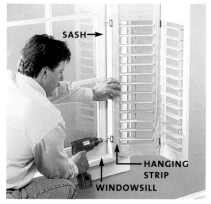

Photo 6. Screw each assembly to the window jamb with 1-1/2 in. wood screws. Predrill pilot holes near each hinge location.

Transform a Doorway with an Arch

An arch is more than just something to walk through. It presents a graceful visual transition from one room to the next and complements the design features of a room. And now, thanks to special building materials, this elegant refinement is easier than ever to build.

Sizing Up the Project

This project involves reshaping a standard rectangular doorway into a curved arch, which means it requires basic drywall and carpentry skills. Depending on where you create the arch, this project might also call for more advanced carpentry, including demolition, wall framing, and, in the case of a new opening in a load-bearing wall, the installation of a header over the doorway. A project requiring these more advanced skills is not dealt with in these pages. Consult a building inspector or structural engineer if your project involves making a brand-new opening in a wall.

Before You Begin

The starting point of this project is a wall with the framing exposed, either because the wall has been newly built or because the existing drywall has been removed. The actual arch-building process is divided into four steps:
- ▷ Construct the wood frame.
- ▷ Hang the drywall.
- ▷ Install the corner bead.
- ▷ Apply the joint compound.

Design Considerations

Make sure the arch you decide to build will fit the basic style of your house. If you're not sure, take photographs of the rooms from both sides of the proposed opening and sketch an arch over the photos.

The arch shown here was built to match existing doorway arches as well as decorative arches over china cabinets. Doorway arches are usually not as deep as the one shown here, which is a full 2 feet deep. Most are only the thickness of a stud wall, or about 4-1/2 inches, but the construction techniques remain essentially the same.

Materials

Two special building materials simplify the arch-building process: drywall sheets only 1/4 inch thick, and flexible plastic corner beading that gives the arch clean, sharp edges.
▷ Thin drywall only 1/4 inch thick flexes easily, making it easier to bend smoothly around an arch without breaking. In some instances, though, including the arch shown here, the curve of an arch is so acute that even 1/4-inch

drywall can't be pressed into place without snapping it. The trick is to score lines across its back side at intervals and snap it along those lines, so that it can be bent to fit around the curve. It's best to use two layers of 1/4-inch drywall to cover the arch, but in a pinch you can use one layer of 3/8 inch or even 1/2 inch if 1/4 inch is unavailable.

▶ Flexible corner beading with a plastic nose like that shown below bends easily around the curve of an arch. The plastic nose protrudes slightly to make a smooth, even corner for the taping knife to follow applying joint compound.

Check home centers and lumberyards for 1/4-inch drywall and flexible corner bead. If you can't find either, consult a local drywall contractor or supply house.

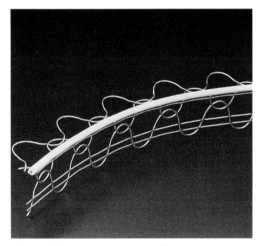

Constructing a curved drywall surface is easier now than it used to be, thanks to flexible arch beading.

This graceful two-foot deep arch creates a distinctive designer touch between kitchen and dining room, where it echoes the inset arches of the china cabinets.

Tools You Need

Tape measure
Straightedge
Saber saw
Hammer
Drill
Drywall saw
Utility knife
Staple gun
Taping knife
Sanding block

Materials

1x4 boards
2x4 boards
3/4" plywood
Plastic corner bead
Metal corner bead
Scrap lumber
Drywall joint compound (setting and regular)
Sandpaper
1-1/4 in. drywall nails or drywall screws
1/2" and 1/4" arch beading

Construct the Wood Frame

This particular arch is a perfect half circle, even though an arch can consist of a smooth curve of any shape. The wood frame supplies the solid foundation for this entire project, so cut it as precisely as you possibly can.

▶ Measure the doorway's width to find the circle's diameter (Photo 1). Then cut a sheet of 3/4-inch plywood to this width.

▶ Scribe a full circle on the plywood so that the circle's edge meets the edge of the plywood (Photo 2).

▶ Carefully cut out the circle with a saber saw (Photo 3). The four arcs left over fit the four upper corners of the doorway, forming the actual arch.

▶ Now measure the distance across the framing of the door opening and subtract 1-1/2 inches from this figure. Cut a series of 1x4 blocking boards to this length.

▶ Nail the 1x4's across the opening, insetting them 3/4 inch to accommodate the 3/4-inch thickness of the plywood arcs (Photo 4).

▶ Nail the four plywood arcs to the 1x4's (Photo 5). Make sure the faces of the arcs are flush with the faces of the door framing.

▶ Screw 2x4 backing boards to the plywood arcs to prevent the thin drywall from bowing inward across the middle of the arch (Photo 6).

Photo 1. Measure the width of the doorway. This is the diameter of the circle that forms the actual arch.

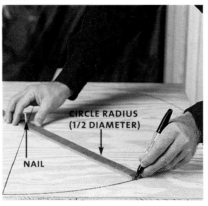

Photo 2. Draw a circle of this diameter on a piece of 3/4-in. plywood cut to match the width of the doorway.

Photo 3. Carefully cut out the circle with a saber saw. Set aside the four corner arcs to be used at a later time.

Photo 4. Nail 1x4 blocking boards to the doorway framework. Leave a 3/4-in. gap on the corner framing for the arcs to fit flush with the corner.

Photo 5. Nail the four plywood arcs that you set aside earlier to the blocking boards. Be sure to fit the arcs tightly into the corners of the doorway.

Photo 6. Screw 2x4 backing boards to each arc, flush with the curved edge, to provide additional support across the middle of the arch to the drywall.

Hang the Drywall

Once the opening has been framed, install regular 1/2-inch drywall over the wall framing, including the plywood arcs.

▶ With a drywall saw, cut out the curve of the arch, using the plywood arcs to guide your saw (Photo 7).

▶ Smooth the edges of the drywall with a coarse file, making it perfectly flush with the curves of the plywood. Work carefully, because small errors here will be magnified later.

▶ Cut a strip of 1/4-inch drywall to the width of the arch. Score a series of parallel lines, 1 inch apart, through the paper on the back side of the drywall (Photo 8).

▶ Carefully turn the piece over. Use a straight board to help snap the back side at about every sixth cut (Photo 9).

▶ With help from a second person, gently lift the piece, push it up into the arch, and nail across one lower edge of it with 1-1/4 inch drywall nails or drywall screws (Photo 10).

▶ With a board long enough to span the entire width of the arch, break the drywall at every score mark and force it tightly into the curve (Photo 11). Nail it to the edges of the plywood every 4 inches as you work around the arch.

▶ Follow the same procedure to install a second layer of 1/4-inch drywall. Don't worry now about slight creases that may appear where the drywall breaks, because these irregularities will be covered later when the joint compound has been applied.

HANG THE DRYWALL

Photo 7. Fasten the 1/2-in. drywall to the wall over the wall framing, then cut out the arch shape with a drywall saw.

Photo 8. Score lines at 1-in. intervals along the back side of 1/4-in. drywall that has been cut to the width of the arch.

Photo 9. Snap the back side of the drywall at about every sixth cut, using a straightedge to ensure a clean break.

Photo 10. Nail the drywall across one lower edge of the arch. Have a helper lift and hold the drywall in place.

Photo 11. Break the back side of the drywall along each scored line, using a straightedge. Nail the drywall to the plywood arcs as you go.

Install the Corner Bead

If you carefully fit the flexible corner bead now you will have crisp edges and corners later. You will also appreciate having as smooth an arc as possible when it comes to the final step of spreading joint compound. Kinks or bulges in the bead will result in an uneven surface on the inside of the arch.

▶ If the flexible plastic bead is not available, you can bend metal corner bead by snipping it at 1-inch intervals (Photo 12).

▶ Hold a piece of flexible corner bead against the corner as it will be installed. Using it as a guide, nail adjacent pieces of metal corner bead so their edges meet the edge of the plastic bead (Photo 13). The metal corners are installed horizontally as shown here, but they are also mounted vertically in the lower portion of the doorway before it enters the curve of the arch. The metal bead protects the fragile drywall corners from traffic passing through the opening and helps you form sharp corners when applying joint compound.

▶ Staple the wire sides of the flexible bead tightly into the curve, being careful not to bend it out of shape (Photo 14). The joint compound will anchor it permanently when it is applied. Compare the gap between the beads along the edges of the arch by running a straightedge across them, checking for a consistent gap between the edge and the inner surface of the arch (Photo 15). You might have to make some adjustments here, but this extra effort now will pay off as the arch is finished.

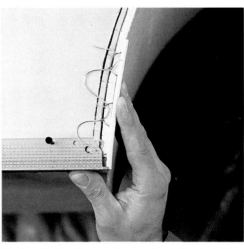

Photo 12. Flexible corner bead with a plastic nose bends into smooth curves. The old method required you to cut metal bead at 1-in. intervals, then bend it.

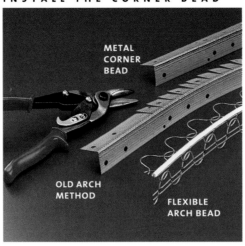

Photo 13. Nail up the metal corner beads for straight sections of wall or door opening, holding up a section of flexible bead to make sure the two types meet.

Photo 14. Staple each side of the flexible bead tightly to the arch at intervals of every 4 in., starting from one end or the other.

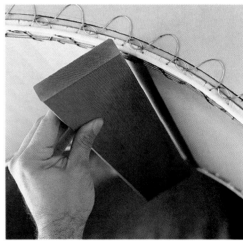

Photo 15. Run a straightedge along the plastic noses of the beading, to be sure the gap between the beads and arch surface is even.

Apply the Joint Compound

This job is best done using two types of joint compound. The first, quick-set compound, hardens in anywhere from about 10 minutes to an hour, depending on what setting speed you choose. Its thicker texture makes it ideal for filling gaps and covering metal parts of the bead, but when it sets, it becomes so hard it can't be sanded smooth. If you use this type of compound as a base coat, apply it no thicker than the level of the plastic nose on the corner bead. Smooth the quick-set compound as much as possible, but don't feel it has to be perfect. Let the next coat take care of that.

Regular joint compound is used on top of quick-set compound to level and smooth the finish. It hardens slowly and is easier to work with. But as it dries it also shrinks, so at least two coats will be required.

▶ Apply quick-set compound to the inner surface of the arch, then drag a straight board along the plastic noses of the bead to level and smooth the compound (Photo 16).

▶ If necessary, apply quick-set compound on the flat walls to fill gaps and other imperfections (Photo 17).

▶ After the quick-set compound is fully dry, administer at least two coats of regular joint compound, smoothing out the last coat in a final surface (Photo 18). Feather the edges of each pass into the earlier coats. If you haven't done this type of work before, practice on a large piece of scrap drywall until you feel confident in tackling the inside of the arch.

▶ Finally, smooth imperfections with sandpaper or a sanding sponge (Photo 19).

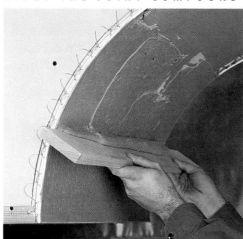

Photo 16. Smooth quick-set joint compound into the arch with a straightedge run along the plastic noses of the corner bead.

Photo 17. Apply additional quick-set compound to the walls with a taping knife to fill large gaps and depressions as needed.

Photo 18. Apply at least two layers of regular joint compound to fill smaller holes and smooth the wall and arch surfaces flat.

Photo 19. Once they have dried, sand the walls and corners lightly to remove rough spots. A 220-grit sponge works well on curves.

Mixing Compound

Quick-set compound comes powdered and must be mixed to the consistency of whipped cream. Some kinds harden faster than others. The 90-minute variety should give you enough time to spread and smooth it.

Install Folding Attic Stairs

Finding extra storage space is always a challenge, yet you probably have hundreds of cubic feet of additional space right over your head in the attic or above the garage. Unfortunately, many attic access panels are small and inconveniently located. Installing a folding attic stairway solves the access difficulty and eases many storage problems.

Sizing Up the Project

This project involves cutting a hole in your ceiling, so it is essential to measure and mark accurately for all cuts.

Putting in an attic stairway requires a moderate level of carpentry skill and framing experience. If you've installed a new door or a skylight, you can tackle this job and complete it in about a day. It is possible to do this project alone, but the job will be much easier with a helper to cut lumber and hand up materials as you go. Hefting the stair unit up into the ceiling opening is also much easier if you have extra pairs of hands to help.

Planning Considerations

▶ Before choosing a spot for your stairs, climb into the attic to look for possible obstructions like ductwork, electrical boxes, and cables. Electrical boxes and cables can be moved fairly easily, but ductwork should generally be relocated by a contractor. The easiest solution is simply to look for another location for the stairs. Wherever you decide to place them, make sure there will be at least 2 feet of room in front of the stairway once it is pulled down.

▶ Determine the type of framing used in the attic. Roof trusses are engineered from smaller pieces of lumber to act as a structural unit. They are usually spaced 24 inches apart from center to center (on center, abbreviated o.c.). In a hand-framed attic, the ceiling joists are independent of the rafters and typically are installed 16 inches apart on center. If you can't determine whether you are dealing with trusses or a hand-framed roof system, consult a carpenter or contractor before buying a folding stairway.

▶ Never cut into a roof truss; this will weaken the entire unit and lead to structural failure. If your attic contains trusses, you'll need to buy a stairway with a 22-1/2 inch wide frame (having a 13-inch tread) to fit into the space between the trusses. You will not be able to put the stairway in a hallway unless the hall runs parallel to the trusses. With a hand-framed attic, buy a 25-inch wide stairway (with a 16-inch tread). You'll have to cut some joists anyway, and the wider stairs will be easier to use.

The project shown on these pages involves a hand-framed joist system, the more difficult of the two types to work with. If you'll be cutting joists, be sure they're supported by walls on each side of the hallway. If a wall is not located within 2 feet of either side of the attic opening, build a support framework as shown in the Ceiling Framing Styles Options box on page 46. You can adjust the position slightly to accommodate ceiling joists so that you cut as few as possible. You will most likely need a building permit for any job that requires you to cut into ceiling joists, so check with a local building inspector before beginning this project.

Determine the size of lumber used for the joists in your attic. They will normally be 2x6's, 2x8's, or 2x10's. You'll have to buy several lengths of the same size lumber to frame the stairway opening.

Before You Buy

Measure the distance from the floor to the ceiling. Stairways normally come in two basic lengths: one for ceilings that are between 7 feet and 8 feet 5 inches high, and another for ceilings up to 10 feet high. Stairways vary in their length as well as pitch, so carefully check the specifications supplied by the manufacturer.

Tools You Need

Adjustable T-bevel
Circular saw
Drywall saw
Flashlight or extension light
Framing square
Goggles, gloves, dust mask
Hammer
Handsaw
Ladder
Power drill and bits
Reciprocating saw
Tape measure

Materials

Foam panel insulation
Framing lumber the same size as the joists
4 metal corner hangers
1/2" plywood
1/2 lb. joist-hanger nails
1 lb. 16d sinker nails
Scrap plywood
2x4's
2 lbs. 3-in. deck screws
Two 3-ft. 1x4's
Wood shims

Frame the Opening

If your attic is framed with roof trusses, frame the stair opening as shown in the Wood Trusses diagram below. For hand-framed joists, proceed as follows. (This project will progress much more quickly if you have one person working from within the attic and another below on a ladder, saving a lot of climbing up and down.)

▶ Select your stair location and mark its center. Drill a hole there and poke a wire coat hanger through it to help you find the location from inside the attic (Photo 1).

▶ Climb into the attic. Check for obstructions and confirm the location you have chosen. Clear away any insulation from the joists over the area that will be cut out. Simply roll up and move batt or blanket insulation. Gather up blown-in insulation in plastic garbage bags and redistribute it elsewhere around the attic. Wear heavy gloves and clothing that covers you well if you are dealing with fiberglass.

▶ Put down sheets of scrap plywood around the area within which you will be working, to avoid stepping between joists and possibly damaging the ceiling below.

▶ Consult the manufacturer's directions to determine what size ceiling opening is needed for the stairs. Mark the size of the rough opening on the ceiling and cut it out with a drywall saw. Wear goggles and a dust mask for protection as you work (Photo 2).

▶ If there are no support walls running perpendicular to the ceiling joists within 2 feet of either side of the rough opening, construct the joist braces shown in the bottom diagram at left.

▶ With a handsaw or reciprocating saw, cut the joists 3 inches back from the rough opening for the ceiling (Photo 3). Be careful not to cut too deeply, down into the ceiling.

▶ Nail helper joists along the length of the uncut joists closest to the cutout (Photo 4).

▶ Cut two pieces of framing lumber of the same dimensions as the ceiling joists to nail to the ends of the cut-off joists, using 16d nails. Then cut two more identical pieces and nail them to the headers you just installed. These doubled headers should now be flush with the edges of the rough opening.

▶ Nail metal corner hangers between the headers and helpers for a strong joint (Photo 5).

Ceiling Framing Styles

Wood Trusses
To avoid cutting wood trusses when installing attic stairs, try to find space in a hallway that runs parallel to the gap between two trusses. Frame the opening by nailing support blocks between the joists to act as a base for the stairway unit.

Ceiling Joists
If there are no walls within 2 ft. of either side of the stairway opening, the ceiling joists will need to be braced. Nail two 2x4's together to form a 90-degree angle, then screw the braces to the ceiling joists with 3-in. deck screws.

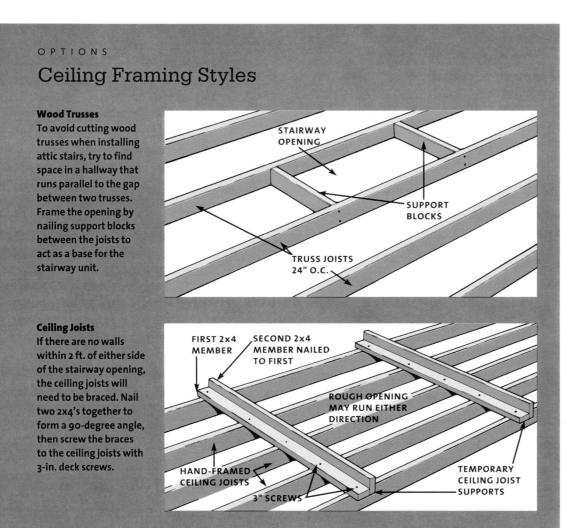

STAIRWAY OPENING

SUPPORT BLOCKS

TRUSS JOISTS 24" O.C.

FIRST 2x4 MEMBER

SECOND 2x4 MEMBER NAILED TO FIRST

ROUGH OPENING MAY RUN EITHER DIRECTION

HAND-FRAMED CEILING JOISTS

3" SCREWS

TEMPORARY CEILING JOIST SUPPORTS

Photo 1. Push a wire hanger through the center of the stair location, then go to the attic and find it. Move electrical lines if they are in the way. If ductwork or pipes interfere, consider relocating the stairs.

Photo 2. Shift the opening's location to accommodate the joist framing so as to cut as few joists as possible. Mark the rough opening for the stairway assembly and cut it to size with a drywall saw.

Photo 3. Cut the ceiling joists 3 in. back from the rough opening in the ceiling. Make sure the joists are supported by a wall below or braces in the attic. Avoid cutting into the ceiling.

Don't Crush Insulation

If you have deep insulation in the attic, don't lay storage items on it—compressing insulation robs it of its insulating value. Instead, build a storage shelf supported by the roof framing.

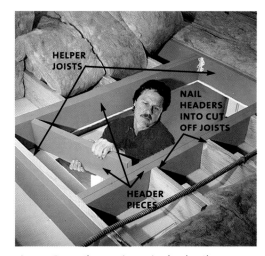

Photo 4. Frame the opening, using lumber the same dimensions as the existing joists. Extend helper joists along the length of the uncut joists to support the headers. Nail the new framing pieces to the cut joists.

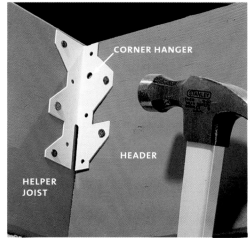

Photo 5. For added strength and stability, nail in metal corner hangers like these, which are available from lumberyards and home centers, on all four corners of the newly framed opening.

Install the Stairway

Helping hands will make maneuvering the stairway up into the attic much more manageable. Nail temporary 1x3 cleats to the new framing on each narrow side of the rough opening so that they overlap the opening by about an inch (Photo 6). These will act as temporary supports for the stairway unit while you fasten it in place from inside the attic.

▶ Attic stairways come completely assembled at the factory. All you have to do is work the unit into the opening and rest it on the cleats. Just make sure you have it facing the right way as you position it.

▶ From inside the attic, center the unit as much as possible within the opening. Then tap shims between the stair unit and the new framing as needed until the unit is properly squared up within the opening.

▶ Drill pilot holes through the stair unit's fastening hardware, then drive 3-inch deck screws into the new framing to secure the unit firmly (Photo 7).

▶ From below, remove the temporary cleats and pull the ladder down. The bottom, hinged, leg will be too long and will need to be cut, so fold it back until the rest of the stairway is in the fully opened up position.

▶ Measure from each leg to the floor. Use an adjustable T-bevel to find and hold the angle from the ladder to the floor (Photo 8).

▶ Mark that distance along the bottom, hinged, leg. Then transfer the angle to the legs with the T-bevel and cut off the excess from the legs (Photo 9). If a tread is in the way, remove it. The bottom of the ladder must make solid contact with the floor to avoid strain on the hinges.

Photo 6. Position the completely assembled new stairway, as it came from the factory, into the rough opening. Screw temporary cleats to the new framing to help hold the unit in place as you work.

Photo 7. Shim the frame until it's square with the opening, drill pilot holes through the points indicated in the fastening hardware, and drive screws through the frame and shims into the new framing.

Photo 8. Fully extend the stairway. Measure along each leg of the ladder to the floor in case the floor is slightly irregular. Use an adjustable T-bevel to mark the angle between the stair legs and the floor.

Photo 9. Transfer the angle from the T-bevel to the legs and cut off the excess. If a stairway tread is in the way of the cut, remove it. The legs must make even contact with the floor to prevent strain on the hinges.

Finishing Touches

To prevent heat loss through the stairway opening, seal the opening, then restore the insulating value of the insulation that was removed to clear the opening.

▶ First, apply self-adhesive weatherseal stripping along the inside edges of the plywood panel where it closes against the stairway opening. Most home centers sell various types of the sort of self-adhesive foam strip insulation needed for this job.

▶ Restore the thermal envelope of the attic by making an insulation box to cover the opening when the stairs are folded up. A frame of light-weight 1/2-inch plywood such as the one shown in the diagram below will be light enough to move aside easily. Cut it to the size of the stairway unit and cover it with 1-1/2 inch polystyrene rigid insulation. Screw sash pulls to the inside of the box to make it easier to move it out of the way as you climb the stairway. Now glue the pieces of foam paneling to each other and to the plywood box with special foam panel adhesive, available at home centers.

▶ Trim the opening of the stairway with door or window casing to match the trim in the rest of the house. Paint the plywood panel on the bottom of the unit and the casing the same color as the ceiling, or else paint the panel and stain the trim. The steps themselves don't need to have a finish.

▶ For convenience and to save on flashlight batteries, install a pull-string light in the attic within easy reach of the opening.

▶ Finally, recognize that folding stairways are steep and are not meant for carrying items as you climb them. Instead, climb the stairs, then have someone below hand boxes and bags up.

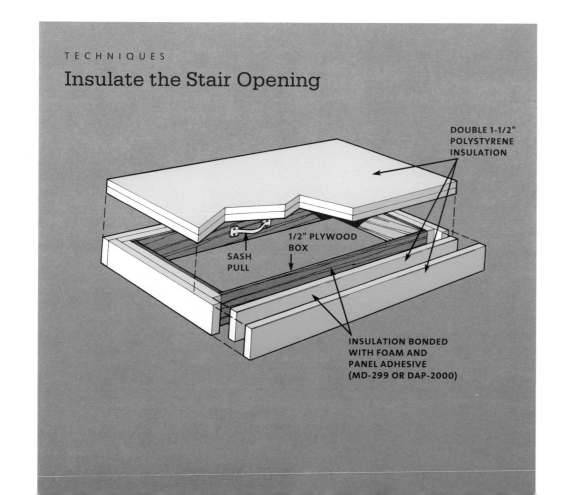

TECHNIQUES
Insulate the Stair Opening

DOUBLE 1-1/2" POLYSTYRENE INSULATION

1/2" PLYWOOD BOX

SASH PULL

INSULATION BONDED WITH FOAM AND PANEL ADHESIVE (MD-299 OR DAP-2000)

Smart Suggestions for Perfect Paneling

The basics of putting up paneling are not difficult. But getting beyond the basics to achieve professional-looking results requires some inside knowledge. Here's a selection of trade secrets.

Hang First Panel Plumb

If the first panel is installed correctly, starting from a corner and with its edge plumb (perfectly vertical), then the rest will follow. Don't rush matters; time spent now means time saved later with the other panels.

Butt the panel into the corner and tack it in place along the upper edge with a paneling nail. Hold a 3- or 4-foot carpenter's level along the panel to make sure the outside edge is plumb (Photo 1). Check the panel at both the top and bottom edges.

If needed, scribe the corner for a tight fit. Once the panel is correctly positioned, drive a nail at the bottom edge to hold it in place.

Scribe for a Tight Fit

Paneling often butts against surfaces that aren't square, such as corners that are out of plumb, resulting in an unsightly gap. Sometimes you can cover the flaw with a piece of molding, but if the gap is too large, using molding becomes impossible.

Tack a panel temporarily in place, making sure that it is perfectly plumb (see Hang Panel One Plumb, left).

Find the widest gap between the panel edge and the surface. Set the legs of a compass slightly wider than this gap. Run the compass down the wall to transfer the contours of the wall onto the panel (Photo 2). A china marker or grease pencil works best for this.

Remove the panel and sand or cut along the scribed line. When cutting, use a fine-tooth saber saw to avoid splintering the panel. The panel should now fit tightly.

HANG FIRST PANEL PLUMB

Photo 1. Use a 3- or 4-ft. carpenter's level to help align the edge of a panel. Check top and bottom edges.

SCRIBE FOR A TIGHT FIT

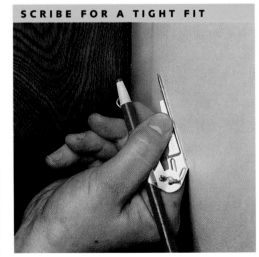

Photo 2. Use a compass with a grease pencil to draw the wall's contours onto the panel. Cut on that line.

Camouflage Gaps

With changes in humidity, paneling can contract, leaving ugly gaps. To prevent openings from showing, paint the wall behind them a color that matches the panel grooves. Prevent shrinking from the start by storing panels in the room where they'll be installed for a few days before you start so they reach the humidity level of the room. Place furring strips between the panels to allow air to circulate.

Lever the Panels

Place a pry bar on a block of wood to act as a lever against the bottom of a panel (Photo 3). This leaves your hands free to nail the panel in place. After lifting the panel, check it for plumb, then tack in a few nails to hold the panel in position so you can remove the jack. Before attaching the panel permanently, check that the top edge fits tightly against the ceiling. If the panel isn't flush there, scribe it as you would an edge, as described in Scribe for a Tight Fit, on page 50.

Use Glue, Not Nails

Mastics hold up panels as well as nails, without making holes. Mastics come in tubes and are applied with a caulking gun. They are easily cleaned with mineral spirits while they are soft.

Apply a 1/8-inch bead of mastic to the wall or furring strips, an inch or two from the panel edges so it won't squeeze out. Make a large X of mastic on the panel back.

Push the panel against the mastic and pound in a few nails along the top edge to hold it. Prop the bottom edge away from the wall (Photo 4).

Once the adhesive is tacky, after about three minutes, push the panel in place. Tap it lightly with a cloth-covered block to set it firmly. Remove the nails at the top.

Install a Drywall Surface

Instead of hanging paneling over bare studs or furring strips on block walls, you can first cover the walls with drywall (Photo 5). It will go up fast; you don't have to tape the joints or cut precisely. Hang 3/8-inch drywall for economy and easier handling:

▶ The wall will be stiffer and more substantial.
▶ You can use mastic to glue down the panels, to avoid exposed nailheads.
▶ The wall will be smoother and flatter. If you plan to use rigid-foam insulation behind the paneling, building codes require that it be covered with drywall as well.

LEVER THE PANELS

Photo 3. Use leverage to lift a panel firmly against the ceiling. Plumb it, tack it in place, then remove the jack.

USE GLUE, NOT NAILS

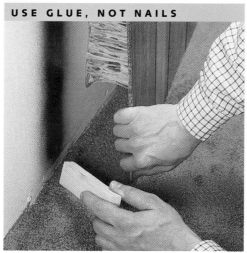

Photo 4. After pressing a panel against the adhesive, prop it away from the wall to allow the mastic to cure.

INSTALL A DRYWALL SURFACE

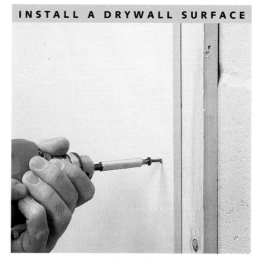

Photo 5. Screw sheets of drywall to furring strips to provide a smooth, flat, solid base for wood panels.

Fill Nail Holes in Trim

The trick to making nail holes invisible is to fill them after you stain and varnish the wood, not before. If you fill the holes before staining, the putty will take the stain differently from the wood, causing the filled hole to stand out. Wood-filling putty comes in many shades; you should be able to find one that closely matches your wood's color (Photo 6). Another trick is to try to nail within the darker lines of the grain, where the nailheads will be less noticeable.

Use the Right Boxes

When running new wiring between furring strips, look for special electrical boxes shallow enough for use under paneling (Photo 7). These 1-inch-deep boxes are designed to fit the common combined depth of 3/4-inch furring strips and 1/4-inch paneling. You must install outlets and switches that are designed to be used with these shallow boxes.

Be careful not to overfill these boxes. The National Electrical Code fixes a limit on the number of wires, connectors, and devices that can safely be put in any such box, and these shallow boxes don't have a lot of room. Consult your local building inspector if you are in doubt.

If you are running ordinary nonmetallic Romex or NM-B cable and it passes through notches in the furring strips, nail a protective metal plate to the strip to guard the wire against nails that might be driven through the wall in the future.

Use Box Extenders

Paneling can burn, so it must be shielded from sparks that might fly from a defective switch, outlet, or faulty wiring. The National Electrical Code requires that you shield paneling with a box extender, which is a metal collar that slips over the outlet or switch and inside the outlet box (Photo 8).

FILL NAIL HOLES IN TRIM

Photo 6. Stain or varnish wood trim before filling nail holes. Then select wood putty of the same color as the finished wood to disguise the nail holes.

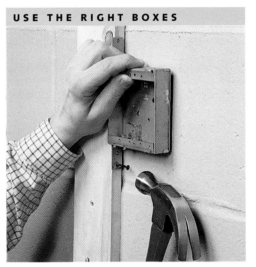

USE THE RIGHT BOXES

Photo 7. Use specially designed 1-in. deep electrical boxes in the narrow spaces between wall and paneling. They require their own fittings.

USE BOX EXTENDERS

Photo 8. Install metal box extenders to hold electrical fixtures away from wood paneling and reduce fire hazards. Such extenders are required by code.

Smart Suggestions for Papering Walls

Hanging wallpaper has become one of the most popular do-it-yourself projects, removed now from the realm of specialists. But here are some tricks and tools from professional paperhangers that will make your wallpaper hang—and look—smoother.

Prepare the Walls

Proper preparation prevents poor performance. While this is true anywhere, it is especially true when wallpapering. Preparing the walls with undercoating, called sizing, is the first task in a good wallpapering job. Consider also a combination primer-sizer, sometimes referred to as a universal primer-sealer. Read the label carefully and consult a knowledgeable salesperson before using one of these for your project.

Sizing performs three important functions:

▶ It acts as a sealer, preventing the wallpaper paste from soaking into drywall or plaster, keeping it on the wall surface where it can do its job.

▶ It makes the walls slightly tacky, to add to the paste's holding power.

▶ It allows you to remove the wallcovering easily later if you need to strip it off and apply a different paper.

Before papering a painted wall, roll on a single coat of sizing. Then, with a brush, cut in close to moldings and ceilings, which are the areas that need sizing the most, since wallpaper tends to start loosening and curling along these edges if it's going to do so at all (Photo 1). If you are papering over existing wallpaper—do so only if the existing wallpaper is smooth and intact—roll on two coats of an oil-base primer, then a coat of sizing. If you will be papering over new drywall or an old wall with large patches of spackling compound, apply one coat of oil-base primer, then sizing.

Sizing is available premixed or powdered. It usually dries clear. Wait the length of time stated by the manufacturer, usually overnight, before hanging wallpaper over the sizing.

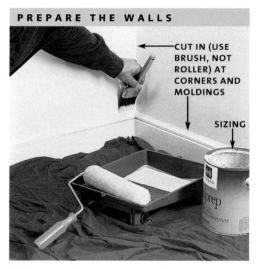

PREPARE THE WALLS

CUT IN (USE BRUSH, NOT ROLLER) AT CORNERS AND MOLDINGS

SIZING

Photo 1. Apply sizing, using a brush to cut in along moldings, corners, and ceilings. Use a roller for the rest of the wall.

Disguise White Edges

When wallpaper is cut to width at the factory, a thin line of the white backing sometimes remains along the front edge. These long white lines ruin the look of a papered wall, especially if the paper has a dark background.

▶ To avoid having to touch up every seam after the paper is hung, quickly and lightly run a marking pen close in color to the background of the paper around both ends of the rolled-up wallpaper before hanging it (Photo 2).

▶ When applying primer to the wall, minimize seam visibility by tinting the primer a color that is close to that of the wallpaper.

▶ If a few seams still remain visible after the paper is hung, use crayons, watercolors, pencils, paint, or eyeliner as touch-up tools after the paper has dried. Experiment first on a scrap piece of wallpaper to find the right color or combination of colors.

Apply Paste Activator

Today, many wallpapers, known as prepasted papers, come from the factory with the paste already applied to their backs. This paste has to be wetted down before hanging the rolls. Paste activators tend to increase the stickiness of the paste, minimizing adhesion problems and seam separations. Paste activators cost more than plain water, of course, but they're especially valuable for beginners, who tend to overhandle the paper and rub the glue off its edges.

Activators are a bit messy, so special steps are called for when applying them. Never use activators in water trays—the rectangular pans used to submerge prepasted papers completely—because they can leave a clear, glossy coat on the surface of the paper. And when you are using an activator, take extra care to wipe down the seams of the installed paper with a sponge and clean water.

Here are some pointers on working with wallpaper paste activators.

▶ Keep one edge of the paper flush with the edge of the table (Photo 3). This prevents activator from getting on the table surface, which would then rub off on the face of the next roll of paper. Also, keeping the paper aligned with the edge of the table provides a firm surface below the entire roll, ensuring consistent coverage.

▶ Place the opposite edge on top of your next strip, known as the next drop of wallpaper, to catch any activator that slops over.

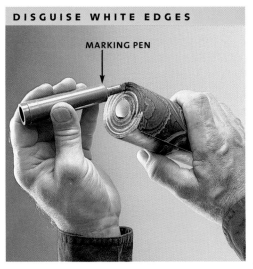

Photo 2. Before installation, use a marking pen or other such tool to color and blend in white edges that may show on the face.

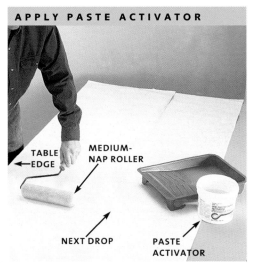

Photo 3. Roll paste activator onto the back of prepasted paper to increase cling and minimize gaps between seams. Keep the table and paper edge flush.

Let the Paper Relax

One of the most important factors in wall-papering is patience. Part of that is simply learning to wait while the paper expands, relaxes, and gets tacky after you moisten the back of the wallpaper.

Folding wallpaper paste side to paste side, called booking, allows the paste to soak into and across the paper evenly. It also provides time for the wallpaper to relax, so that it's easier to handle, and easier to expand to its final dimensions. Prepasted, vinyl-coated papers can grow up to 1/2 inch in width after the backing is completely soaked.

To book wallpaper before you hang it, follow the four steps here.

▶ Fold the paper back onto itself, sticky side to sticky side, from both ends. Make the folds on the ceiling end of the drop longer than the folds at the floor end so you can tell at a glance which end goes up when you start to install the wallpaper (Photo 4).

▶ Follow the manufacturer's recommendation for resting booked papers, which is usually for about 10 to 15 minutes.

▶ Loosely roll each drop and place it inside its own plastic bag. The watertight interior will provide a moist environment for the paste and prevent the edges from drying out.

▶ Try to establish a rhythm, keeping one drop booked as you hang the preceding one.

Align the Seams' Edges

Do not simply slap an entire drop against the wall, then try to push and shove the seams together. This can stretch the paper, resulting in open seams as the paper dries and then regains its shape. Instead, unfold only the top part of the drop and leave the bottom half still booked, so that it's less likely to grab the wall.

▶ Start installing the drop about a foot from the ceiling, laying it seam to seam with the previous drop as much as possible. Hold the other edge of the paper away from the wall so that it doesn't grab the wall.

▶ Match the pattern at eye level, where it's most noticeable (Photo 5). Work the seam of the drop down the wall as far as you can reach, then use a smoother to flatten the paper across the width of the upper part of the drop.

▶ Unbook the bottom of the paper and repeat the procedure.

▶ If you get off track or create a large crease, pull the entire drop away from the wall and start over. You can remove and reposition a given drop two or three times before its paste starts to lose its stickiness. If the back side appears to be drying out, rewet it with paste activator and try again.

LET THE PAPER RELAX

LARGE FOLD AT TOP

DROP ⟶ BOOKING IN PLASTIC BAG

Photo 4. Book the wallpaper, folding it paste side to paste side, then roll it up and set it aside in a plastic bag for about 10 minutes to expand and relax.

ALIGN THE SEAMS' EDGES

HOLD THIS EDGE AWAY FROM WALL

MATCH PATTERN AT NORMAL EYE LEVEL

Photo 5. Install the paper seam to seam while holding the other edge away from the wall. Match the pattern exactly at eye level for the best fit.

Roll the Seams

Resist the temptation to roll the seams too hard, too many times, too quickly after the paper has been installed. Wait until the paste has had a chance to set up and get tacky, say about 30 to 45 minutes, then roll the seam lightly, only once. Rolling too vigorously results in a visible sheen or roller mark that is especially noticeable on vinyl-covered papers. And rolling too soon forces wet paste out and away from the back edge of the paper.

If a seam needs to be adjusted slightly, use a lightly dampened sponge—instead of your fingers—to adjust it, before rolling the joint (Photo 6). The sponge prevents fingerprints or indentations and helps distribute the pressure over a wider area.

Use a Broad Knife and Sharp Blades

For crisp, straight cuts when trimming wallpaper, cut against sharp, straight surfaces. A drywalling broad knife and a utility knife with snap-off blades are ideal for papering projects.

▶ Remove paint blobs along door and window moldings and the caulk along baseboards. Use a scraper or sandpaper to even out rough areas along woodwork. With a broad knife turned at an angle, scrape and remove material from a 1/8-inch wide line along the corner of a textured ceiling before installing wallpaper right up to the ceiling (Photo 7).

▶ Dull the sharp edge of a 5- or 6-inch broad knife with sandpaper to prevent it from tearing into the wallpaper.

▶ Press the blade into the corner between a wall and the ceiling (or between a wall and door trim, window trim, and so forth) to keep the wallpaper from lifting and tearing and to provide a straight guide for the cut (Photo 8). Cut along the width of the broad knife. Then, without moving the cutting blade, leapfrog the broad knife ahead and continue the cut. Don't press so hard that you cut through the underlying drywall tape.

▶ Keep a sharp blade in the utility knife at all times. If you wait for the point to become dull, it will shred the paper instead of cutting it. Snap off the blade and push a fresh, sharp one forward. Don't be surprised if you find yourself changing blades a dozen times while papering just a single room.

ROLL THE SEAMS

PUSH SEAM TIGHT WITH DAMP SPONGE

Photo 6. Roll the seam just once, lightly, after the paste has had time to set up. Use a sponge to make minor adjustments to seams.

USE A BROAD KNIFE AND SHARP BLADES

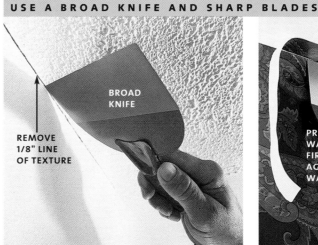

BROAD KNIFE

REMOVE 1/8" LINE OF TEXTURE

Photo 7. Scrape away ceiling texture for 1/8-in. from the corner. Also remove paint and caulk with a broad knife or sandpaper.

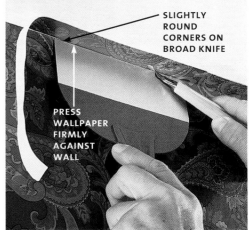

SLIGHTLY ROUND CORNERS ON BROAD KNIFE

PRESS WALLPAPER FIRMLY AGAINST WALL

Photo 8. Make crisp cuts by creasing the wallpaper against the ceiling or moldings, then cutting along a broad knife with a sharp razor knife.

Overlap the Corners for a Neater Look

You will rarely find walls with perfectly square inside corners, even in new construction. The underlying 2x4 studs can be bowed or crooked, the walls themselves might not be perfectly plumb, and the drywall or plaster materials may dip and bulge.

To compensate for all these potential problems, install the wallpaper in two pieces for tighter, neater-looking inside corners. (This technique works equally well for outside corners, although the paper actually pulls an outside corner tighter as it shrinks.) Using two drops to turn an inside corner serves several purposes. For one, it lets you establish a fresh, plumb starting line for the next stretch of wallpaper after turning a corner. And because wallpaper shrinks as it dries, this technique prevents a large piece from pulling away from the corner days or weeks later. Detached, peeling corners not only look unsightly but are easily torn by even a slight nudge from furniture or people.

▷ Measure in three places from the edge of the last full-width drop to the corner (Photo 9). Then cut the paper for the last drop 1/8 inch wider than the largest of these measurements, using a 4-foot straightedge or level as a guide for the razor knife (Photo 10).

▷ Now hang this first piece, wrapping the approximately 1/8-inch excess (it will be more in some places) around the corner. Press the paper firmly into the corner, slitting it for a tight fit where it laps against the ceiling and baseboard.

▷ Measure the width of the remaining half of the drop you just cut, then draw a plumb line on the adjacent wall that distance from the corner.

▷ Install this second piece, matching the pattern in the corner and laying the other edge exactly on the plumb line (Photo 11).

▷ Finally, run a small bead of vinyl seam adhesive at the corner to secure the overlap if it's necessary, especially if you are using solid vinyl papers, which cannot stick to each other without the adhesive.

OVERLAP THE CORNERS FOR A NEATER LOOK

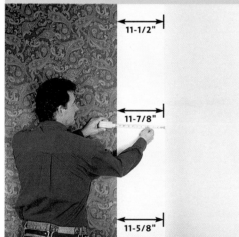

Photo 9. Measure from the edge of the last drop over to the corner in three different places, to allow for the variances that exist even in new construction.

Photo 10. Cut a drop of booked wallpaper 1/8 in. wider than the largest measurement you just took. Use a 4-ft. straightedge or level.

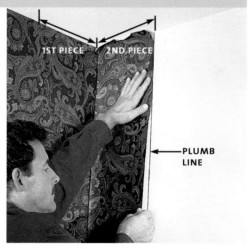

Photo 11. Overlap the seams at the corner and line up the edge of the second piece with the plumb line. Apply adhesive to secure the overlap as needed.

Paper-Over Fixture Covers

A great wallpaper job looks even better when you paper-over the plastic switch plates and outlet covers in the room.

▶ Turn off the electricity at the main circuit panel or fuse box whenever you are working around an outlet or switch. Water, metal tools, and electricity don't go together. Leave a note on the panel so that no one will turn the power back on inadvertently while you're working. (See "Is the Power Really Off?," page 112.)

▶ Once the power is off, remove the plate you want to cover, wash it in warm, soapy water to remove dirt and oils, and after it dries lightly scuff its face with extra-fine sandpaper. Brush on a coat of sizing and let it dry overnight.

▶ Hold the plate in place against the wall. Make a light mark on it to indicate the position of an easily matched part of the pattern. Hold a scrap of wallpaper over the plate to test whether you can match the pattern against the wall and still have enough paper left to overlap the plate (Photo 12). If so, carefully trim this scrap so it overlaps the plate by about an inch on each side.

▶ Activate the paste on the scrap, then place it over the plate again, taking care to match the pattern on the scrap precisely where you marked the plate. Hold the paper in that exact position and carefully remove the cover and paper from the wall.

▶ Double-check the pattern match against the mark on the plate, then cut the corners at a 45-degree angle. Crease and fold the paper along the back of the plate (Photo 13). Hold the edges down with a thin bead of seam adhesive.

▶ Trim the switch or outlet opening after the wallpaper has dried (Photo 14). Use the cutouts in the plate to guide the razor knife.

PAPER-OVER FIXTURE COVERS

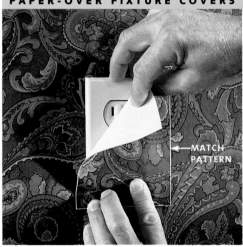

Photo 12. Match the pattern of a wallpaper scrap with that of the surrounding wall. Wet and position the scrap. Gently remove the wallpaper and plate.

Photo 13. Cut the corners first for crisper folds, then bend the edges around the back of the plate and secure them with seam adhesive.

Photo 14. Cut out and remove the excess wallpaper with a razor knife, using the openings in the wall plate to guide the blades.

Leave Pieces Loose for Fine-Tuning

The wider a window is, the more difficult it is to make the pattern and seams line up by the time you reach the far side. However, if you position the last two or three pieces loosely, you can make adjustments on two or more pieces while lining up the pattern and widths exactly. Be sure to book the individual pieces for equal lengths of time so that the pieces will expand to the same widths.

▷ Install the side piece numbered 1 in the accompanying photo, then the upper pieces 2 and 3 (Photo 15). Trim them along the ceiling and moldings, then roll the seams.

▷ Using an easily recognizable part of the pattern as a starting point, draw a horizontal line under the window with a 4-foot level.

▷ Now install piece 4, lining up the pattern along this horizontal line.

▷ Lightly position pieces 5 and 6. Then, using the horizontal line as a guide, adjust these pieces until their patterns match and the seams fit tightly without gaps or an overlap.

▷ Finally, once the patterns and widths are aligned, finish smoothing out and trimming pieces 5 and 6.

LEAVE PIECES LOOSE FOR FINE-TUNING

HORIZONTAL LINE FOR PATTERN MATCH

LEAVE THESE LOOSE FOR ADJUSTING

Photo 15. Adjust pieces 5 and 6 before installing and trimming them once and for all. The horizontal line acts as a guide to keep the pattern lined up.

Revive Interior Woodwork

Tools You Need
Brushes
Cotton rags
Drop cloths
Sanding sponges

Materials
Mineral spirits
Varnish
Wood putty

Before stripping and refinishing natural woodwork, take a closer look: you may be able to revive it instead. Mineral spirits and new varnish can clean and brighten wood at a fraction of the cost, time, and mess of having to strip it.

Ready to revive

CHECKING AND BUBBLING

Ready to strip

Sizing Up the Project
This project requires only some elbow grease and a few simple tools. Essentially, it involves cleaning the wood with mineral spirits and roughening up the surface of the old finish so it will accept a new coat of varnish.

Evaluate the Condition of the Woodwork
Most woodwork is finished in either varnish or polyurethane. Mineral spirits will have no effect on polyurethane, but if your woodwork has a varnish finish and is in generally good condition, it's a likely candidate for reviving.

Compare the woodwork to the photos at left.

▶ If the finish looks like the surface in the top photo—dark, maybe, but no major flaws—the woodwork is a candidate for easy cleaning and lightening with mineral spirits.

▶ If the finish looks more like that in the bottom photo—with checked, alligatored, or bubbling deterioration—it's beyond reviving. You have no choice but to strip off the old finish entirely and apply a new one.

The Process of Revival
Before you do any work, test the process in an obscure area. If you don't like the results, stop and consider alternatives such as stripping and refinishing. Divide the work into manageable sections like one room at a time. Be sure to follow the safety procedures outlined in the Techniques box on the facing page.

▶ Protect the floor and furniture with drop cloths, which are cheap. Do not try to cut corners in time or expense in such matters.

▶ Use a sanding sponge, which works best because it cleans and sands at the same time. And, because the sponge conforms to the contours of the wood, you can clean detailing without a host of other specialized tools (Photo 1). For particularly fine detailing, use a stiff-bristle toothbrush dipped in mineral spirits.

▶ Do not scrub woodwork too hard with the sanding sponge. Apply just enough pressure to degrease and scuff the finish so it will accept a new coat of varnish. Too much pressure will remove the finish down into the stain, causing the wood to look blotchy. Then you'll have to restain the light areas to match the rest of the finish.

Photo 1. Scrub the surface of the trim with a sanding sponge dipped in mineral spirits. Do not press too hard, to avoid sanding all the way through the finish.

Photo 2. Wipe down the surface to remove residue, using a clean cotton rag soaked in mineral spirits. Let the surface dry before you do the final finishing.

Photo 3. Stain spots where the finish is worn away. Use oil-base stains, blending them for an exact color match. Let the stain dry thoroughly before varnishing.

Photo 4. With a sash brush, apply two coats of an oil-base varnish so it's compatible with the original finish. Let each coat dry completely; sand between coats.

▶ Wipe away residue with a clean cotton rag and mineral spirits (Photo 2). Let the surface dry before proceeding.

▶ If you do have to spot-stain some areas, you may need to blend stains to get a good color match (Photo 3). If possible, remove a small section of the trim to take to a paint store and buy a custom-blended stain that matches closely. Otherwise, blend your own. Buy a few cans in colors that match the woodwork as closely as possible, making sure they are all from the same manufacturer, and mix them. Experiment in an out-of-the-way area.

▶ Before varnishing, fill any small holes in the trim with wood putty that is colored to match as closely as possible.

▶ Brush on two coats of an oil-base varnish for the finish coats, letting the first coat dry completely and then sanding lightly between coats (Photo 4).

TECHNIQUES

Working Safely with Mineral Spirits

As effective as mineral spirits may be on old woodwork, it is a flammable, toxic solvent that must be handled with great care. Follow the manufacturer's instructions for its use, and observe the following safety precautions.

▶ Ventilate the work area well, preferably with a door open at one end of the room and an exhaust fan in a window to draw air through and out of the room.

▶ Don't smoke, and turn off all pilot lights and flames throughout the house.

▶ Wear polyvinyl alcohol or neoprene rubber gloves, goggles, long pants, and a long-sleeved shirt.

▶ For added protection, wear a good-fitting organic vapor respirator approved by the National Institute for Occupational Safety and Health (NIOSH). Be aware that there are some health risks associated with wearing a respirator, so secure your doctor's okay before using one.

▶ If you spill the container of mineral spirits, turn off the fan and call the fire department at once. Vapors from a 1-gallon spill can be dangerous.

▶ Spread out rags and sponges soaked with mineral spirits to dry outside, away from children, pets, and flames. Once they have dried thoroughly, toss them out with the garbage.

Lay Carpet Like a Pro

Soft underfoot, plush, colorful—carpet is all these things. Putting it down was once a job best reserved for the pros, but with the techniques shown here you can now achieve professional-looking results on your own.

Sizing Up the Project

Shown here is laying, stretching, and seaming jute-backed carpet in a medium-sized room. If you're a beginner, start with a room less than 12 feet in width. Because most carpet comes in 12-foot widths, this eliminates seaming long pieces of carpet. Not covered here are carpeting stairs and oversized rooms or how to install glued-down carpet, or the more difficult laying of Berber carpets. Stay away from Berber carpet for your first project—it's tough to stretch, seam, and match patterns in it.

Before You Begin

Accurate measurements are key to successfully carrying out this project.

▶ Measure along each wall, including inside closets, then sketch the room on graph paper, showing each dimension. Plan so that transitions from one type of flooring to another, whether from one color of carpet to a different one or from carpet to wood or tile, fall under a closed door. Include these small carpet outcroppings in the plan. Add 3 inches in every direction to allow enough carpet to cut and tuck.

The actual dimensions of a 12-foot wide roll of carpet can range from 11 feet 10 inches to 12 feet 2 inches. If the room is up to 11 feet wide by 13 feet 6 inches long, you're safe ordering a 12- by 14-foot piece of carpet. But if you have a room wider than 12 feet in both directions, you'll have to seam pieces together or order carpet in the less common 15-foot width. If you're a beginner, go with the 15-foot size rather than attempting a long seam that would be visible in the open part of a room. If not done right, this seam may bulge up or separate.

Besides carpet, there are some other supplies to buy at this stage.

▶ Order the equivalent amount of carpet padding to cushion the carpet from compression against the hard flooring below.

▶ Purchase enough tackless strips to go around the perimeter of the room. These strips hold the carpet taut against the walls. (The term "tackless" is misleading. The strips are nailed to the floor, and plenty of tacklike points stick out of these strips. The term comes from the fact that these strips allow you to secure carpet to the floor without driving tacks through the carpet, as was once done.)

▶ Secure tackless strips to concrete floors with masonry nails. For added strength, run onto the bottom of each strip a bead of construction adhesive or an adhesive designed specifically for securing tackless strips to concrete. Use drywall screws or nails to fasten the strips to a wood floor.

Prepare the Floor

First, remove doors from their hinges, and take up heating registers from the floor. Refasten squeaky floor boards or plywood with drywall screws driven into the floor joists (Photo 1).

▶ Nail tackless strips fingertip distance (1/4 to 3/8 inch) from the wall or molding, with the pins leaning toward the wall (Photos 2 and 3). Add drywall nails to the strips so that short strips are secured by at least two nails to prevent twisting. In long pieces, drive a nail in each end as well as one in the middle. Follow the contours of the walls closely, even around the floor tracks of bifold closet doors.

▶ Position the first length of carpet pad with one edge flush against a tackless strip. Place the scrim, or smooth side, up so that the carpet can slide over it during installation.

▶ Secure the padding around the perimeter of the room with staples every 4 inches. Use the tackless strip as a guide to cut the pad length-wise (Photo 4). Butt the edges of subsequent lengths of padding, then staple and trim them.

▶ Over a concrete floor attach sections of carpet padding to one another with duct tape along the underside. Secure padding to the floor at the perimeter with double-faced tape.

Photo 1. Remove doors from their hinges and refasten squeaky areas of the floor with drywall screws. Then sketch the room on graph paper to determine the amount of carpet to order.

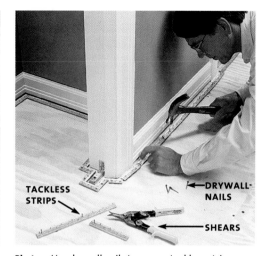

Photo 2. Use drywall nails to secure tackless strips around the perimeter of the room fingertip distance (1/4 to 3/8 in.) from the wall. Cut strips with shears. Drive extra nails into short pieces so each has two.

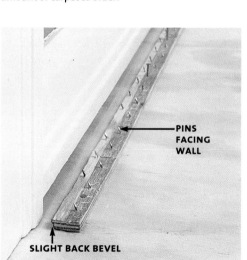

Photo 3. Face tackless strips so the pins angle toward the wall. A slight back bevel increases the carpet's grip after it is tucked between the baseboard and strip.

Photo 4. Install carpet pad with the smooth side up. Use the edge of the tackless strip as a cutting guide. Staple the pad every 4 in. along walls and seams.

Tools You Need

Carpet knife or trimming tool (rented)

4-ft. straightedge

Hammer

Linoleum tool

Power stretcher, extension tubes (rented)

Seaming iron (rented)

Staple gun, staples

Tape measure

Knee kicker (rented)

Materials

Carpet

Carpet padding

Drywall screws and nails (wood flooring)

Tackless strips (wood flooring)

Masonry nails (concrete flooring)

Construction adhesive (concrete flooring)

Duct tape, double-faced tape (concrete flooring)

Metal or wood transition strips

Seaming tape

Cut and Fit the Carpet

If the new carpet is more than 2 feet wider than the room, rough-cut it to size outdoors or in a large area before bringing it into the room in which it is to be installed. How you cut the carpet will depend upon how it has been made.

Cutting Carpet

▶ Always trim cut-pile carpet—the kind with individual tufts—from the back side.
▶ Cut carpet with loops, called loop-pile carpet, from the front, to make sure all the loops are sliced across a cut. Trim the carpet so at least 1-1/2 inches will lap up each wall.

Making a Seam

Making a short seam, like one inside a closet, should be manageable for a beginner. However, attempting anything more visible on the first try could prove an expensive lesson. Practice making seams on carpet scraps first.

▶ Edges to be joined at a seam must be cut perfectly straight. Use a 4-foot straightedge and a sharp carpet knife to do this (Photo 5). Carpet that comes directly from the factory rarely has straight edges.
▶ Rough-cut the closet piece to size, making sure the carpet pile leans in the same direction as the room carpet. Seaming a small piece is best done outside the closet. This not only leaves room to work but avoids the problem of starting and ending with the seaming iron up against a wall or door jamb.
▶ Butt the two straight edges together. Then check that the backings fit together tightly along their entire length.
▶ Cut seaming tape the length of the seam, then center the tape beneath the joint (Photo 6).

▶ Warm up the seaming iron (see the box Tools of the Trade on page 66) for 5 to 10 minutes, then set it on top of the tape and under the carpet at one end of the seam. Wait 15 to 20 seconds or until the glue on the tape melts, then slide the iron forward for about one length of the iron (Photo 7).
▶ Inspect the tape to make sure the glue has in fact melted as you embed the two halves into the glue. Don't touch the tape or iron—they're hot! You have only about 20 seconds before the glue hardens to adjust the pieces and push the halves together.
▶ Press down the carpet behind the iron as you move down the seam. Slide a large, flat weight such as a toolbox tray over the area just joined to hold the seam flat.

CUT AND FIT THE CARPET

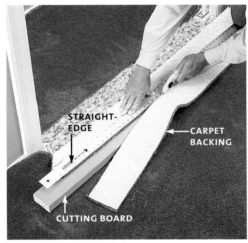

Photo 5. Cut and fit the carpeting, allowing about 1-1/2 in. of excess to lap up the walls. Evenly cut the edges of the carpet that are to be seamed together.

Photo 6. Position and center seaming tape under the edges to be joined. These pieces were temporarily removed from the closet for easier seaming.

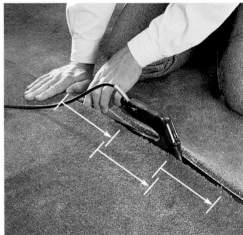

Photo 7. Melt the carpet edges together. Let the iron rest 15–20 seconds, then slide it forward an iron length. While the glue is hot, press the backing down.

Sequential Plan for Stretching Carpet

Stretch away from trouble like doorways and other openings by starting here at the entry door corner (AB) and finishing in corner CD diagonally across from it.

1 Set the carpet onto the tackless strips in corner AB at the bottom left.

2 Position the stretcher with its heel at Wall A and head near corner BC, adding extension tubes as needed to reach within 4 inches of Wall C.

3 Work back along Wall B pressing the carpet onto the tack strip as you go.

4 Stretch across to the opposite wall (D).

5 Use the knee kicker to bump the carpet into the back, sides, and front of the closet.

6 Working perpendicular to stretch 4, finish Wall D.

7 At 90° to the last stretch, finish the last wall (C).

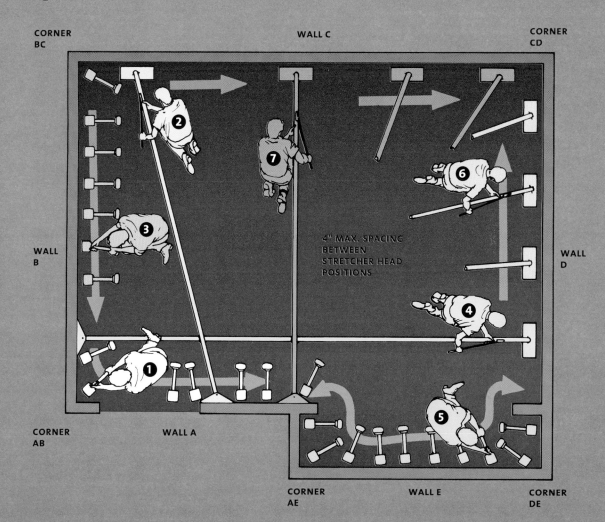

Tools of the Trade

In addition to a hammer, straightedge, and other ordinary hand tools, professional carpet installers use the specialized tools shown below to obtain top-quality results. You can, and should, use these tools, too. A seaming iron melts glue on the seaming tape when joining edges of carpet; a trimming tool, once mastered, is a faster, more accurate substitute for a carpet knife; a power stretcher and extension tubes are used between tackless strips; a stair tool can be used in place of a hammer head for setting carpet backing onto tackless strip pins; a knee kicker is used for bumping and tightening carpet onto tackless strips or stretching carpet in confined spaces.

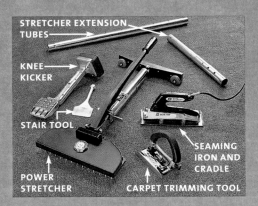

STRETCHER EXTENSION TUBES

KNEE KICKER

STAIR TOOL

POWER STRETCHER

SEAMING IRON AND CRADLE

CARPET TRIMMING TOOL

Stretch and Fasten the Carpet

If you don't stretch the carpet, it will eventually stretch on its own, resulting in a carpet that wears out quickly and is full of dangerous, unsightly humps.

The trick is to "stretch away from trouble," that is, away from doorways, stairways, free-standing radiators, and other obstacles. In the room shown here and in the Sequential Plan for Stretching Carpet on the previous page, this meant starting at the entry door corner and finishing in the corner diagonally across from it.

Make relief cuts in the corners and around openings so the carpet can lie flat and conform to the floor and wall. Let enough carpet extend into the doorways so that seams or transitions will be under the doors. Go ahead now and lay the carpet over heating registers, then use a carpet knife later to cut out the opening.

Making the First Stretch

▶ With a hammer head, press the carpet backing onto a tackless strip 5 feet in each direction from the doorway (Photo 8) . Press hard; you'll feel and hear the carpet backing pop onto the tackless strip pins. Pound over the pins that are in the doorway.

▶ Position the power stretcher with its heel a few feet away from the door and the head angling into the adjacent corner (Photo 9). Add and adjust extension tubes so that when the stretcher handle is halfway down the head is 4 inches from the wall.

▶ Press down firmly on the handle; don't throw your weight against it, but don't push so softly that it just flops down, either. You should see the carpet stretch about 1/2 inch.

▶ With a hammer, set the backing over the tackless strip pins directly in front of the stretcher head.

▶ Use the knee kicker (see the box at left) to bump the carpet lightly so it catches on the tackless strip along Wall B (see the diagram on the previous page) parallel to the stretcher pole (Photo 10). Always use a hammer to press the carpet backing onto the pins.

Stretching Around the Room

Follow the order shown in the Sequential Plan for Stretching Carpet (page 65) to complete the carpeting of the room. Stretch the carpet perpendicular to the first stretch and press it onto the tackless strip. Then use the knee kicker to bump the carpet into the back of the closet and into the sides and front.

▶ Once the carpet has been secured along walls A, B, and E, use the power stretcher, positioned first straight on and then at angles, to stretch and set the carpet at the remaining walls, D and C.

▶ Reposition the stretcher often; never leave more than a 4-inch gap between stretcher head positions. The final stretch will be at the corner diagonally across from where you started.

Trimming, Tucking, and Transitions

The key to easy, clean trimming is to have a sharp knife. You can use a utility knife, but a carpet knife, available where you buy the carpet, will be best for the job.

▶ Trim the carpet around the perimeter of the room, leaving exactly 1/4 inch excess (Photo 11). Cut less and the edges will show, leave more and there may be a hump when tucking the carpet under the baseboard. Also, shaving off just a little bit more is tough and time consuming. Use a carpet knife like that shown here or, better, a trimming tool (see Tools of the Trade on the facing page).

▶ Tuck the carpet between the tackless strip and the baseboard molding, using the back of a linoleum knife (Photo 12).

▶ Finally, where carpet meets vinyl or tile, use metal transition strips (available at most home centers or flooring stores) to cover the joint. Where carpet meets wood, use metal or wood transition pieces as you like.

Photo 8. Press carpet backing onto tackless strips by rubbing it hard with a hammer head. Do this for 5 ft. in each direction from Corner AB (see the bottom left corner of the diagram on page 65).

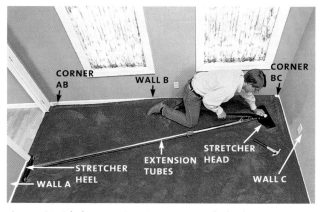

Photo 9. Stretch the carpet into Corner BC. Set the heel against the molding (Wall A), the head 4 in. from the opposite wall. Press the handle until the carpet is taut. With a hammer head, set the carpet onto pins.

Photo 10. With a knee kicker, gently bump carpet onto the tackless strip along Wall B. Continue stretching, bumping, and setting the backing in the order shown on page 65.

Photo 11. Trim the carpet from the back side, allowing exactly 1/4 in. to run up the baseboard. A trimming tool (page 66) does a better job than the carpet knife shown here.

Photo 12. Neatly tuck the carpet into the space between the baseboard and the tackless strip, pressing it down with the curved back edge of a linoleum knife.

enhance home systems

Extend Cable TV to Every Room
Enjoy cable TV in every room, without paying the cable company to install the extensions.
70

Hang a Ceiling Fan
Cool a room economically with a ceiling fan—you won't even need to go into the attic to install it.
74

Cool with a Whole-House Fan
A whole-house fan is great for cooling your house without running the air conditioner.
78

Accent a Room with Track Lighting
New options in track lighting can transform a room.
84

Wire-In Motion Sensor Lights
No more fumbling for keys in the dark with lights that switch on when and where you need them.
108

Install a No-Scald Shower Faucet
Sudden changes in water temperature can be dangerous. Ensure that you aren't burned.
114

Upgrade Your Kitchen Sink and Faucet
Replacing a sink and faucet with bright new fixtures is easy.
120

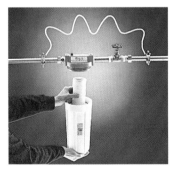

Filter Your Drinking Water
If your water tastes bad or contains lead, put in a filter for tasty, clean water right from the tap.
126

Install a Central Humidifier
A whole-house humidifier improves health and comfort during the dry winter season.
88

Add a Space-Saving Microwave
Gain counter space, ventilate the kitchen, and consolidate your cooking appliances with one unit.
94

Smart Suggestions for Saving Energy
These six conservation ideas will help you save energy and money.
98

Automate Your Garage Door
Once you have an automatic garage door opener, you'll wonder how you lived without it.
102

Simplify Plumbing with a Shutoff Valve
Add a shutoff valve to your system to make future repairs easier.
130

Add an Outdoor Faucet
It's a quick and easy job to add an outdoor water supply closer to where you need it.
132

Extend Cable TV to Every Room

Cable television reception in every room in the house is no pipe dream, and you don't have to wait between 9:00 A.M. and 5:00 P.M. for the cable company's representative to show up to have it installed. With only a small expenditure of money and time, you can watch your favorite shows no matter where you are in the house.

Sizing Up the Project

This project requires no permit, there aren't any building codes to follow, and there's no waiting for an inspector to approve your work. It allows you to have as many cable TV extensions (called legs) in your house as you like, as long as you continue to pay for the basic cable service every month. (In some cable-service areas, premium channels such as HBO and Showtime need a separate signal-decoding box at each TV set.)

The hardest part about adding cable TV extensions is running the cable itself into the rooms. Pulling coaxial cable—a single strand of copper wire wrapped in a plastic sheath (see the diagram on page 73)—through walls can be difficult and frustrating. If possible, drill a hole in the floor and push the cable through from the basement or a crawl space. In some cases it's easier to run the cable along the outside of the house, drill through the siding and interior walls, and pull the cable through. You will need a fish tape and a helper if you choose this route. If you do this, paint the cable to match the house and place a small dab of caulk around the hole where it enters the house.

Before You Begin

Find where the cable service enters your house. This is the best place to add extensions.

In some cases, the connection is located on the outside of the house and comes from an overhead cable similar to an electrical power line. If you do have an overhead cable TV line, be careful as you work—it's usually very close to the power lines to the house. At other times the service will be an underground cable, with the connections either inside or outside the house. If you're not sure which type of service you have, call your cable TV company.

Special Tools and Materials

The tools and materials for this project are available at electronics stores and full-service hardware stores. Before buying the coaxial cable itself, contact your cable TV company to find out what type of cable they use. It's best to use one that is rated the same as theirs, to reduce the chance of reception problems. Most cable TV companies will sell you the cable they use at a reasonable price per foot.

Buy a few extra feet of cable and an extra package of connectors so you can practice stripping the cable and crimping on the connectors a few times before you start the installation.

If you buy screw-on connectors, you won't need to purchase a crimping tool like the one shown in Photo 5 on page 73. The screw-on kind may not hold as well as the crimp-on type, but the crimp-on type can be used only once.

Choose a Hookup Method

The process of adding cable TV branches throughout your home is best approached by first discussing the different types of electronic multiple-TV hookups, and then explaining step by step how to secure the connectors to the various units.

Using Splitters and Amplifiers

A splitter is an electronic device that divides or splits the incoming cable TV signal. The splitter then produces new signals, which are transmitted to the TV sets through the extension cables. The number of signals depends on the type of splitter you use.

Two-, three-, four- and even eight-way splitters are available (Photo 1). Be aware, however, that each time the signal is split there's a possibility that the signal quality will degrade, causing poor cable reception on all the TVs on those lines. As a general rule, the smaller the number of split signals, the better.

▶ If you find that the reception isn't what it used to be after installing a splitter, boost the incoming signal before it's fed into the splitter by installing a signal amplifier. An amplifier requires power from a standard 120-volt household circuit, so install it and the splitter inside the house. The top diagram on the next page shows how to run multiple cable extensions using an amplifier and a four-way splitter.

▶ The amplifier should be rated at 25dB (decibels) and have a bandwidth (the range of TV signal transmissions it can pick up and boost) between 45 and 900 MHz (megaHertz) so that all the channel signals (both UHF and VHF) will be boosted. But if an original incoming signal is bad, installing an amp won't help. Consult your cable service provider if this is the problem.

Using Taps

Rather than splitting a signal, a tap redirects it within the device. The signal then leaves either through the tap's terminal to the first TV or through the out terminal to the next TV (Photo 2). A tap is the best way to send the original cable signal to one or two additional TVs, because it involves the least amount of work while providing excellent reception.

To calculate how many taps to buy, count the number of TV sets to be hooked up and subtract one from the total. That is: two TVs require one tap and three TVs require two taps. The bottom diagram on the next page shows how to hook up multiple TV sets using taps.

There is one drawback to using taps: Most electronics stores don't stock them. You can buy them from electronics parts suppliers that offer mail-order service, but many of these companies have a minimum order amount.

Tools You Need

Cable-stripping tool
Crimping tool
Drill
Fish tape (if necessary)
Screwdrivers

Materials

Coaxial cable connectors
Coaxial shielded CATV cable
Splitters or taps

CHOOSE A HOOKUP METHOD

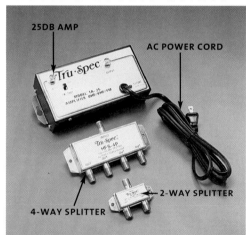

Photo 1. Splitters are available with different numbers of outgoing signal terminals, the most common being 2-way and 4-way. A 120-volt amplifier boosts the signal to compensate for the loss of strength when split.

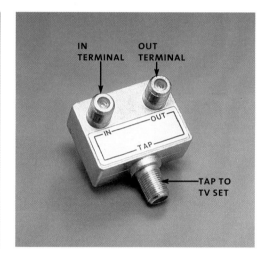

Photo 2. Consider a tap as an alternative to a splitter, especially for just one or two additional sets. It takes the least effort, is the cheapest, and on top of that gives excellent reception.

Hookup Methods for Cable TV Splitters

Amplifier and Four-Way Splitter
This sequence shows how to run multiple cable extensions to an amplifier and a four-way splitter. Install the amp to your standard 120-volt household circuit to boost the incoming reception when it's not up to par after installing a splitter.

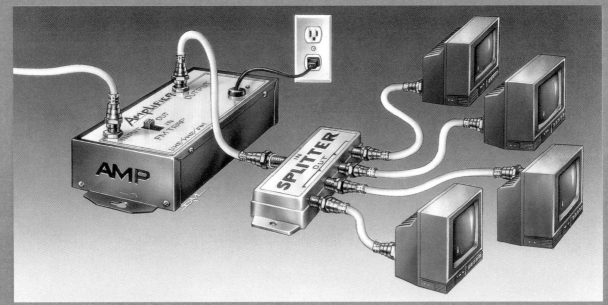

Tap-to-TV Splitter
The best, and cheapest, way to hook up multiple TV sets is to use taps like those shown here. To hook up two TVs, use one tap; three TVs, two taps, and so forth.

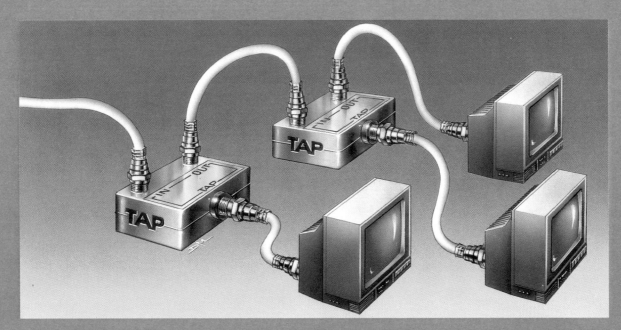

Make Cable Extensions

Work carefully when stripping coaxial cable and securing the connectors.

▶ Be sure not to nick the copper wire in the center of the cable when you strip the plastic sheathing, metal braid, and insulator. Even a slight nick weakens the wire. If the copper wire breaks, redo the connections. The illustration at the right shows how coaxial cable is stripped for use with crimp-on connectors, using a tool like that shown in Photo 3.

▶ Slip on a crimp-on connector (Photo 4). Make sure the connectors are securely crimped onto the cable, but don't squeeze too hard. If you do, you'll crush the cable and ruin the connector. You can tell when the connector is properly crimped and secured when the shape of the crimped connector matches the shape formed by the crimping tool's jaws (Photo 5).

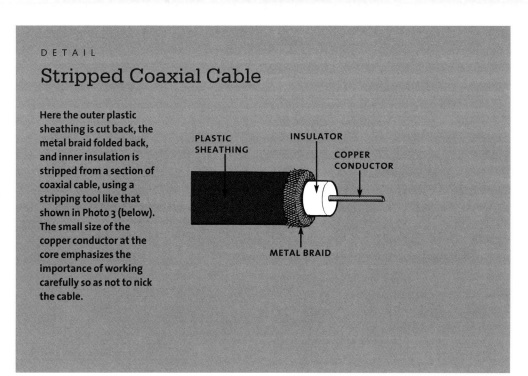

DETAIL

Stripped Coaxial Cable

Here the outer plastic sheathing is cut back, the metal braid folded back, and inner insulation is stripped from a section of coaxial cable, using a stripping tool like that shown in Photo 3 (below). The small size of the copper conductor at the core emphasizes the importance of working carefully so as not to nick the cable.

PLASTIC SHEATHING
INSULATOR
COPPER CONDUCTOR
METAL BRAID

MAKE CABLE EXTENSIONS

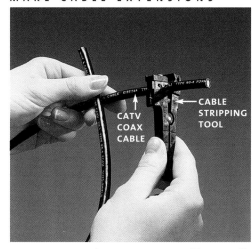

CATV COAX CABLE
CABLE STRIPPING TOOL

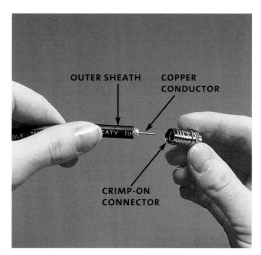

OUTER SHEATH
COPPER CONDUCTOR
CRIMP-ON CONNECTOR

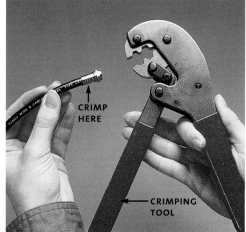

CRIMP HERE
CRIMPING TOOL

Photo 3. To expose the copper wire in a cable, strip off the outer sheathing, braid wrap, and insulator. Don't nick the copper wire. Check the connector's package for the amount of insulator and braid to strip.

Photo 4. Slip a crimp-on connector over the stripped cable. Make sure that the metal braid contacts the connector and the copper wire is long enough to make a good, solid connection.

Photo 5. Crimp the connector onto the cable with a crimping tool. Some connectors require crimping in two places. Don't squeeze too hard; that will crush the cable and ruin the connector.

Hang a Ceiling Fan

Want to add an elegant touch to a room's decor, or keep a hard-to-cool room comfortable without running the air conditioner? Bedroom, kitchen, or family room—any room will be more comfortable and inviting with a ceiling fan.

Sizing Up the Project

The fan shown on these pages is installed using wiring from an existing light fixture. Hanging a fan where there is no fixture involves running new cable to the fan and from the fan to a light switch, steps that are not shown here.

This project involves removing the existing fixture box, mounting a fan-support bracket in the ceiling, and making the necessary wiring connections. There is no need to cut into the ceiling or wall.

Preliminary Considerations

There's a wide selection of styles, colors, and finishes available to fit just about everyone's taste and room decor. Even if you have low ceilings, there are flush-mounted fan models that may still work for your house. (See more about space requirements on the next page.)

The Electrical Code

The National Electrical Code is specific on how a ceiling fan is to be installed. You must not hang a ceiling fan from an existing electrical box, which cannot support the weight. You need to remove the old box and bracket and install a fan-support brace kit, available at hardware stores and home centers. Such a kit can be installed either from above (in the attic) or from below (in the room) without having to cut a new hole in the ceiling. (See Sources, "Ceiling Fan Support Brackets," page 190.)

Switch Loops and Pull Chains

Many wall switches are configured in what's called a switch loop, in which the power from the service panel enters the light fixture and is then channeled down to the wall switch. In such a case the white wire, which is normally neutral, becomes a hot wire from the fixture to the switch. The black wire then carries the current back to the fixture when the switch is on. (Electricians remember this setup with the doggerel line "white down, black back.") In a switch loop, you cannot operate both the fan and its light (if it has one) from the same switch. In such a case, it's often easier to operate the fan with a pull chain.

If you want to operate the fan and an at-tached light using two separate switches, a third wire must be installed from the switch to the fan, a job that's often difficult and may be best left to an electrician.

If the light switch lacks the words "on" and "off" on the toggle, it is either a three-way or a four-way switch, meaning that the fixture is controlled from more than one location. In this case, consult an electrician on the proper way to wire the fan.

Space Requirements
The fan must meet certain space requirements.
▶ There must be at least 24 inches between the fan-blade tips and the nearest wall.
▶ The bottom of the fan (or its light, if there is one) must be at least 7 feet from the floor to allow people to walk under it safely. If some members of your household are taller than average, or if, for instance, you're in the habit of lifting your arm over your head when you put your shirt on in the morning, you may want to consider a higher-mounted fan.
▶ Consider also the effect a fan may have on the look of its room. A large fan will make a small room seem crowded, whereas a small fan in a high-ceilinged room will be not only incon-spicuous but inefficient.

Ceiling fans come in every imaginable configuration: with one globe, like this one, or multiple lights; with full wood blades, as here, or with cane inserts; flush mounted to the ceiling, or with extension tubes like this, for high ceilings.

Tools You Need
Electrician's tape
Hacksaw
Hammer
Screwdrivers
Wire stripper
Wrench

Materials
Cable clamps
Fan-support brace
Plastic or fiberglass electrical box

Hang the Fan

Turn off the power to the circuit before doing any work. Tape a warning sign on the main circuit panel so that no one will turn on the circuit before it is safe to do so.

Caution

Follow the manufacturer's directions carefully when attaching the fan's blades. A fan that is out of balance can spin out of control and become a hazard.

Removing the Old Light Fixture

▶ Take down the old fixture itself.

▶ Put a piece of tape on the incoming hot wire (black) and the outgoing hot line of the switch loop (white). This will help you keep the wires straight when they have to be reconnected later (Photo 1). The incoming white wire is the circuit neutral; the outgoing black wire is the switch return wire.

▶ The green or bare copper ground wires will later be secured together with a pigtail to the fan's grounding points, which are either a wire or a screw.

▶ Now remove the existing metal box, if there is one, by unscrewing the middle screw and fastener (Photo 2). You won't be able to remove the box completely, but pull it down from the ceiling. If the old box is plastic or fiberglass, you can break it apart with pliers or a screwdriver and hammer to remove it. Wear protective glasses while doing so.

▶ Loosen the cable clamp screws and pull the cable out of the clamps. Remove the box.

▶ Cut the old support bracket with a hacksaw and remove it.

Installing the Hanger Brace Bar and Fixture Box

▶ Install the new hanger brace by working it up into the hole and turning it perpendicular to the joists (Photo 3).

▶ Place the feet of the brace on the ceiling and turn the bar, which extends the screw within the bar. Small teeth on the brace ends bite into the joists, creating secure support. Make sure the brace remains centered over the opening.

▶ Feed the cable through the knockouts in the new fixture box and secure it to the box with cable clamps.

▶ Finally, attach the fixture box to the brace, as per the manufacturer's directions (Photo 4).

Mounting the Fan

The various models of ceiling fans are installed using slightly different methods, but most follow the same basic procedures. Most models feature a hanging hook to suspend the fan while you work, leaving both hands free to make wiring connections.

Now refer to the manufacturer's instructions for exactly how to wire the unit. If your home has aluminum wiring, have an electrician who's certified to work with this type of wiring do the entire installation.

▶ Create a ground pigtail from the ground wires in the electrical box ground, then secure it to the ground wire in the fan hanger bracket and to the fan motor ground wire, using plastic wire caps (Photo 5).

▶ Connect the wires according to the manufacturer's directions (Photo 6). Remember, the incoming black is hot, the incoming white neutral. The white leaving the box to the switch becomes hot in a switch loop, and the black that runs from the switch to the fan becomes hot when the switch is on. If the fan has a light, there might also be a red or light-blue wire.

▶ Once you are done, have the finished work inspected by an electrical inspector.

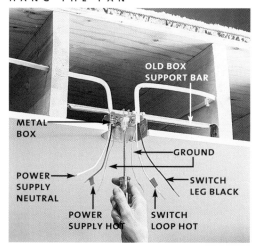

Photo 1. Tape the black wire (incoming hot) and the white wire, which were connected inside the box, to the switch (switch loop hot). These wires deliver power to the wall switch and must be reconnected later.

Photo 2. Remove the old metal ceiling box by unscrewing the center fastener, loosening the cable clamp screws to release the cable, and pulling out the box. Cut off the old support bar with a mini-hacksaw.

Photo 3. Work the hanger brace bar through the ceiling opening. Place the feet of the bar on the ceiling and turn the bar until the legs are secure against the joists. Keep the brace centered over the opening.

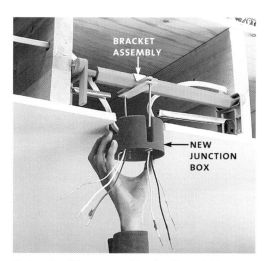

Photo 4. Feed the power cable wires through the knockouts in the box, then secure the cable to the box with the cable clamps. Attach the new junction box to the hanger bracket assembly.

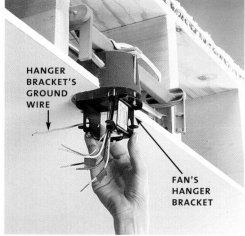

Photo 5. Mount the fan's hanger bracket on the new junction box. Follow the manufacturer's instructions to make the ground connections between the incoming and outgoing cables and the fan hanger bracket.

Photo 6. Make the wiring connections according to the manufacturer's directions, keeping in mind that the white wire between the switch and the fan serves as a hot wire in a switch loop.

Cool with a Whole-House Fan

A whole-house fan is an economical, energy efficient, effective way to keep cool. Except for the hottest, muggiest days of summer, you can keep your house comfortable without running the air conditioner.

Sizing Up the Project

Installing a whole-house fan requires you to cut a hole in the ceiling to accommodate the fan housing. Since you don't need to cut into your home's structural framework, only basic carpentry is required to finish the project. Much of the work is done in the attic, including tapping an electrical source for power. If you are not comfortable with electrical work, hire an electrician to do this portion of the job. Installing a timer or thermostat will require extra wiring. The fan used in this project has two speeds and is operated by a pull chain, although an optional timer is available.

Before You Begin

A whole-house fan is designed to be used when the outside air is cooler than that inside, as for example when entering a stuffy house at the end of a hot day. The fan pulls cooler, outside air in through the windows, which are left open 2 to 3 inches, and draws warm air from the house into the attic, as shown in the schematic on the next page. The warm air in the attic is then exhausted under pressure through soffit, ridge, and gable vents (see "Vent Your Roof the Right Way," page 170).

The fan itself is concealed inside the house, generally in a ceiling, by a louvered panel. The weighted louvers remain closed when the fan is off but are drawn open when it is turned on.

Electrical Considerations

Because this project involves electrical work, consult your local building authorities to determine if a permit is needed. If your house has aluminum wire, detectable by its grayish color, the hookup to the house circuit must be done by a licensed electrician certified to work on aluminum wiring. Always have completed electrical work inspected by an electrical inspector.

Choosing the Size, Capacity, and Location

Whole-house fans, available at home centers, lumberyards, and heating and cooling equipment suppliers, come in different sizes to accommodate rafter or truss framing in the attic. (See "Install Folding Attic Stairs," page 44, for a discussion of attic framing.) These fans are rated by their capacity to move air, measured in cubic feet per minute (cfm).

The fan shown here was designed to be installed over rafters, so it measures 34 by 32 inches, because rafters normally are 16 inches apart, center to center. The fan fits atop three joists with little overlap, which means there's no need to cut into the ceiling joists or rafters, always a tricky and sometimes a dangerous procedure. The fan rests on and is secured to the ceiling joists. (With trusses, which are usually spaced 24 inches apart on center, the fan would be sized accordingly.)

Determining the correct size fan to buy involves only a little basic calculating.
▶ Add up the house's total square footage of living space by multiplying its overall exterior dimensions (length times width) for each floor, not including the basement and attic. (A whole-

house fan won't force cool air down into the basement, which is likely to be cooler than the rest of the house anyway, and it pulls warm air into the attic.) For example, a single-story house that measures 35 by 40 feet contains 1,400 square feet of living area.

▶ Now take this total square footage and multiply it by 3 (1,400 x 3 = 4,200). Such a house needs a fan that can move 4,200 cubic feet of air in one minute (CFM). It will replace the air supply of the whole house in approximately three minutes.

If you live in a warm or very humid climate, multiply the square footage by a factor of 4 instead of 3, as for example 1,400 x 4 = 5,600, and get a fan with a 5,600 cfm rating that will exchange all the air in about 2 minutes.

Working in an Attic

Before you begin the actual work of preparing for and installing the fan, consider some of the conditions that apply to working in that setting.

▶ Provide adequate light. A portable, hanging trouble light, sometimes called a drop lamp, works well.

▶ Place 1 x 12-inch boards across the joists to walk and kneel on. If you slip off the narrow top edge of a ceiling joist, your foot—and maybe the rest of you—will go through the ceiling.

▶ Attics are dusty and dirty. Wear a long-sleeved shirt, gloves, and a dust mask when pulling back insulation.

▶ Keep an eye on the outside temperature. In warm weather, attics get extremely hot very quickly. Take a cool-down break before you suffer heat stroke.

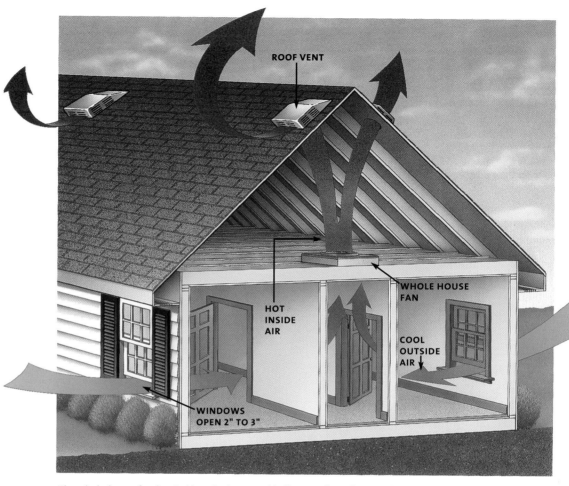

The whole-house fan, located here in the central hallway, pulls cooler outside air in through windows left open 2 to 3 in. and exhausts the warmer house air through roof vents. Such a fan works well on the warm but not sweltering days when it's not necessary or desirable to air condition.

Prepare the Ceiling

For this type of fan to work effectively, it must be centrally installed on the upper level of the house, usually over a hallway leading to the bedrooms. Pinpointing the exact location for the fan will involve some trips between the attic and the house.

Once you've decided where your fan will be, you will need to transfer the location chosen for the fan from inside the hallway to the corresponding point in the attic.

▶ Poke a straightened clothes hanger up through the center of the hallway ceiling into the attic, pushing it all the way through any insulation (Photo 1).

▶ Inside the attic, pull back the insulation in the vicinity of the wire and check between the ceiling joists for obstructions such as electrical boxes, conduits, heating and cooling ducts, and plumbing vents or lines.

▶ Find the ceiling joist closest to the wire. Let this joist support the center of the fan.

▶ With a drywall saw, cut rectangular openings about 3 inches by 12 inches through the ceiling along each side of the center joist (Photo 2).

▶ After cutting these holes, go back down into the hallway.

Install the Fan

The following steps can be carried out by one person, except for the step in which the fan is moved into the attic.

Cutting Out the Ceiling

Most whole-house fans come with a cardboard template the size of the opening for the louver panel, not of the fan. The template shown in Photo 3 has printed lines across its middle to help align it under the center ceiling joist.

▶ Center the template, then tack it to the ceiling with a few roofing nails.

▶ Use a drywall saw to cut through the ceiling along the edge of the template (Photo 3). Wear a dust mask and safety goggles, because dust and small pieces of drywall will fall out.

▶ Cut completely around the template, and then remove it. The drywall won't fall out yet, because it's still secured to the middle of the ceiling joist.

▶ Finish the cuts along the edge of the center ceiling joist, but don't remove the small portion still attached to the joist before checking the fan's installation instructions. Some models require this strip of drywall to help stabilize the louver panel. If the fan's instructions don't require the use of it, remove the strip and any screws or nails there.

PREPARE THE CEILING

Photo 1. Locate the wire pushed up from the hallway. Pull back the insulation and check for obstructions. Use wide boards to walk on and kneel on in the attic.

Photo 2. Cut 3 x 12-in. openings on both sides of the center ceiling joist. The board running perpendicular to the ceiling joist is the top plate of the hall wall.

Positioning the Fan

After cutting the hole in the ceiling from below in the hallway, return to the attic.

▶ Attach the brackets (usually two) that secure the fan to the ceiling joist.

▶ Have a helper pass the fan up to you through the ceiling opening.

▶ Set it on the center joist and adjust it over the opening (Photo 4). Its weight should hold it in position as you proceed with the next steps of the installation.

Select the Power Source

The first step in wiring up your new fan is to identify an appropriate source of power.

Finding the Power

With the fan being located in the attic, the easiest way to route power to it is generally to tap in to the nearest electrical box, which will often be the hallway's ceiling light. If the light is operated by a switch whose toggle lacks the words "on" and "off," it is a three-way or four-way switch, controlled from more than one location. Find another power source.

Some houses built from about 1963 to 1975 used aluminum wiring, which is required by the National Electrical Code to be fastened to copper wires only with the correct type of connectors needing a special connecting tool. Call in a qualified licensed electrician for this part of the job.

Many ceiling lights have a power supply cable coming in from the service panel. In the junction box where the lines connect, a cable enters the box, another exits the box going to another room, and a third one runs to the wall switch to form a switch loop. (For further information on switch loops, see "Hang a Ceiling Fan," page 74.) Most of the time, however, there is no way to tell just by looking whether a cable is the incoming power, part of a switch loop, or a cable going on to another light or perhaps another electrical outlet.

To check the power on a live circuit the electricity must be on, so work carefully.

▶ Turn the light switch off. Drop the light fixture down from the ceiling, but don't pull any wires out of the electrical box—the power is still on, even though the switch is turned off.

▶ Using a multitester, touch one of its probes to the bare copper ground wires. If the ground wires are sheathed in green plastic, insert the probe inside the wire cap so it touches the bare copper ends of the wires.

▶ Carefully put the other probe inside the wire cap that secures the hot wires, which generally are black but can be any color other than white, bare copper, or green. You should get a voltage reading on the multitester, indicating that the cable has incoming power and you can tap into it. If there's no voltage reading, look for another power source like a ceiling light in a bedroom.

Tools You Need

Adjustable wrench

Drill

Drywall saw

Dust mask, safety goggles, protective clothing

Hammer, roofing nails

Multitester voltage tester

Screwdrivers

Straightened clothes hanger

Materials

Fan kit including template

Screws and plastic anchors or spring-loaded hollow-wall anchors

INSTALL THE FAN

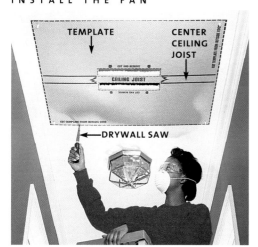

Photo 3. Position the template for the louver panel and cut completely around its edge. Use its center cutout areas to center and align it on the central joist.

Photo 4. Position the fan housing by placing it on the center ceiling joist so the motor is right over the joist. Center the fan itself over the opening in the ceiling.

Checking a Circuit's Capacity

If the box contains an incoming power cable, perform a quick test to make sure the new fan will not overload the circuit.

▶ A 15-amp circuit such as one for a hall light can handle up to 1,800 watts. This particular fan motor draws 4.5 amps or 540 watts at 120 volts, so it uses less than one-third of the circuit's full load capacity.

▶ Add up the wattage of all the other electrical appliances on the circuit, including each light bulb, radio, television, and so forth. In this case, the total wattage must be less than 1,260 watts (1,800 – 540 = 1,260), but preferably much less. The National Electrical Code recommends that the continuous load on a circuit be less than 80 percent of its capacity. In this instance, the appliances on this circuit totaled 1,020 watts, so the circuit had sufficient capacity. Unplug and move smaller appliances to a different circuit if necessary. If you can't locate a circuit with enough capacity to support your fan or if you feel uncomfortable about calculating a circuit's capacity, contact a licensed electrician.

Install New Cable

After finding a power source, remove the hall light fixture in preparation for running new cable from the electrical box to the fan motor (Photo 5). Check the fan manufacturer's instructions for the recommended gauge of cable for the fan. If the recommended cable is larger than the house wiring, stop and call in a licensed electrician, because the fan will probably need its own circuit. The gauge number is embossed on the sheathing of the plastic cable of the box wiring. Smaller gauge numbers indicate larger cable.

Now proceed as follows to run the new cable and make the connections.

Running the New Cable

▶ Turn off power to the light at the main service panel; turning off the light switch does not shut off the power. Put a note on the service panel so that no one turns the power back on inadvertently while you are working.

▶ Remove the light carefully so that the wires are pulled down from the electrical box.

▶ Double-check that the power is off by touching one probe of the voltage tester to the ground wires. Touch the other probe to the copper ends of the black wires. If the tester's light comes on, there's still power to the light from another circuit. Determine which circuit is on and shut it off before you work with wiring.

▶ Repeat the test, this time touching the probes to the ground wires and then the white wires. If the light doesn't come on in either test, the circuit is off and the line is safe to work on. Remove the wire caps from the exposed wires (Photo 6).

▶ Remove one of the electrical box's unused knockouts. If the box is metal, install a cable connector. The connectors themselves can be metal or plastic. If the box is plastic or fiberglass, no connector is necessary; they're built in.

▶ Feed cable through the connector so that the wires extend 6 inches beyond the face of the box after you cut away the plastic sheathing, a requirement of the National Electrical Code. The cable must be long enough to reach the fan and go into the fan's switch box.

▶ Secure the cable to the joist with electrical cable staples. One staple is required within

12 inches of where the cable enters or exits a metal box and within 8 inches of where it enters a plastic or fiberglass box. After that, tap in a staple every 4-1/2 feet, according to code.

Making the Connections

If the house has metallic-sheathed wiring (type BX or AC "armored cable" or conduit), the wires' color scheme and grounding connections might differ from what is described here. Check with an electrician if you're not sure.

▶ Connect the black and white wires of the new cable to the black and white wires in the fan switch box (Photo 7).

▶ Attach the bare copper ground wire of the new cable to the metal fan switch box with a ground screw.

Final Touches

Once the electrical hookups are complete, drill holes through the joist to accommodate the nut, bolt, and washer used to secure the saddle bracket, then bolt down the brackets (Photo 8).

▶ Fill the gap between the ceiling and the bottom of the fan frame by installing cardboard baffles, which come with the fan (Photo 9). Screw the baffles onto the fan frame. Cut the baffles, as needed, to extend between the ceiling joists down to the drywall or plaster ceiling. Don't place insulation over the fan frame or blades.

▶ Install the louver panel in the hallway ceiling (Photo 10). Most panels are secured to the ceiling joists and drywall or plaster with drywall screws and plastic anchors. For a more reliable grip, drive the screws into joists if possible, and try to use hollow-wall anchors between joists.

INSTALL NEW CABLE

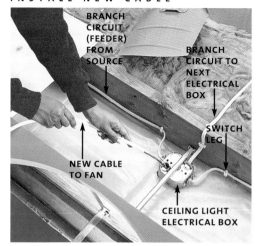

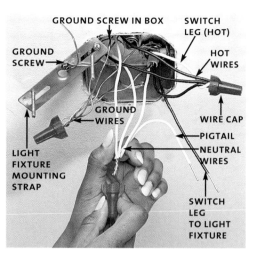

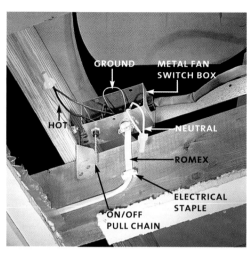

Photo 5. Run a new electrical cable between the electrical box and the fan. Check the fan's instructions for the correct cable and connector sizes.

Photo 6. Connect the wires of the existing power supply (in and out of the box), the switch leg cable (for the hallway light switch), and the new fan cable.

Photo 7. Connect the power cable wires to the wires in the fan's switch box. Screw the copper ground wire to the metal fan switch box with a ground screw.

FINAL TOUCHES

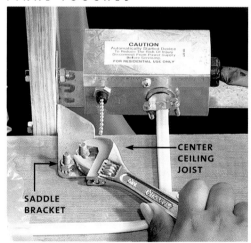

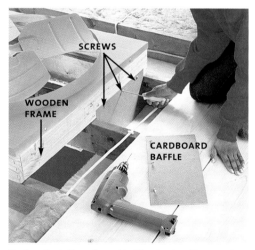

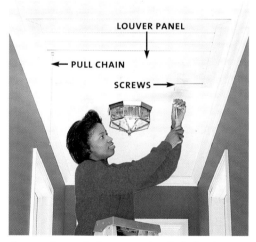

Photo 8. Make sure the fan is centered before you drill holes in the joist. Then secure the saddle brackets to the center ceiling joist with nuts and bolts.

Photo 9. Install cardboard baffles to close the opening between the fan frame and the ceiling. The baffles are usually screwed to the fan frame.

Photo 10. Secure the louver panel to the hall ceiling with drywall screws, preferably into the joists. Use hollow-wall anchors between the ceiling joists.

Accent a Room with Track Lighting

Track lighting can transform the feel of a room as thoroughly as a fresh coat of paint and new furnishings. And the new halogen bulbs that nearly duplicate sunlight will spotlight your favorite artwork or architectural details with all the vividness of the best museum or model-home lighting.

Sizing Up the Project

Installing track lighting requires only basic electrical and mechanical skills. This project involves disconnecting an existing light fixture and connecting its wires to the track lighting's feed where power enters the track system. After that, you simply mount the tracks on the ceiling. The lights snap into grooves in the ceiling tracks and require no additional wiring.

Before You Begin

Many track light systems operate with everyday incandescent bulbs, but you might want to consider installing a system that uses halogen bulbs. These new lights provide a brighter, more focused beam that makes accent lighting more vivid than ever. Halogen lights also last up to three times longer than ordinary incandescent bulbs. And they have reflective backs and improved focusing that let you use lower-wattage bulbs to save energy.

As you plan a track lighting system, follow these steps.

▶ Find the nearest ceiling light or electrical fixture controlled by a wall switch. This is a potential power source to tap into. (Some track lighting systems feature on-off switches built in to the individual fixtures, which provides even more lighting options.)

▶ Consult an electrician if you have old knob and tube wiring with fabric insulation. This old wiring makes it tough to distinguish hot from neutral wires and could have frayed insulation. Also, you may have no ground wire, or some wires may be too short to connect.

▶ Check that either the circuit has a ground wire or the electrical box is grounded. You might have to hire an electrician to determine this unless you feel comfortable doing so yourself (see "Hang a Ceiling Fan" on pages 74–77 for more information on wiring).

▶ Look in the electrical box for aluminum wiring, notable for its grayish color. If you have this kind of wiring, you'll have to hire a specially qualified electrician to make the connections.

▶ Measure the height of the ceiling. Track lights hang down as much as 6 inches, so if the ceiling is less than 8 feet high, as it might be in a basement, this can present a problem.

▶ Decide whether you want to control the lights with a conventional on-off switch or a dimmer. Some dimmers are compatible with track systems, including the low-voltage transformer systems. However, certain low-voltage transformers require a special dimmer, which is available from lighting retailers.

Give some thought to how you want to use the room and what objects in it, such as plants or artwork, you want to highlight to help you decide how many lights to buy.

You can select track fixtures that use standard 120-volt household power. These are ideal for general lighting, because they create a wider, less focused beam of light. In the same track, you can use low-voltage (12 volt) halogen fixtures with their own transformers.

Each manufacturer has a track designed for its own fixtures. Don't try to mix brands or modify the fixtures of one manufacturer to fit those of another.

Keep in mind when planning your layout that track is sold in 2-foot increments, usually up to 12 feet long. Longer runs can be fashioned with connectors. Connectors in various patterns will let you run track in as many as four directions, including diagonally, from the electrical box.

Track lights no longer resemble large coffee cans with floodlights in them. Today's tasteful but powerful halogen lights will revitalize your accent lighting more efficiently than ordinary incandescent lighting.

Glass Shield

Every low-voltage bulb must have a glass lens over it for safety. Occasionally a bulb may shatter and the lens will prevent glass fragments from falling out.

Install the Lighting System

Shut off the power to the light circuit at the main service panel before starting. Then post a note at the panel to alert others not to turn the power back on again prematurely.

Removing the Old Light

▶ Carefully remove the old fixture (Photo 1). The wires inside the electrical box must extend at least 6 inches beyond the box when they are pulled out fully.

▶ Check the wires with a voltage tester, touching one probe to the ground wire, or known ground, as you touch the other probe to the black (hot) and white (neutral) wires, in turn. If the bulb lights in either case, the power is not off. Go back to the service panel and switch off circuits until you determine that no power is entering the box.

▶ Twist off the electrical connector and straighten the exposed ends of the wires. Clip the exposed ends so that 3/8 inch is exposed to fasten to the terminals of the feed connector.

Testing the Layout

▶ Position the track and connectors on the floor directly beneath their planned locations, making sure the feed connector is directly under the electrical box. This helps you visualize how much space the lights will take, so you can adjust the layout accordingly.

Keep the track at least 2 feet from the wall. This will result in better ambient room light and it will also provide better light for accenting artwork or wall shelving.

▶ Once you are satisfied with the track layout, dangle a plumb bob from the ceiling until its weight is centered over the feed box, then over each end of the track and the track's corners.

▶ Now transfer these points onto the ceiling with a pencil. Use painter's tape (a blue masking tape that won't leave adhesive residue) to mark the location of the tracks on the ceiling. This is particularly important to do where the tracks change direction.

Wiring the Track

Fasten the wires to the feed connector according to the manufacturer's specifications (Photo 2). The neutral (white) wire connects to the silver-colored screw, and the hot (black or red) wire connects to the brass- or copper-colored screw. Connect the ground wire to the bracket as shown in the photo.

Do not tuck the wires into the box yet, because the track must still slide in above them.

Anchoring the Track

The track has a groove or other marks to identify its hot and neutral sides. Be careful not to reverse these. On many models the connectors are made to fit the track in only one way, so if you try to put the track in backward the connectors will point the wrong way.

Toggle bolts are ideal for securing tracks to a drywall ceiling but won't work with other types of ceiling, like plaster over concrete, as is found in multiple-unit buildings. Use fasteners that are appropriate for your surface.

▶ Clip the track into the hanger bracket and position it along your tape marks on the ceiling.

▶ With a pencil, mark the locations of the factory-drilled holes on the ceiling (Photo 3).

▶ Disconnect the track from the bracket and, at the marks, drill holes into the ceiling of a size recommended for the anchors. Each section of track up to four feet long needs two fasteners. Secure longer tracks at least once every 4 feet.

▶ Hang and bolt the first track, then slide in a connector, which happens to be a 90-degree corner connector in this case (Photo 4). The connectors are not anchored to the ceiling but are held in place with a setscrew.

▶ Continue anchoring sections of track and installing connectors until the layout is done.

▶ Affix the supplied caps at the ends of the track runs to prevent electrical shocks.

▶ Now double-check that all the track connectors are secure.

Mounting the Fixtures

The light fixtures have contact prongs at their tops that let you slide them onto the track in only one way, to ensure correct contact with the hot and neutral lines. Once the fixture is installed, rotate it in any direction you desire.

▶ Push the end of the fixture into the track, then turn and lock it into place (Photos 5 and 6). Install the canopy below the electrical box. A low-voltage halogen fixture is connected directly to a transformer that locks into the track in exactly the same way as the line-voltage lights.

▶ Finally, turn on the power and test the system. You can add track any time, but don't exceed 1,440 watts on a 15-amp circuit or 1,920 watts on a 20-amp circuit. Count all lights and appliances, including TVs, stereos, fans, and the like on the circuit. (See "Cool with a Whole-House Fan," page 82, for more on how to calculate circuit loading.)

OLD LIGHT FIXTURE

Photo 1. Shut off power at the main panel, test to ensure it's off, then remove the light fixture. Take out only the electrical connections to the fixture.

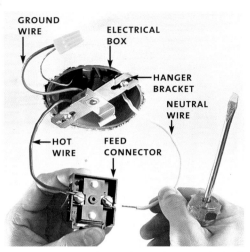

GROUND WIRE

ELECTRICAL BOX

HANGER BRACKET

NEUTRAL WIRE

HOT WIRE

FEED CONNECTOR

Photo 2. Connect the hot and neutral wires to the feed connector and wire in the ground wire to the hanger strip. Don't tuck the wires into the box yet.

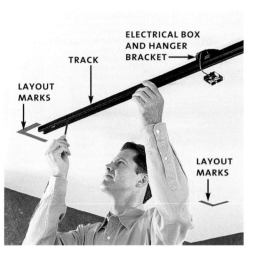

ELECTRICAL BOX AND HANGER BRACKET

TRACK

LAYOUT MARKS

LAYOUT MARKS

Photo 3. With painter's tape mark the locations of the fasteners that connect the track to the ceiling. Use at least one fastener every 4 ft.

Hot Tip

Halogen bulbs get very hot. To avoid burns, take care not to touch them while adjusting their positions.

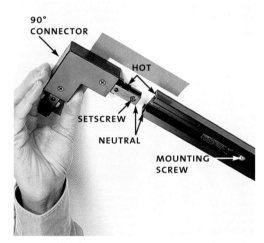

90° CONNECTOR

HOT

SETSCREW

NEUTRAL

MOUNTING SCREW

Photo 4. Slide the 90° corner connector into the track, and then tighten the setscrew to hold it firmly in position. Make sure it's aligned with the track.

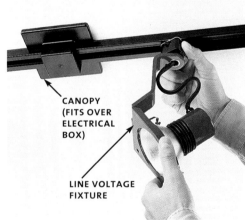

CANOPY (FITS OVER ELECTRICAL BOX)

LINE VOLTAGE FIXTURE

Photo 5. Twist the fixture connector into the track. To maintain polarity between hot and neutral wires, the connector is designed to twist in one direction only.

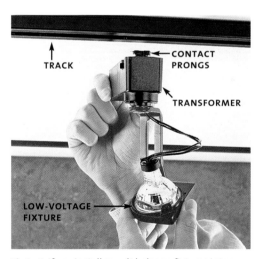

TRACK

CONTACT PRONGS

TRANSFORMER

LOW-VOLTAGE FIXTURE

Photo 6. If you install 12-volt halogen fixtures into a 120-volt track, buy a transformer with the fixtures. Some have their own built-in transformers.

Install a Central Humidifier

Dry winter air brings many problems, from parched skin to static electricity shocks, loosened furniture joints and gaps in hardwood flooring. If you have had to cope with such symptoms of dryness in your house, adding a central humidifier to supply moisture to the air as it is heated could be the answer to these problems.

Sizing Up the Project

Installing a central humidifier involves a number of skills: cutting sheet metal, installing low-voltage electrical wiring, and doing some simple plumbing. You must cut an opening in the furnace ducting to install the humidifier and make wiring connections between a transformer, the humidifier unit, and a humidistat (a device that measures the amount of moisture in the air, as a thermostat gauges temperature). Finally, you have to tap into a nearby plumbing pipe with a saddle valve to supply water for the humidifier.

If your house has no ductwork and is heated by hot water or electric baseboards, you cannot install a central humidifier. You'll have to rely on spot humidifiers placed in key locations.

Before You Begin

It is important to begin by understanding the basic theory of how a whole-house humidifier works, especially if your exposure to the subject extends no further than a portable one-room unit or a pan of water on a radiator.

How a Central Humidifier Works

A whole-house humidifier mounts on the heating ductwork near the blower, on both furnaces and heat pumps. (The term *furnace* will be used throughout these pages, but the instructions also apply to a heat pump.) Whenever the furnace blower switches on, the low-voltage electricity circuit that operates the humidifier is also activated (see the Central Humidifier Installation Plan on the next page). The humidifier operates when the humidistat senses that the air in the house is too dry. You can control condensation on windows by setting the humidistat lower.

There are three types of whole-house humidifiers that are available:

▶ A bypass humidifier, the type installed in these pages, features a drain and relies on a bypass duct (shown in gold, opposite) that circulates warm air through a wet grid inside the humidifier. Water trickles through the grid while the unit is on, with the excess draining out through a tube into a nearby floor drain.

▶ The bypass type without a drain works like the first example, except that in it water in a pan moistens a revolving element, which the air then passes through. This type must be cleaned every few weeks so that algae and bacteria don't grow in the standing water.

▶ In the third type, a spray humidifier injects a fine mist directly into the ductwork when the blower turns on. Avoid this type if the water in your area is very hard, that is, it contains a lot of minerals. The use of hard water in this type of humidifier allows a white powder to build up on the blower, furnace burners, and ductwork, which in turn can show up on the inside of the house and furniture.

You can buy a good humidifier at a home center, but if you have no experience with sheet-metal work and electrical wiring or have little understanding of how a furnace operates, consider buying from a heating supply dealer. He or she will help you select the proper size unit for your house, supply the bypass ducts (which often do not come with the unit), and offer advice to head off installation problems.

Required Maintenance

Humidifiers are no more maintenance-free than any other system in the home. The following maintenance routines should thus be carried out either at the start or end of each winter.

▶ First, shut off the humidistat, the power to the furnace, and the water supply.

▶ Next, wash the inside of the housing and parts with detergent to stop the growth of algae, fungus, and bacteria.

▶ Replace the humidifying element annually.

▶ Turn the humidistat down and close the damper at the beginning of the cooling season if you have central air conditioning.

Sizing Up the Furnace

A furnace has two main ducts: a warm-air supply duct (red in the diagram, right), which carries the heated air from the furnace to be distributed by the house's ductwork, and the return duct (blue in the diagram), which brings cool air back. Two other common furnace layouts are shown in the bottom right detail.

It's best to install the humidifier on the return-air duct of the heating system. If it's mounted on the supply side, a leak would risk damage to expensive furnace parts. And don't put a humidifier where it might freeze.

In some houses, the furnace and ductwork are crammed into a restricted space so you can't reach the wide side of the return duct. In such a case, mount the humidifier on the narrow front surface of the return air duct or on its back, using special adapter fittings.

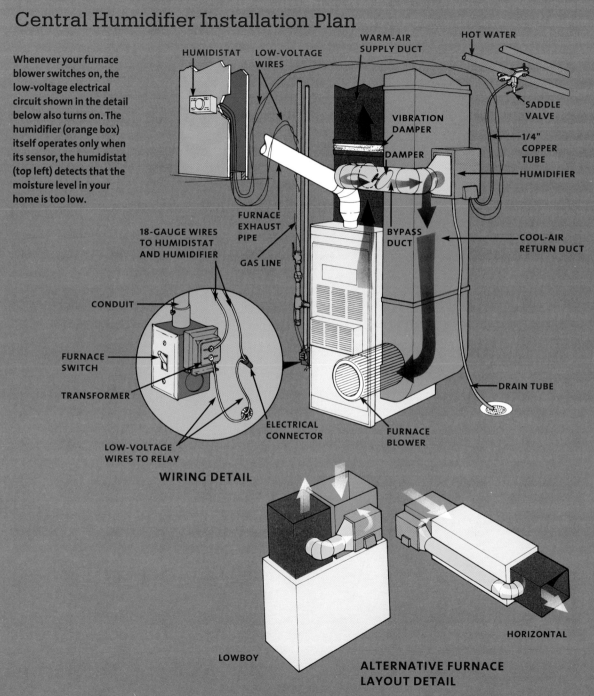

DIAGRAM

Central Humidifier Installation Plan

Whenever your furnace blower switches on, the low-voltage electrical circuit shown in the detail below also turns on. The humidifier (orange box) itself operates only when its sensor, the humidistat (top left) detects that the moisture level in your home is too low.

HUMIDISTAT LOW-VOLTAGE WIRES WARM-AIR SUPPLY DUCT HOT WATER

VIBRATION DAMPER

DAMPER

SADDLE VALVE

1/4" COPPER TUBE

HUMIDIFIER

FURNACE EXHAUST PIPE

18-GAUGE WIRES TO HUMIDISTAT AND HUMIDIFIER

GAS LINE

BYPASS DUCT

COOL-AIR RETURN DUCT

CONDUIT

FURNACE SWITCH

TRANSFORMER

LOW-VOLTAGE WIRES TO RELAY

ELECTRICAL CONNECTOR

FURNACE BLOWER

DRAIN TUBE

WIRING DETAIL

LOWBOY

HORIZONTAL

ALTERNATIVE FURNACE LAYOUT DETAIL

Tools You Need

Adjustable wrenches

Drill

Hammer

Metal-cutting shears

Screwdrivers

Torpedo level

Materials

Humidifier unit, humidistat

No. 6 sheet-metal screws

No. 18 low-voltage wire

1/4" flexible copper tubing, compression fittings

Relay switch

Saddle valve

Sheet-metal duct work, starting collar, elbows, boots

Wire caps

Mount the Humidifier

Always begin by turning off the electrical power to the furnace at the main service panel. Don't merely shut off the switch on the side of the furnace, because you must work inside that switch box later. And, to be safe, tape a note on the service panel to warn others not to turn the circuits back on prematurely.

▷ Position the paper template that came with your unit at about eye level on the return duct; in other words, above the furnace but below the vibration damper in the warm-air ductwork (Photo 1). This allows you to make the bypass duct as short as possible yet still avoid obstacles. Be sure the cutout is level or water won't trickle through the system as designed. A small torpedo level is useful at this point.

▷ Drill holes for the sheet-metal mounting screws as positioned on the template.

Metal-cutting shears come in three varieties: left cutting, right cutting, and straight cutting. You will need straight-cutting shears no matter which type of unit you install. However, to avoid having to buy both a left-cutting and a right-cutting set, plan your cuts in advance. If the furnace is positioned so that you can cut the bypass hole in only a clockwise direction, buy right-cutting shears; if counterclockwise, buy left cutting. Unfortunately, sometimes you may need both, in which case you might consider borrowing or renting a set.

▷ Cut the mounting hole with metal-cutting shears. Wear heavy leather gloves to avoid metal cuts (Photo 2).

▷ Screw the frame of the unit in place (Photo 3), checking again to make sure that it's level.

MOUNT THE HUMIDIFIER

Photo 1. Identify the warm-air supply (red) and cool-air return (blue) ducts. Level the paper template on the return duct, mark the cutout, and drill mounting holes.

Photo 2. Cut the humidifier mounting hole in the return-air duct with sheet-metal shears. Wear heavy leather gloves to protect your hands.

Photo 3. Mount the humidifier frame to the cool-air return duct with sheet-metal screws. Make sure that it's perfectly level.

Cut the Bypass

Mark the position for the round hole for the bypass duct in the warm-air supply duct. Use the starting collar, shown in Photo 5, to mark the correct hole size.

▶ To start a cut in sheet metal, drive a corner of a screwdriver tip through the metal with a hammer (Photo 4).

▶ Cut the hole inside the line to make sure the collar won't fall through the hole.

▶ Push the starting collar, tabs first, into the hole, then bend over the tabs to hold the collar in place (Photo 5).

The bypass duct consists of two elbows (the size depending upon the unit), sections of straight pipe, a transition boot, and a damper (see Photo 6 and the Central Humidifier Installation Plan on page 89). The damper is a round, flat sheet-metal plate that fits inside the duct. During the air-conditioning season, it is rotated to the closed position to seal off the bypass.

▶ In a straight section of pipe, drill a hole large enough so you can poke the damper screw through and attach the handle.

▶ Round duct comes in 2-foot flat sections that are bent into a tube shape and snapped together at seams along their length. Trim these sections to length, taking care to make straight 90-degree cuts before snapping the pieces together.

▶ Assemble and secure all the duct joints with three 1/2-inch No. 6 sheet-metal screws at each joint, and then wrap duct tape around the joint at the humidifier.

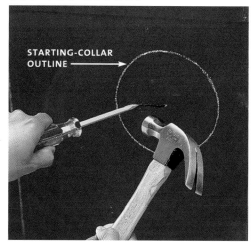

Photo 4. Mark the supply duct and slice a starting cut with the edge of a screwdriver and a hammer, avoiding a heat exchanger unit or coil.

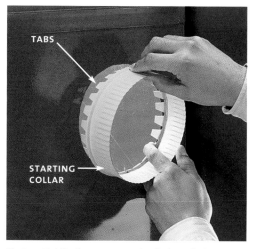

Photo 5. Cut the bypass mounting hole with shears, then push the starting collar, tabs first, and bend the tabs over to mount the starting collar.

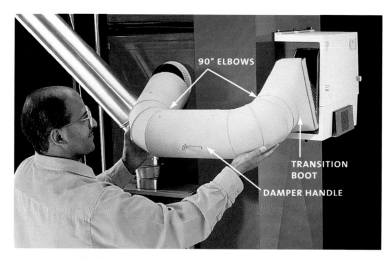

Photo 6. Assemble the bypass duct, including a damper. Attach it to the collar and humidifier with 1/2-in. No. 6 sheet-metal screws.

Electrical Wiring

Standard Voltage Connections

Mount the transformer on the furnace switch box. Attach its hot (black), neutral (white), and ground (green) wires to the corresponding wires from the main panel. Secure the low-voltage and relay wires.

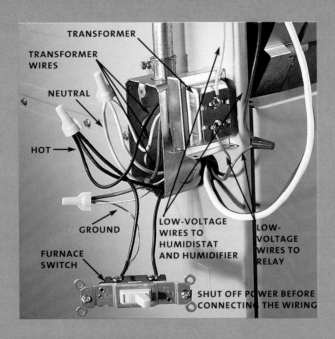

TRANSFORMER

TRANSFORMER WIRES

NEUTRAL

HOT

GROUND

FURNACE SWITCH

LOW-VOLTAGE WIRES TO HUMIDISTAT AND HUMIDIFIER

LOW-VOLTAGE WIRES TO RELAY

SHUT OFF POWER BEFORE CONNECTING THE WIRING

Low-Voltage Connections

Ideally, the humidistat should be mounted on an inside wall near the thermostat. Run an 18-gauge wire from a transformer post to the humidistat and on to the humidifier. Connect the other wire to a furnace relay and the humidistat, then extend it to the humidifier as shown.

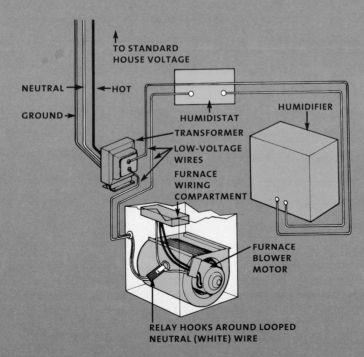

TO STANDARD HOUSE VOLTAGE

NEUTRAL

HOT

GROUND

HUMIDISTAT

TRANSFORMER

LOW-VOLTAGE WIRES

FURNACE WIRING COMPARTMENT

HUMIDIFIER

FURNACE BLOWER MOTOR

RELAY HOOKS AROUND LOOPED NEUTRAL (WHITE) WIRE

Hook Up the Electrical Power

Humidifier wiring involves two kinds of circuits. A standard 120-volt house circuit powers the transformer mounted on the side of the furnace's switch box (see Standard Voltage Connections, left). A low-voltage (24 volt) circuit runs from the transformer to a relay (a type of switch available from a heating supply dealer), then to the humidistat and to the water control on the humidifier itself (see left).

Making the Standard Voltage Connections

▶ Connect the transformer to the "hot" (black), neutral (white), and ground (green or bare copper) wires in the switch box as shown at left. This ensures the transformer will stay on.

▶ Join the relay wires to the low-voltage wires as shown at left.

▶ Open up the blower compartment on the furnace, unscrew the metal bracket from the relay, and loop the white neutral wire leading to the blower motor through it (Photo 7). The relay will now turn on whenever it senses current flowing through the neutral wire, so whenever the blower is running the low-voltage circuit will also have to be on.

Making the Low-Voltage Connections

Buy two 18-gauge wires (these will be marked with a Class 2 insulation rating) for this portion of the wiring. Ideally, mount the humidistat on an inside wall near the thermostat. If you can't snake the wires through the house walls, mount the humidistat on the return-air duct above the humidifier. To do this, cut another hole in the duct, for humidity sensing, and buy a mounting bracket from a heating supply dealer.

▶ Connect one wire to a low-voltage terminal on the transformer and one to a relay wire. Then run them to the humidistat (Photo 8). Cut the wire you connected to the relay wire and attach its ends to the humidistat terminals. Continue the wires on to the humidifier, connecting them there to the two wires on the unit (see Low-Voltage Connections Diagram, on the facing page).

Tap a Water Line

The water supply to a humidifier runs through flexible copper tubing from a nearby hot-water line. (Hot water evaporates faster than cold and thus increases the humidifier's effectiveness.)

A saddle valve lets you tap into the water line without cutting pipe. It connects to flexible copper tubing that runs to the humidifier. The humidifier's instructions will give the proper tube size, usually 1/4 inch around the outside (O.D.).

▶ Attach the tube to the humidifier with a compression fitting (Photo 9). Be careful not to overtighten it; just go about half a turn past finger-tight.

▶ Assemble the saddle valve and tighten it around a nearby copper or plastic hot-water pipe (Photo 10). Once the valve is attached, turn the handle to puncture the pipe, then unscrew it. This releases the plunger to allow the water to flow. With galvanized pipe, remove the valve fitting (leaving the clamps in place) and drill a 3/16-inch hole through the pipe wall. (Remember to turn off the water and drain the line first.) Then refasten the valve fitting.

▶ Attach the 1/4-inch supply tube to the valve as you did to the humidifier. Then open the valve and check for leaks.

▶ Finally, connect the plastic drain tube to the humidifier and run it to the nearest floor drain. Turn on the water and check for leaks.

Test Your New Humidifier

To test your new installation, open the saddle valve, turn the electricity back on, open the damper, set the humidistat to high, and adjust the thermostat so the furnace blower switches on. After a few minutes you should see a trickle of water coming out the drain tube. If not, take the cover off the humidifier to see if water is trickling down the element and air is moving through the bypass. If all is as it should be, reset the humidistat to the desired humidity level.

HOOK UP THE ELECTRICAL POWER

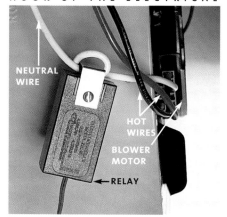

Photo 7. Open the blower compartment and hook the relay over a loop in the neutral (white) wire that leads to the blower motor.

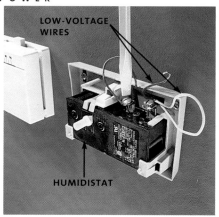

Photo 8. Connect the low-voltage wires from the relay to the humidistat terminals. Then connect both wires to the humidifier.

TAP A WATER LINE

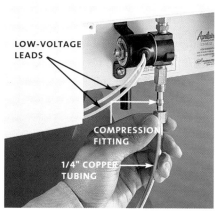

Photo 9. Connect a 1/4-in. outside diameter water supply tube to the humidifier with a compression fitting. Do not overtighten.

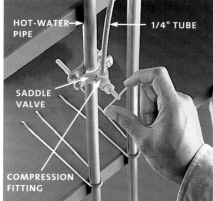

Photo 10. Connect the 1/4-in. tube to the saddle valve and turn the handle to puncture the copper or plastic hot-water pipe.

Add a Space-Saving Microwave

Tools You Need

Drill, bits

Fish tape

Screwdrivers

Stud finder

Tape measure

Wire cutters and strippers

Materials

Combination microwave oven/exhaust hood unit

12-gauge electrical cable

20-amp receptacle and electrical box

Lag screws

Toggle bolts

Tired of a cluttered kitchen counter with no room to work? You can gain about 3 feet of counter space without getting rid of any appliances, simply by installing a microwave oven underneath the cabinet over the range.

Sizing Up the Project

This project requires you to remove the existing range hood, disconnect the electrical source between the old hood and the kitchen light fixture, and run a new, dedicated 20-amp circuit between the main electrical service panel and a new microwave oven/range hood unit.

To mount the unit, you must fasten a mounting plate to the wall, using at least one wall stud. Some instances might require modifying the existing exhaust ductwork.

If you feel uncomfortable running a new electrical circuit, hire an electrician for this portion of the job. The remainder of the project requires only basic do-it-yourself skills.

Before You Begin

A combination microwave oven and exhaust hood is a convenient appliance. It not only lets you exhaust the moisture and kitchen odors just like a conventional vented range hood but also puts all of your cooking appliances—range, oven, and microwave—in one central area.

Venting Options

Most combination microwave and exhaust hood units can be either vented back into the kitchen, like a ductless range hood, or connected to the existing range hood's exhaust ductwork (the type of installation shown here). The opening for the exhaust can be out either the top or the back of the unit, depending on how the original range hood was vented.

Mounting Options

These units attach to the wall or wall cabinet in different ways, depending on the brand. One frequently used mounting method involves attaching two mounting brackets to the underside of the cabinet, and then sliding the microwave onto the brackets.

The other method, which is the one shown here, uses a mounting plate that attaches to the wall, with the microwave secured to the plate. This mounting plate is the same size as the back of the microwave unit and is mounted using a template supplied with the unit.

Duct Placement Options

Don't purchase the new microwave unit until you've removed the old range hood and measured the distance from the wall out to the center of the exhaust duct. For step-by-step instructions on removing the range hood, see the following section, Prepare the Space.

Even though microwave units come in a standard 30-inch width, the distance from the back edge of one microwave to the center of its exhaust duct will vary from one manufacturer to another. The closer you can make the new unit match the old, the easier the installation.

For example, if the distance from the wall to the duct's center is 3-1/2 inches and from the back of the microwave to the center of its exhaust duct is 4-1/2 inches, the difference is only 1 inch. With gaps this small and up to 2 inches, you may not have to add ductwork elbows; you may be able to simply shift the ductwork in the hole in the cabinet to connect it to the microwave. A larger gap, however, means that you will more than likely have to do some work on the duct. If the measurements differ by more than about 2 inches, you'll have to cut the back of the cabinet housing the exhaust duct or purchase additional ductwork elbows.

The edges of ductwork are sharp, so wear heavy gloves if you have to adjust it.

Prepare the Space

Turn off the power to the range hood at the main electrical service panel before beginning this project. Leave a note on the panel to warn others in your household not to turn the power on while you're working.

▶ Disconnect the range hood's motor wires from the electrical service wires. These wires are usually underneath a protective cover located next to the hood's filter. Straighten out the service wires and any loops at the ends of each so the hood doesn't snag when you remove it.

▶ Remove the screws and pull the hood away from the existing exhaust ductwork (Photo 1). Range hoods are usually secured to the cabinet with a screw in each corner.

▶ With the old hood removed, measure the distance from the wall to the center of the exhaust duct (Photo 2). Jot down this measurement to take with you when you buy the unit.

▶ Locate the wall studs within the opening, using a stud finder, and mark their locations with a pencil (Photo 3).

PREPARE THE SPACE

Photo 1. Turn off the power at the main panel. Then disconnect the electrical wires and screws and remove the range hood.

Photo 2. Measure from the back wall to the center of the exhaust duct. Adjust the ductwork or new elbows to line up the new unit.

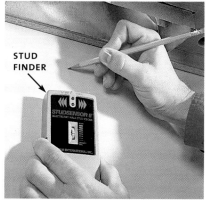

Photo 3. Locate the studs along the back wall and mark their locations. Later you will attach the mounting plate to at least one of them.

Mount the New Unit

The new microwave unit will require its own separate 20-amp circuit and standard receptacle (Photo 4). It is not hard-wired like the old range hood. The unit draws 12 to 14 amps of power, depending on the manufacturer, so even though a 15-amp circuit would be sufficient, a 20-amp new line will provide excess capacity to accommodate a more powerful unit you might want to install later.

For a 20-amp circuit, use cable with 12-gauge wires, including a ground wire. If possible, run most of the length of the cable from the service panel through an attic or crawl space to reach the kitchen, then fish it to the cabinet directly above the microwave to install the receptacle. This lets you conceal the receptacle. The power cord for the unit is usually 18 to 24 inches long, which gives you some leeway on where you install the receptacle. Again, if you are not confident undertaking this step, hire an electrician.

Disabling an Old Circuit Leg

Many range hoods receive their power from the same circuit as the overhead kitchen light. (At this point the light should not turn on, though, because you shut off the power to the range hood circuit.) That leg of the circuit is no longer needed, so the wire should be disconnected. There's no need to pull the cable out of the ceiling and wall, however, if you follow the procedure outlined here, which is the one approved by the National Electrical Code.

▶ Test the wires at the light fixture with a circuit tester to ensure that the power is off. Make sure the tester's leads have made good contact. Disconnect the range hood's power cable from the light fixture's junction box.

▶ Cut the disconnected wires back by 3 to 6 inches and push the wires up into the ceiling area. Make sure they will not flop back down and make contact with the junction box.

▶ Now go to the other end of this cable, where it was connected to the range hood, and pull the cable out of the cabinet. Cut these wires back the same 3 to 6 inches. Then push them into the wall cavity, again being sure they cannot flop back and make contact with any part of the electrical system. What remains now is a harmless, dead length of cable in the wall and ceiling.

Attaching the Mounting Plate

Most combination microwave oven/exhaust hood units come with mounting templates and easy-to-follow mounting instructions. There are usually two templates: one for the underside of the top cabinet and one for the wall.

▶ Use pushpins to hold the templates in place on the cabinet and wall.

▶ Drill holes in the wall according to the template's instructions (Photo 5).

▶ Remove the templates and attach the mounting plate to the wall (Photo 6). This unit's plate is secured with one toggle bolt at each corner.

▶ Secure the plate to at least one wall stud with a lag screw (Photo 7). Make sure this lag screw is centered in the stud, since it will be supporting a lot of weight.

Installing the Microwave Range Hood

Lift the microwave oven into the opening and hang it on the lower lip of the mounting plate (Photo 8). Make sure the mounting plate hooks are in the slots on the microwave's housing. It will be useful to have a helper to support the unit at this point.

Now, with the unit secured on the hooks, push it up against the mounting plate. Insert the two mounting rods into the holes in the mounting plate and tighten them (Photo 9).

Finally, attach the vent grille and plug in the unit. Test it after turning the circuit back on again at the main panel. If all is well, you're ready to start cooking.

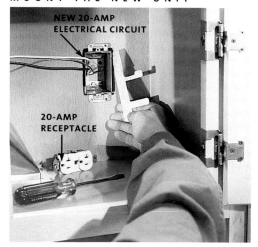

Photo 4. Run a new, separate 20-amp circuit and install a 20-amp grounded receptacle inside the wall cabinet. Hire an electrician if necessary.

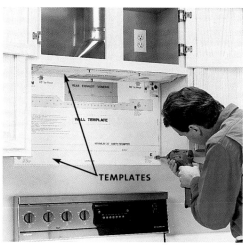

Photo 5. Drill the holes required for the mounting plate by following the directions on the cabinet or wall templates that are given.

Photo 6. Attach the mounting plate to the wall with one toggle bolt in each corner. This type of bolt expands behind the wallboard for a firm grip.

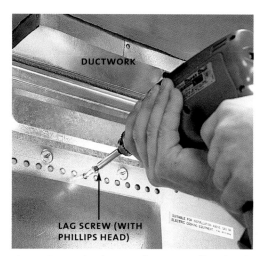

Photo 7. Secure the plate to at least one wall stud with a lag screw. Center the lag screw on the stud and use more than one if the stud spacing permits.

Photo 8. Lift the oven onto the lip of the mounting plate. Make sure the slots in the back of the unit are secured to the hooks on the plate.

Photo 9. Screw the mounting rods into the holes in the mounting plate. Attach the vent grille, plug in the power cord, and test the unit.

Smart Suggestions for Saving Energy

Energy conservation is still one of the best ways to save money. By making your house more energy efficient you ease the burden on your heating and cooling systems, increase your family's comfort, and make a sound financial investment, too.

Watch the Thermostat

This practice is a tried-and-true money saver. Adjusting your thermostat to 68 degrees Fahrenheit in winter and 78 degrees in summer is still one of the best ways to save energy (Photo 1). It costs nothing to do, and you save from 2 to 3 percent of your heating and cooling bill for each degree of change.

To maintain your family's comfort at the new, lower, setting in winter, dress for the temperature and control drafts by pulling the drapes over the windows to make your house warmer. In summer, shade the windows from the sun with awnings or other such devices to keep your house cooler. In all seasons, however, be aware that changing the thermostat's settings affects the health of elderly persons and infants.

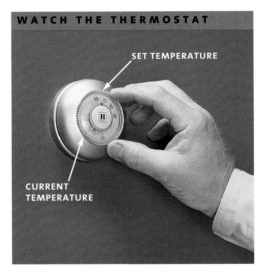

Photo 1. Remembering to change the setting on your home's thermostat to 68° F in winter and 78° F in summer is the simplest way to save money on energy.

Set a Clock Thermostat

One way to shave a significant amount off your fuel bill is to turn down the thermostat at night or when you leave the house and to shut off the air conditioner when you're away. The discipline it takes to make these setbacks routine can be replaced by installing programmable setback

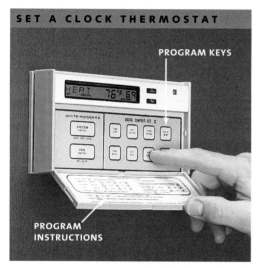

SET A CLOCK THERMOSTAT

PROGRAM KEYS

PROGRAM INSTRUCTIONS

Photo 2. Program a clock thermostat so that it automatically adjusts your home's temperature according to your daily or weekly schedule.

thermostats that remember to do the work for you. The cost of the initial investment will be repaid fairly quickly by the 10 to 20 percent savings in energy.

Programmable digital thermostats, which contain miniature computers into which you punch your daily schedule, are the most common type of clock thermostat (Photo 2). Some of the more complex models are programmed by the week, meaning that you can set different times for weekends, for instance, when you might be sleeping late and spending more daytime hours at home. Digitally controlled thermostats run from easy to moderately difficult to install, depending on the complexity of the mechanism.

You can also buy a mechanical, clock-operated thermostat, which uses plastic pins in slots to preset the times at which to turn the furnace or air conditioner on and off.

Maintain Furnace Filters

Filters for furnace or air-conditioning returns are designed to protect the unit's blower motor from dust and dirt and make it last longer. When the filter becomes clogged, this reduces air flow through the heating and cooling ducts, which in turn makes the motor work harder, reducing the efficiency of the furnace or air conditioner. The savings of efficient filters comes not so much from lowered utility bills, which would likely cover the ongoing cost of

new filters, but more importantly from helping the blower last longer.

Instead of buying just one filter, purchase half a dozen at a time from the hardware store or home center, so you have them on hand. Then routinely replace the filter every one to three months (Photo 3).

MAINTAIN FURNACE FILTERS

COLD-AIR RETURN

FURNACE

FILTER 16x35x1"

NEW FILTER

Photo 3. Replace dirty filters regularly so that your furnace or air conditioner will run more efficiently and help the blower last longer.

Seal Around Air Ducts

Research shows that large energy losses—in the range of 10 to 40 percent—are caused by heated or cooled air leaking from the ducts that carry the treated air to various parts of the house and return it to the furnace, air conditioner, or heat pump. The leakage occurs at the duct joints in "unconditioned" areas outside the insulated perimeter of the house such as an attic, crawl space, unheated basement, or exterior wall. The duct tape that is often used to seal joints in venting is only a temporary solution, because eventually it dries out.

Ducts generally run in hard-to-reach areas, and you usually have to pull back insulation for access to the joints (Photo 4). To seal small cracks, use either caulking tubes of special duct sealant, available from heating supply stores, or silicone caulk. For larger gaps, apply the same type of fiberglass mesh tape as is used for drywall. Spread duct sealant over the tape with a putty knife. For the greatest effectiveness, buy the duct sealant in 1-gallon cans.

Convert the Shower Heads

From 10 to 20 percent of the energy loss from any house literally goes down the drain, in the form of hot water. About half that total comes from the shower. By converting from an existing 5-gallon-per-minute shower head, a flow that is typical in older systems, to a 2-1/2-gallon-per-minute model, you use less hot water and save the heating cost (Photo 5). For various reasons, some older shower heads don't put out a full 5 gallons per minute. Many houses have low water pressure and clogged pipes or shower heads, all of which act to reduce water flow. To check yours, turn the shower on and fill a bucket for exactly 30 seconds. Then measure the amount of water and double that total to find the shower's output per minute. If it measures about 5 gallons per minute, change the shower head to a low-flow model.

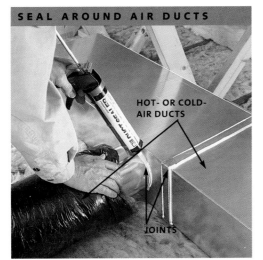

SEAL AROUND AIR DUCTS

HOT- OR COLD-AIR DUCTS

JOINTS

Photo 4. Seal the joints in heating and cooling ducts where they run through accessible areas in the attic or a crawl space. Use special duct sealant or caulk.

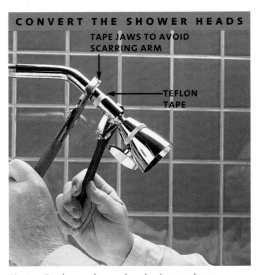

CONVERT THE SHOWER HEADS

TAPE JAWS TO AVOID SCARRING ARM

TEFLON TAPE

Photo 5. Replace a shower head using 5 gal. per minute or so with a new, low-flow model that has a capacity of only 2-1/2 gal. per minute.

Reset the Water Heater

The typical 40- to 60-gallon tank of a home water heater is like a hot-water radiator that continually gives off heat, which in the case of the water heater is wasted.

You can reduce water-heater energy loss in the following two ways.

Covering a Heater with an Insulating Blanket

Buy a special fiberglass blanket to wrap around your water heater. To do this safely, carry out the directions that come with the blanket, being especially careful to observe the following:

- ▷ Do not insulate the top of the water heater.
- ▷ Don't cover the air intakes of gas burners.
- ▷ Leave the controls and all valves exposed.
- ▷ Don't cover any warning labels (Photo 6).

Lowering the Water Temperature to 120° F

Older water heaters were commonly set at 140 degrees F so the hot water would last longer, even though 120-degree water is still hot enough to scald you. (See also "Install a No-Scald Shower Faucet," pages 114–119.) Unless you have an automatic dishwasher that requires a higher temperature, lower the temperature of your hot water to 120 degrees.

The temperature-setting knobs on many water heaters aren't calibrated in degrees (Photo 7). If you can locate an owner's manual, look up the temperature settings. Otherwise, find a high-temperature thermometer such as a candy or meat thermometer, if it is calibrated in degrees, and run hot water onto it. The point at which the temperature eventually stops rising is the water-heater setting.

RESET THE WATER HEATER

Photo 6. When you install a water-heater insulation blanket, take care not to obstruct safety valves, air intakes, or warning labels.

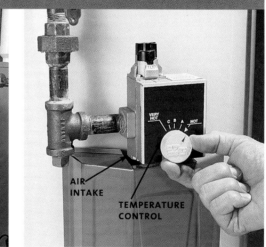

Photo 7. Reduce your water heater's temperature at the control knob to 120° F rather than the usual 140° F to save noticeably on heating costs.

Automate Your Garage Door

If you've ever had to leave the comfort of your car to open a garage door in the pouring rain or freezing cold, you can appreciate how nice it would be to have the door open for you with the press of a button. Installing an automatic garage door opener is the answer.

Sizing Up the Project

This project involves installing a new or replacement garage door opener for an overhead garage door, which is the most common type, and adjusting the opener controls properly for safety. The job requires only basic do-it-yourself skills to mount a support bracket on the header support over the garage door, assemble the opener unit and hang it from an overhead bracket, and then connect the mechanism to the garage door.

If no overhead mounting bracket is already in place, you will have to add one that is supported by the garage's framing. And if a grounded electrical receptacle is not within easy reach of the power unit, you will have to extend a circuit into the garage's ceiling or rafters.

This project can be completed by one person, although having a second pair of hands would be a great help at certain steps.

Before You Begin

Most overhead garage doors are sectional doors, because they have horizontal panels that are hinged together and roll up along a pair of tracks. There are also one-piece "kick out" garage doors. Door openers can be installed on both types in much the same way. Openers use one of two techniques to pull the door open: a chain-link drive or a screw drive. Both work well, but a chain-link drive tends to do better in extremely cold weather conditions.

Before you start this project, do the following.
▶ Watch the door as it's going up, to be sure of having at least 3 inches of space above the highest point to which the door travels.
▶ Check that there is a grounded electrical outlet within 3 feet of the new opener's motor. Some codes even specify that openers must be wired directly to an electrical box, so check your local requirements.

▶ Inspect the garage door's rollers and hardware. If any of the hardware is worn or damaged, replace it—the door must travel smoothly to operate well.

▶ Note whether the garage door's springs are broken or damaged. The door must be properly balanced, with the right amount of spring tension so that it's easy to open and close. Replace broken or damaged springs. If the door relies on torsion springs (see the Garage Door Installation Plan on page 105), which are wrapped around an axle mounted directly above the door opening, these will have to be replaced by a professional.

▶ On a fiberglass, hardboard, metal, or lightweight wood door, plan to add bracing (see the detail in the Installation Plan) to strengthen the top panel of the door where the bracket is attached. Otherwise, the opener can rip the bracket right out of the door itself.

▶ Measure the height of the door when it's closed so you can buy the correct length opener. Standard-size openers at home centers are made for doors up to 7 feet 6 inches high. If your door is taller, buy an opener that is appropriate to its length.

▶ Measure the width of the door, to match the horsepower of the opener to the door's size. Openers with 1/2 or 1/3 hp work with all residential overhead doors, but a 1/4-hp opener should be used only on a single door that is 9 feet wide or less.

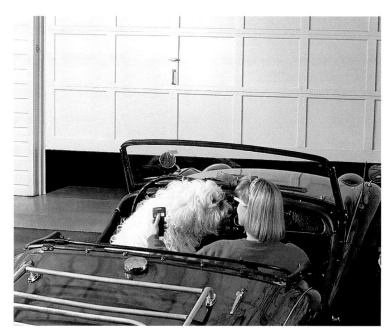

Without an automatic opener, the weight of this large sectional garage door might prove a strain to lift by hand. An opener also adds safety and convenience.

Test and Adjust Regularly

Many accidental deaths and injuries have occurred from children being trapped under closing garage doors. Most of these cases occurred because the owners failed to test and adjust their door openers properly. Once you have installed your opener, test and adjust it monthly, according to the instructions supplied by the manufacturer.

Before you purchase an opener, be sure it complies with the Consumer Product Safety Act of 1990, which requires that openers meet the UL 325 safety standards. Look on the box or in the product literature for the compliance documentation. In addition, as of January 1, 1993, all newly installed openers must be equipped with a safety reversing feature and have electric or optical sensors that will reopen a closing door if there's an obstruction.

Assemble the Opener

Back all cars out of the garage, clear away obstructions near the sides of the door, and remove all ropes and locks from the door.

Hooking Up the Rail

Assemble the rail that runs from the power unit to the header bracket (Photo 1 and the Garage Door Installation Plan, opposite). The exact order of assembly varies by manufacturer, so follow the instructions that came with the unit. Chain-drive and screw-drive openers both assemble in basically the same way.

Positioning the Rail

For best operation, the rail must be positioned in the very center of the door.

▶ With the door closed, find the top midpoint of the door itself—not the door opening—and draw a 6-inch vertical line on the door header, which is the large, horizontal support above the door.

▶ Next, determine the highest point of travel of the door's top edge. You will have to watch from the side or the back of the garage to see this. Then measure the distance from this point to the floor and make a tick mark on the header. Above that mark, add the distance required for

the rail to clear, which can be found in the unit's instruction manual. Draw a horizontal line at this height along the header (Photo 2). The intersection of this line and the center vertical line marks where to install the header bracket.

▶ If the door uses torsion springs, as in Photo 2, and they're in the way of the marks, move the header bracket up until the rail clears the spring.

▶ Drill holes and screw the header bracket in place with lag bolts. Don't skimp on the bolts—use as many as the manufacturer recommends.

ASSEMBLE THE OPENER

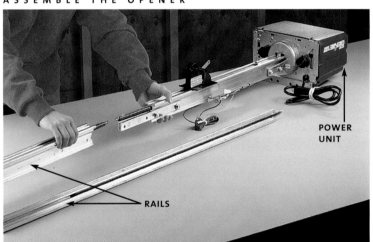

Photo 1. Connect the rails and power drive assembly according to the manufacturer's directions. Chain-drive and screw-drive assemblies fit together in basically the same way.

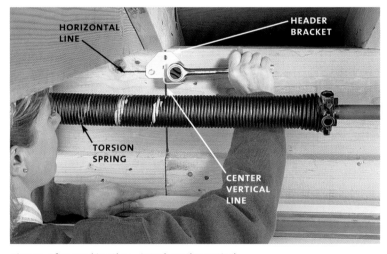

Photo 2. After marking the point where the vertical and horizontal guide lines intersect, fasten the header bracket at that point. If a torsion spring is in the way, move the bracket up.

Garage Door Installation Plan

Many accidental deaths and injuries have occurred when children have been trapped under closing garage doors. A tragedy like this can be averted if you test and adjust your door openers properly. Once you have installed your opener, test and adjust it monthly.

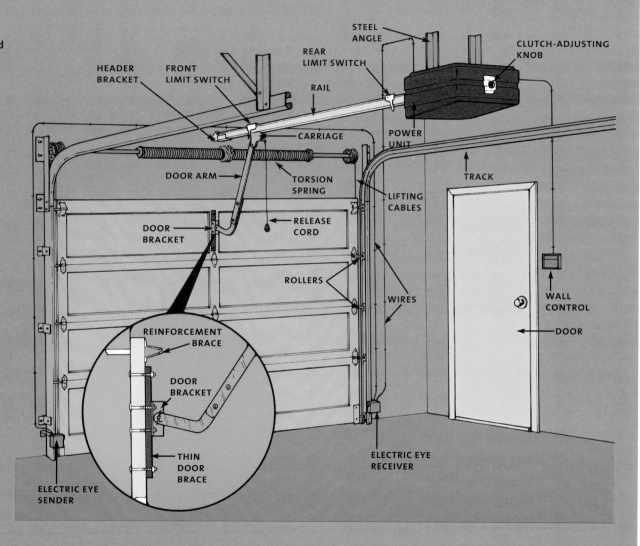

Tools You Need

Adjustable wrenches or socket wrenches

Carpenter's level

Drill

Hammer

Screwdrivers

Stapler

Stepladder

Tape measure

Materials

1/4–1/2 hp door opener

Door-panel bracing

Overhead mounting bracket (as needed)

Replacement door rollers and hardware (as needed)

Replacement springs (as needed)

Install the Rail and Power Unit

At this stage, it would be handy to have a helper to hold the long assembly in place while you work at each end.

Hanging the Rail and Power Unit

▶ Fasten the end of the rail to the header bracket. If you are working by yourself, rest the power unit on top of a 6-foot ladder placed underneath the area where it will be mounted.

▶ After securing the rail to the header bracket, lift the end of the power unit and tie it temporarily so that it's approximately level, or have a helper hold it at that height (Photo 3). Now raise the door.

▶ Lower the power unit and rest the rail on top of the door. Position the rail above the center line of the door and put spacer blocks under the rail to level it (Photo 4).

▶ Once the rail is level, fasten the power unit with lag bolts to nearby rafters, ceiling joists, or collar ties, using a perforated angle iron or blocks of wood (Photo 5). On a finished ceiling, screw a 2x4 to wood framing in the ceiling, then hang the angle iron from it.

▶ Move the rear limit switch (visible to the right in Photo 5) along the rail until it is about 12 inches away from the power unit, as shown in the diagram on the previous page. Now remove the spacer blocks and close the door.

Connecting to the Door

If the door needs reinforcement, add that before connecting the bracket to it. Parts are available from garage door dealers. However you choose to reinforce the door, do so over the whole vertical height of the top door panel.

▶ Position the door bracket as close as possible to the height of the upper garage door rollers, then attach it to the door (Photo 6). Secure it with bolts, not screws.

▶ Finally, fasten the door arm between the bracket and the carriage so it's as close to perpendicular as possible, as in Photo 6. Then set the front limit switch about an inch from the front of the carriage.

INSTALL THE RAIL AND POWER UNIT

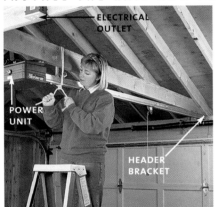

Photo 3. Temporarily fasten the opener in its approximate position after attaching the front of the rail to the header bracket.

Photo 4. Align the rail with the midpoint of the door. Add spacer blocks as necessary to ensure that the rail is kept level.

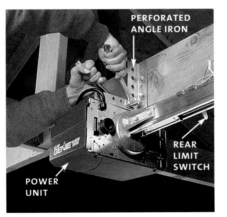

Photo 5. Anchor the power unit to solid framing like rafters, ceiling joists, or collar ties. Use a perforated angle iron or wood blocks.

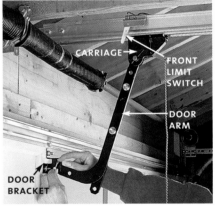

Photo 6. Using bolts, not screws, attach the door arm to the door bracket. Then center the door bracket on the door.

Connect and Test the Controls

Before undertaking this last stage, review Test and Adjust Regularly, on page 103.

Adding the Controls

The electric eye's sender and receiver need to be mounted about 6 inches above the floor, alongside the door tracks (Photo 7).

▶ Run the wires from the sender's eye to the receiving eye and then to the power unit. Secure the wires a few inches away from the roller track, using insulated staples. Avoid damaging the wires while stapling them down.

▶ Run the wires from the power unit to the wall control. Then mount the wall control up out of the reach of children.

▶ With the door completely closed, engage the carriage in the track.

Adjusting the Door

It's time now to plug in the opener for a test run.

▶ Set the clutch so there's just enough power to move the door (Photo 8). If the door closes too hard, it won't reverse properly when it hits an obstruction. Not all models adjust in the same manner as that shown in the photo, so check the owner's manual before setting the clutch on your new model.

▶ If the door doesn't close all the way, move the front limit switch forward. And if the door reverses when it hits the floor, move the front limit switch away from the door, toward the carriage. If the limit switch is installed correctly, this adjustment should make the door stop exactly where you want it to.

▶ To raise the door to its full upward position, adjust the rear limit switch in small increments. If you set the limit switch too far back, the door will damage the opener.

Testing Your Opener's Safety Features

All garage doors sold since 1993 must have an automatic-reverse feature and sensors to detect when an object is in the way of the closing door. Here's how to test these features.

▶ Place a 2x4 (some localities require a 1-inch board) under the center of the doorway and close the door. If the door reverses when it hits the 2x4 or smaller board, it needs no further adjustment. If it doesn't reverse, set the front limit switch 1/16 inch forward and try again. Keep moving the limit switch like this until the door reverses upon striking the board.

▶ Test the electric eye by placing a solid object in its path while closing the door. If the door reverses, the electric eye is working. If nothing happens, check the unit's electrical connections—the opener won't work without the electric eye sensor.

Test the opener monthly to make sure that its reversing functions are working properly. Test the beams often. The door, tracks, and hardware need to be checked for wear and lubricated periodically , according to the manufacturer's instructions.

CONNECT AND TEST THE CONTROLS

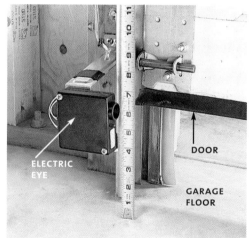

Photo 7. Position the electric eye's sender and receiver about 6 in. above the floor and alongside the door tracks. Keep the wires away from any moving parts.

Photo 8. Adjust the clutch on the power unit so it has just enough force to move the door. A sensitive setting minimizes the impact on an obstruction.

Wire-In Motion-Sensor Lights

A motion sensor that automatically switches on outdoor lights exactly when and where you need them is the perfect convenience to welcome visitors to your home at night, usher you up the walk, and ease concerns about intruders entering your yard.

Sizing Up the Project

If you are able to mount the new motion-sensor lights on existing outdoor light fixtures, this project calls for only basic electrical skills. If there is no box where you wish to install the lights, however, you will have to extend a circuit and mount a new box, either recessed in the wall or surface mounted. In some cases, you might have to replace the existing electrical box with a larger one or add a ground wire to an ungrounded system.

If your house has aluminum wiring, which is grayish in color, hire an electrician who is specifically certified to work with aluminum wiring to do the entire installation.

Check with local building authorities to see whether an electrical permit is needed, and inquire about any special local rules. Then be sure to have the work checked by an inspector when you are finished.

Understand How Motion Sensors Work

Motion detectors are small electronic eyes that detect the infrared heat waves radiated by moving objects such as people, animals, and cars. When the detector identifies an object moving across its field of view, especially warmer objects, it electronically flips a switch that turns on lights. The lights remain burning anywhere from 1 to 20 minutes, depending on how the timer is set. The lights automatically turn off then unless the detector continues to sense movement.

A motion detector has a field of view limited to a wedge-shaped area about 100 degrees wide and extending not much beyond 50 feet. It must therefore be carefully aimed at the zone you want to cover. And since the detector senses the motion of animals as well as of people, it will react to the movement of the family dog standing 15 feet away as readily as to the approach of an adult 45 feet away. In fact, a motion sensor will sometimes react even to wind-blown leaves or a passing car. Most such nuisance triggering, which can be irritating to both you and your neighbors, can be solved by adjusting the device's sensitivity and aiming it accurately.

The motion sensor connects to the lights it controls in a variety of ways, depending on the type of light used. Most often, the sensor is connected to a waterproof cover plate that holds one or two light bulb sockets (see the Location and Light Styles Diagram, page 111). Most sensor lights are designed to replace an existing outdoor light while still letting you operate the light in the normal way. The manufacturer's instructions tell you how to shut off the sensor when it's not needed. In addition, many motion sensors detect the onset of daylight and automatically deactivate themselves.

MOTION
DETECTO

MOTION DETECTOR
SENSITIVITY ZONE

Whether you are coming home with your hands full or negotiating a wintry sidewalk, you'll appreciate having a motion sensor to light your way and to provide added home security.

Position the Lights

To prevent moisture from seeping into the sensor and light sockets and ruining them, locate the fixture so that it is under cover or buy a fixture that has bulb seals (see Photo 6 on page 113), and angle the light downward.

Aim the motion sensors to cover walks leading to the front and back doors and driveway (see the schematic on the facing page). Other areas that would benefit from sensor lights are patios, decks, and any potentially hazardous locations such as around stairways and swimming pools. If improving security is a priority, aim the motion sensors to cover all the approaches to your house, including fence gates and patio doors. Also aim them at darker areas of the yard near dense trees and bushes where intruders might hide.

It's best to mount motion sensors 6 to 10 feet above the ground, positioned so that most movement will pass across their sensitivity zone rather than directly toward them. But, you won't always be able to do this if you want to reuse existing light locations. One solution is to install a remote motion sensor some distance away from the lights themselves (see Sensor Styles No. 3, opposite). The wires connecting the sensor to the light are low-voltage and therefore not dangerous, so there is no need to enclose them in metal or plastic conduit.

Electrical Considerations

Sometimes the electrical box of an existing light fixture presents problems. For one, it might not contain a ground wire (bare copper or one with green insulation) or other grounding method such as metal conduit. The National Electrical Code requires that all exposed metal parts of

lights be grounded, so check with your electrical inspector to determine if you will have to run a new cable with a ground wire. If you run new electrical cable outdoors, it must be encased in approved protective conduit and be connected in weatherproof electrical boxes.

Many electrical boxes no longer meet the minimum size required by code. Follow the guidelines at right for calculating box size. This method sometimes overestimates the minimum size, but it does simplify the calculation. To install the light shown on page 113, the old box was too small and had to be replaced with a larger one. The size of a plastic box in cubic inches is stamped on the side.

To determine box size, first calculate what the wire requirements will be:

Wires entering box (neutral and hot)	= 2
Ground wires (combined total)	= 1
Clamps	= 1
Sensor and lights	= 2
Total number of wires	= 6

Next, calculate what the space requirements per wire will be:

14-gauge wire = 2 cubic inches/wire
12-gauge wire = 2.25 cubic inches/wire

For this project, using 14 gauge wire, 2 cubic inches per wire x 6 wires equals 12 cubic inches of box required. Because the box's volume is 16 cubic inches, it's large enough.

Tools You Need

Adjustable wrench

Screwdrivers

Voltage tester

Wire cap connectors

Materials

Motion-sensor kit

Conduit or cable as needed

Floodlights; decorative, remote, or back-plate lights

Low-voltage wiring

Silicone caulk

Weatherproof electrical boxes

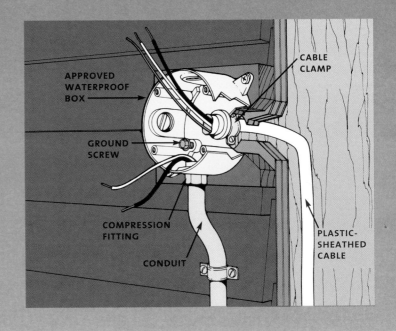

DIAGRAM

Connecting a Surface-Mounted Box

Connect a waterproof surface box either from the wall side, with plastic-sheathed cable, or from the outside, with cable run inside approved conduit.

APPROVED WATERPROOF BOX

CABLE CLAMP

GROUND SCREW

COMPRESSION FITTING

CONDUIT

PLASTIC-SHEATHED CABLE

Locations and Light Styles

Locations

Position sensors and lights to cover approaches to the house, commonly used areas, and dark, shadowy parts of the yard. Floodlights are the most versatile and cast the most light.

The numbers in the illustration at right refer to the styles below.

DARK OR DEEPLY
SHADED AREAS

③
FRONT WALK
AND FRONT
DOOR

DECK

BACK WALK
AND BACK DOOR

PATIO

A DRIVEWAY AND GARAGE

Caution

Do not let your ladder or body touch overhead power lines. They could deliver a lethal shock.

Light Styles

The most effective motion sensor lighting systems use a combination of floodlights (1) and decorative lights (2).

Sensor Styles

Remote sensors (3) let you mount the sensor and light in different locations. Backplates (4) allow you to convert existing or standard fixtures into motion detector lights.

1. FLOODLIGHT   2. DECORATIVE

3. REMOTE   4. BACK PLATE

Is the Power Really Off?

Before you begin working with electrical wiring, make sure the power is turned off. To test a wall switch, turn off the circuit breaker or fuse, remove the cover and ears, and withdraw the switch. Don't let the screw terminals touch metal. Touch the circuit tester leads to the switch terminals and to each terminal and the grounding-wire terminal. If the power is off, the circuit tester will not light.

To test a receptacle, insert the leads of a circuit tester into the slots where the plug goes. The circuit is on if the tester's bulb lights. If it does not, this may mean only that the tester's leads were too short or too thick to reach far enough for good electrical contact; it does not mean that the power is off. Check further by removing the receptacle's face-plate screws and mounting ears at the top and bottom, gripping the ears, and pulling the fixture straight out, being careful not to let its terminal screws touch metal. Now touch one lead of the tester to a brass screw terminal where a red- or black-insulated wire is connected, the other to a silver screw having a white-insulated wire. If the circuit is off, the tester's bulb will not light. Check also between the brass/black- (or red-) wire terminal and the terminal where the bare or green-insulated grounded wire is connected, and between the silver/white-insulated wire terminal and the grounding-wire terminal. If the tester's light glows in either case, the power is still on.

To test a cable, remove the twist connectors from the wire's ends. Hold only the insulated parts; don't touch bare wires before ensuring the power is off, and don't let the wires' ends touch. Touch one lead of the tester to the bare end of the white-insulated wire and the other lead to the tip of the black-insulated wire. Test between each of these wires and the bare or green-insulated grounding wire. If the tester lights in any case, the power is on, so turn off other breakers or fuses until the circuit tester fails to light.

Install the Light

All motion-sensor lights are installed in essentially the same way, although each type and brand has its own variations. Read the installation instructions supplied by the manufacturer, then follow the general guidelines here.

▶ Turn off power to the light circuit at the main service panel, then remove the light fixture, but don't undo any wiring connections yet (Photo 1).

▶ Test to see that the power really is off, following the directions in the box at left.

▶ If necessary, install a new electrical box, making sure the incoming cables are securely clamped (Photo 3). See the formula on page 110 to determine box capacities.

▶ Run the wires through the light fixture's rubber gasket and connect them from the light to the cable wires, according to the manufacturer's directions (Photo 4).

▶ The cover of an outdoor electrical box must be waterproof. Most use a rubber gasket to seal the gap between the box and the light fixture (Photo 5). Seat this gasket carefully. If it rests against a rough surface, also seal the edges using silicone caulk.

▶ Now aim the sensor at the field you want covered. Because heat from a light bulb can confuse the sensor, keep the bulb and sensor as far apart as possible (Photo 6).

▶ Turn the power back on to test so that you can adjust the sensor.

▶ Finally, adjust the sensitivity of the sensor to avoid nuisance triggering from normal passing traffic, animals, pools of water, air conditioners, heating vents, and trees and shrubs (Photo 7). If part of the sensor's field of view must be blocked to avoid false alarms, cover that portion of the sensor with tape (Photo 8).

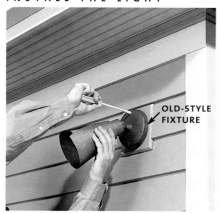

Photo 1. Turn off the power at the main panel and unscrew the old fixture. Tape a note to the panel so no one turns the power on again.

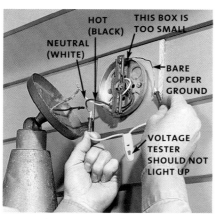

Photo 2. The current is off if the tester doesn't light when you've touched its leads to wires as given in the text.

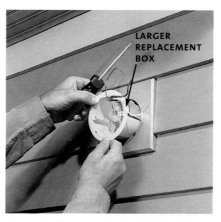

Photo 3. Replace an undersized electrical box or surface-mounted waterproof box. Plastic boxes have their size imprinted on them.

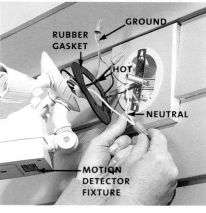

Photo 4. Run the wires through the rubber gasket, then mount the fixture according to the manufacturer's directions.

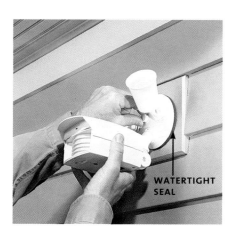

Photo 5. Screw down the fixture, making sure the rubber gasket seals the edges to keep out moisture. Add silicone caulk if necessary.

Photo 6. Aim the sensor at the zone you want covered, then point the bulbs toward that area. Keep the bulbs away from the sensor.

Photo 7. Test and fine-tune the sensor, using the sensitivity and time controls described in the manufacturer's instructions.

Photo 8. If necessary, cover a portion of the lens with any kind of opaque plastic tape to narrow the field of view.

Install a No-Scald Shower Faucet

The morning shower is always relaxing, until the water temperature suddenly turns freezing cold or, worse, scalding hot. This problem is easily solved with a no-scald faucet that automatically reacts to pressure changes in the hot and cold water lines to keep the water temperature almost constant—within 2° F in some models.

Sizing Up the Project

To replace a single-handle bath and shower faucet with a no-scald shower faucet, you must cut existing copper pipes and solder the new faucet in place, or use solvent and cement especially formulated for use with plastic pipe.

If your house has no panel giving access to the shower plumbing, you will have to cut a hole in the wall, preferably from the back side, in another room or a closet. If no access can be gained there, you will have to cut through from inside the shower and replace wall tiles. A new faucet cannot be installed from inside a fiberglass shower, since cutting through the fiberglass creates irreparable damage.

In a shower with separate hot and cold faucets, the no-scald faucet combines both into one. The holes in the wall left over from the old faucets are covered by a special plate available from most home centers or plumbing supply stores. It is important to make sure that the cover plate you buy will span the distance between the two old handles; otherwise you will be left with an open hole in the wall.

In this project, shutoff valves, called ball valves, are added to the plumbing so that you can repair the faucet in the future without turning off the water to the whole house.

Don't try this project unless you have experience at soldering or plastic-pipe fitting, especially since much of the work has to be done in a tight space. (For step-by-step procedures on pipe soldering, see pages 134–135 of "Add an Outdoor Faucet.")

How No-Scald Faucets Work

Sudden swings in the temperature of a shower occur when water is drawn all at once from elsewhere in the house. An operating dishwasher or washing machine takes its share of the hot water, making the shower water suddenly too cold. Or worse, a flushed toilet steals a share of the cold water quickly, making the shower too hot. The resulting shock, which may just be irritating to most of us, can be dangerous to the elderly, children, and anyone who might not be able to react quickly enough to keep from receiving a serious burn.

A standard shower faucet is not designed to react to changes in water pressure created in other parts of the system. A no-scald faucet, more properly called a pressure-balancing faucet because it controls both the hot and cold water, automatically reacts to pressure changes in the hot and cold water lines and keeps the water temperature very nearly constant. As the valve reacts to changes in pressure you feel only a slight drop in water delivery at the shower head. These faucets are now even required by some building codes in new houses and large remodeling projects.

If possible, buy a no-scald faucet made by the manufacturer of your existing faucets. Although this isn't absolutely necessary, in some cases it makes the installation work easier.

New models of pressure-balancing no-scald faucets are able to keep the shower-water temperature within a range as narrow as 2° F.

Tools You Need

Adjustable wrench

Drywall saw

Hammer

For copper piping: tube cutter or mini-hacksaw, propane torch, fireproof cloth

Pipe wrench

Screwdrivers

Utility knife

Materials

Emery cloth

Flux

Lead-free solder

Plastic pipe solvent, cement and plastic pipe fittings (as needed)

Prepare the Plumbing

Begin by turning off the water supply at the house's main inlet valve. Then open the lowest faucet in the house, followed by all the other faucets, to drain the lines. Soldering copper requires the pipes to be free of water.

Create Working Space

▶ Remove the old faucet trim and unscrew the tub spout (Photo 1). Then remove the handle and the cover plate (Photo 2 and "Removing a Single-Handled Faucet," right).

▶ Now move around to the back side of the shower. Many installations have an inspection door behind the shower, often in a closet. Remove this door and set it aside.

▶ If there is no access door, or if it does not expose the faucet body, cut through the drywall to make working space (Photo 3). Locate the wall studs with a flashlight and a measuring tape, working through the hole on the bathroom side. Then cut the drywall down the center of the studs, to simplify reuse of the drywall when you're done.

CREATE WORKING SPACE

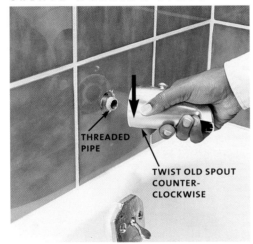

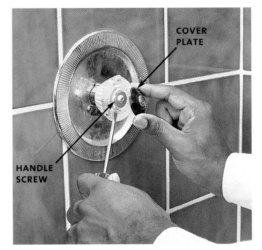

Photo 1. Twist off the old tub spout, turning it counterclockwise. If you can't do this by hand, use a pipe wrench. Don't worry about damaging it.

Photo 2. With a screwdriver, pry off the original decorative plate covering the screw in the center of the handle. Unscrew the handle and the trim plate.

Photo 3. Cut the drywall by repeatedly scoring it with a utility knife down the center of the studs. Work carefully so you can reuse it later.

Cut the Pipes

Now cut the riser leading to the shower head, the hot- and cold-water supply pipes, and the pipe leading to the spout in a bathtub (a shower stall will not have a spout).

▶ Mark the pipes for cutting. Then, with a small tubing cutter or mini-hacksaw, cut the hot and cold water pipes in the wall opening (Photo 4). Cut the riser pipe to the shower head about 2 inches above the old faucet body.

▶ After making these three cuts, lift out the old faucet. In some cases you might have to remove the piping to the spout first, to allow the whole assembly to be removed.

▶ Finally, nail 2x4 support blocks between the studs, just above the spout pipe and the faucet assembly. These pieces will act as support sections after the new faucet is installed.

CUT THE PIPES

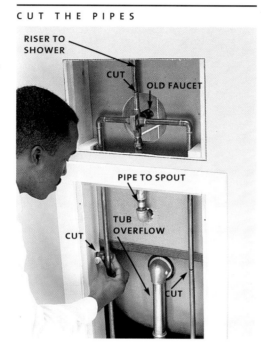

Photo 4. Cut the old pipe with a compact tubing cutter (shown) or a mini-hacksaw. Choose an area that gives you plenty of room to work.

DIAGRAM

Removing a Single-Handled Faucet

Cut the copper supply pipes inside the wall, as well as the riser pipe to the shower head. Replace the spout and supply pipe. If the supply lines are galvanized pipe, unscrew them at the nearest fitting.

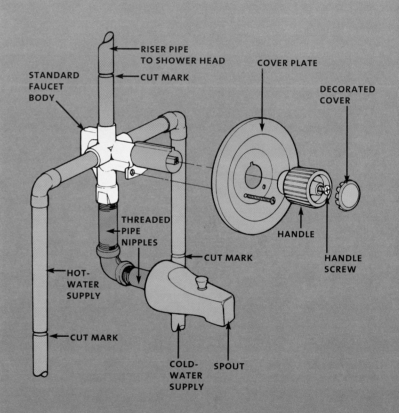

Connecting Galvanized Pipe

Use the fittings shown to make a transition from old galvanized supply pipes to copper or plastic. Include a new shutoff valve if there isn't one there already.

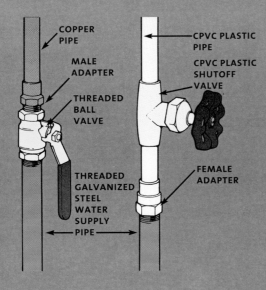

COPPER PIPE

MALE ADAPTER

THREADED BALL VALVE

THREADED GALVANIZED STEEL WATER SUPPLY PIPE

CPVC PLASTIC PIPE

CPVC PLASTIC SHUTOFF VALVE

FEMALE ADAPTER

Shifting a Faucet

Position the new valve according to the manufacturer's directions. You might have to offset pipes so they will fit correctly, as shown.

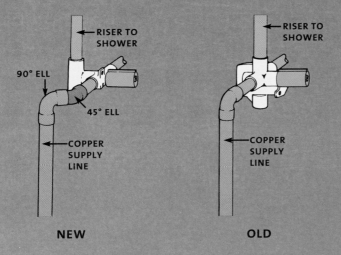

RISER TO SHOWER

90° ELL

45° ELL

COPPER SUPPLY LINE

NEW

RISER TO SHOWER

COPPER SUPPLY LINE

OLD

Install the New Faucet

Put in the shutoff valves before installing the new faucet, so you can turn the water back on to the rest of the house. Solder them to copper lines if that's what you have, or see Connecting Galvanized Pipe, top left, if you must join them to galvanized steel or plastic pipes.

Correct positioning of the new faucet body is critical. Most new, single-handled shower faucets come with a plastic spacer fastened to the faucet body. The spacer must align with the surface of the wall, ceramic tile, or fiberglass. Read the manufacturer's directions carefully in planning this step. Even though you may be using the same brand for the replacement faucet, you might have to offset the hot- and cold-water pipes to bring the new faucet body into alignment with the face of the ceramic tile (see "Shifting a Faucet," bottom left).

▶ Measure and cut the new pipe and fittings. Dry-fit them, then recut the pipe as necessary, making sure the faucet is centered on the waste and overflow lines (Photo 5).

▶ Once all the parts fit, disassemble the pipes, apply flux, reassemble the unit, strap the assembly firmly to the 2x4 support blocks, and solder the joints. Before soldering, open the valve to avoid pressure buildup and to avoid burning any rubber or plastic seals there might be in the faucet body. Hold a fireproof cloth or a metal plate between the flame and any adjacent wood, and keep a bucket of water or a fire extinguisher nearby in case of fire.

▶ Once you finish soldering the copper connections, turn on the water and look for leaks.

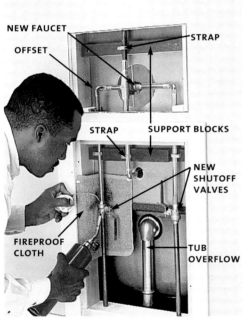

Photo 5. Set the new faucet body into the proper position, then attach the new pipe and fittings to it. Strap the pipes to wood support blocks. Solder the new connections, protecting flammable materials.

Finish Up

Install the new cover plate, handle, shower head, and bath spout (Photo 6). A slip-on-style bath spout works best as a replacement for the old one. This kind slides over the plain-end copper pipe stub until it fits firmly against the wall and is tightened down with an Allen wrench, visible in the photo on page 115. If you have replaced a two-faucet system, install a new cover plate wide enough to conceal the old holes (right). Run a bead of silicone caulk around the edges of the faucet cover plate and the spout.

If necessary, replace the drywall or ceramic tiles that were cut out. However, to make future repairs easier, consider building an access door rather than simply replacing the drywall. Shore up the cut-out drywall by applying metal J-bead to its edges. Then frame the opening in wood to provide a surface for attaching hinges and latches. Finish off the opening with wood trim, even if it will be concealed in a closet.

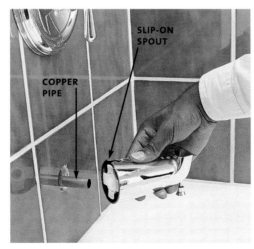

Photo 6. Install the new cover plate, then the handle, shower head, and bath spout like this slip-on model. Finally, caulk around them.

Cover Plate for a Two-Handled Faucet

Use this special cover plate if you are replacing a two- or three-handled faucet (8 in. apart at most) with a single-handled pres- sure balancing faucet. Remove the old faucets, cut the proper-size hole for the new one, and use the plate to cover the old faucet holes.

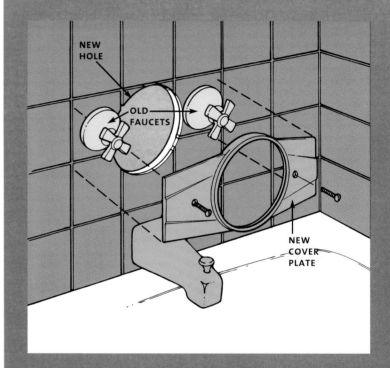

Upgrade Your Kitchen Sink and Faucet

Instead of putting in just another stainless-steel sink and chrome faucet, as found in so many other houses, add a splash of color to your kitchen by installing a sink and faucet in bright new designer colors.

Sizing Up the Project

To complete this project, you must disconnect the existing plumbing hookups below the kitchen sink and lift the old sink out of the countertop. Installing a new sink and reconnecting the plumbing require only basic skills and careful measuring.

Before You Begin

Before ripping out the old drain and water supply lines, take a photo or draw a sketch to use as a reference. The current setup is usually a good road map to follow when installing new sink and drain lines. However, dimensions may change with the new fixtures, so you may have to install new drain lines from the sink and new water supply tubes to the faucet.

If the new sink needs to accommodate a garbage disposer or you're adding a dishwasher, or both, the installation will be slightly different from the one shown here, requiring some additional drain pieces and different plumbing fittings. The Typical Sink Plan Diagram on page 123 shows a sink with a garbage disposer and built-in dishwasher. Most installations are similar to this generic version.

If your water supply lines are copper or plastic, plan to use compression fittings for the new water lines. If the supply lines are galvanized pipe, buy a fitting that's threaded on one end for the galvanized pipe and has a compression fitting on the other for the supply tubes. Measure the outside diameter (o.d.) of the galvanized supply pipe, since the fittings come in different diameters for different pipes.

From beneath the countertop, measure the size of the sink opening carefully before buying a new sink. If the replacement unit is going to be smaller than the existing opening, you'll have to replace the countertop. And if the upgraded sink is larger, you can try to enlarge the counter opening with a jigsaw, but this involves delicate cutting. It's better to find a sink that fits the old opening.

Most new sinks come with four large factory-drilled holes along the back edge. The first three holes from the left are for the water supply lines or the two threaded faucet body pieces on the faucet. The hole on the right is for the spray attachment that comes with many faucets, a soap dispenser, hot-water dispenser, or the air gap for a dishwasher (seen in Photo 4, page 122).

Remove the Old Sink

Before starting to work, shut off the water supply to the faucet. If there are shutoff valves on the supply lines, close them. Shutoff valves are not required by code, but they are a convenient feature you should have on all sink water supply lines. (See "Simplify Plumbing with a Shutoff Valve," page 130).

If the supply lines have no shutoff valves, turn off the water at the main valve, which will be somewhere in the house downstream from the water meter. Then open the kitchen faucet and a faucet on a lower level, such as in a basement sink, to drain the entire system above the kitchen faucet. If the house is built on a slab, open an outside water faucet instead.

Disconnecting the Sink

Work from front to back in removing the old setup, taking out the old drain lines first, then disconnecting the faucet supply tubes from the water supply lines. Have a bucket and rags handy. How you disconnect the faucet's supply tubes from the water lines will vary according to the type of connection you are dealing with.

▶ Disconnect the old drain lines by loosening the slip nuts with groove joint pliers (Photo 1).

▶ If the supply lines are galvanized, the connections can be undone with a pipe wrench.

▶ If the supply lines are copper, the connections could be sweat-soldered. In this case, cut the pipe with a tubing cutter or hacksaw. If the slip joints are compression fittings, simply unscrew them with an adjustable wrench (Photo 2).

Taking Out the Sink

Don't bother disconnecting the old faucet from the sink; it's easiest just to lift out the entire sink and faucet all at once.

▶ Stainless-steel sinks are secured to the countertop with four clips attached to the underside of the countertop. Using a hex-head ratchet screwdriver, loosen the screw bolts holding the clips in place (Photo 3), then lift out the sink.

▶ If the old sink is porcelain, it may be held in place simply by adhesive and its own weight. If so, run a putty knife between the sink edge and the top side of the countertop to break the adhesive seal, being careful not to scratch the countertop, then lift out the sink. Clean off sealant residue around the opening in the countertop with a putty knife to provide a clean surface for a new bead of sealant, applied later.

REMOVE THE OLD SINK

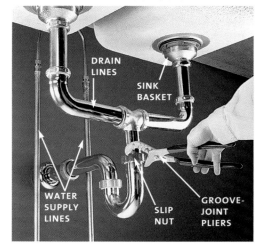

Photo 1. Disconnect old drain lines by loosening slip nuts with groove-joint pliers or a pipe wrench. Be ready with a bucket and rags.

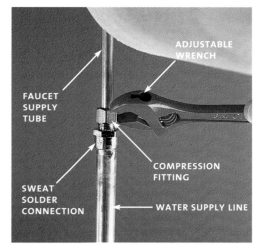

Photo 2. Disconnect the water supply lines and faucets. Loosen compression fittings with an adjustable wrench. Cut soldered fittings with a hacksaw or tubing cutter.

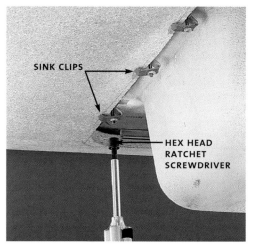

Photo 3. With a hex-head ratchet screwdriver, remove the four sink clips that secure stainless-steel sinks to the underside of the countertop.

Attach the New Faucet

Rather than trying to attach a faucet to your new sink while working in the confined space below the sink, attach it before you install the sink (Photo 4). (Don't install the sink baskets yet, however. The drain holes in the bottom of the sink provide a good way to hold on to the sink while setting it in place.)

Preparing the Faucet

▶ Attach the flexible metal supply tubes to the threaded faucet body. Many faucets use a coupling nut to make this connection (Photo 5).

▶ Other faucet styles come with flexible-copper supply tubes preattached at the factory. Connect these soft copper tubes directly to the water supply line valve after the sink is in place, just like the flexible metal supply tubes. If the supply tube that is provided is too short, use an extension supply tube. Connect the tube with compression fittings on both ends to the faucet and the water supply line.

▶ Attach the spray hose, if there is one.

Preparing the Sink

If the new sink is enamel over cast iron, you'll need a helper to put the sink in place—a cast-iron sink weighs about 80 pounds and is awkward to maneuver. Do not apply the adhesive until the sink is ready to be installed.

▶ Set the sink into the countertop opening by holding it through the drain holes. Do not lower it by holding the faucet, which you can damage.

▶ Center the sink, then draw a light pencil line on the countertop along each side and its front edge. Use these marks to position the sink once the adhesive is applied.

▶ Now lift out the sink and faucet by grabbing the unit through the basket holes. (Do not grab by the faucet.)

▶ After putting a piece of cardboard on the countertop to avoid marring the sink, turn the sink and faucet over and set them on the cardboard with the faucet hanging over the edge of the countertop.

▶ Apply a 1/4-inch bead of silicone adhesive around the underside of the sink edge (Photo 6). This adhesive prevents water from running between the sink and countertop and bonds the sink to the countertop.

ATTACH THE NEW FAUCET

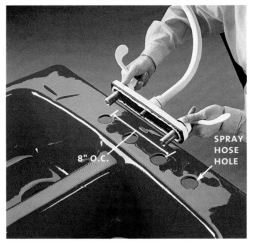
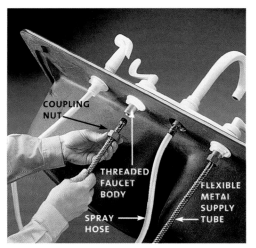

Photo 4. Install the new faucet onto the sink before installing the sink, so you won't have to do this later in the cramped area under the sink.

Photo 5. Attach the faucet supply tubes to the threaded faucet body. A coupling nut secures the supply tube to the threaded stem.

Photo 6. Place a piece of cardboard between the sink and countertop to protect them. Apply a 1/4-in. bead of silicone adhesive to the bottom edge of the sink.

Typical Sink Plan

Most installations with a garbage disposer and dishwasher are similar to this generic version. Use this schematic as a guide if your kitchen has either of these appliances.

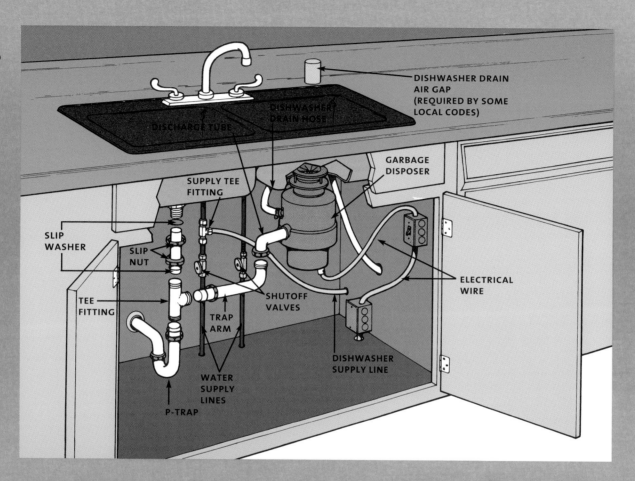

DISHWASHER DRAIN AIR GAP (REQUIRED BY SOME LOCAL CODES)

DISHWASHER DRAIN HOSE

DISCHARGE TUBE

GARBAGE DISPOSER

SUPPLY TEE FITTING

SLIP WASHER

SLIP NUT

ELECTRICAL WIRE

TEE FITTING

TRAP ARM

SHUTOFF VALVES

P-TRAP

WATER SUPPLY LINES

DISHWASHER SUPPLY LINE

Garbage Disposers and Noise

Because all disposers work by having a spinning plate force food waste against a grinding ring to pulverize it, noise is often a problem, even with the best units.

You can lower the noise level by installing a cast-iron sink rather than the lighter stainless steel or enameled-steel sinks that are noisier.

Mount the Sink

With the adhesive applied, proceed immediately to install the sink.

▶ Lower the sink into position and line up its edges with the pencil mark guidelines (Photo 7). Run your fingers along the edge of the sink to smooth out any adhesive that oozes out. Leave the sink until the adhesive has had time to cure, about 30 minutes. If you try to install the sink baskets right away, you'll shift the sink as you tighten the baskets' locknuts.

▶ Place a 1/4-inch thick (about the diameter of a pencil) rope of plumber's putty around the entire underside of a sink basket lip to seal the gap between the lip and the recessed area of the sink basket hole.

▶ After the adhesive has set, fit the sink baskets into the holes in the bottom of the sink, positioning a rubber washer and a cardboard or fiber gasket between the basket and the metal locknut (Photo 8 and Photo 9). It's important to have the cardboard or fiber gasket between the rubber washer and locknut, to prevent the rubber washer from being twisted out of shape as the locknut is tightened. If the sink basket doesn't come with a cardboard or fiber gasket (Photo 9), cut one out of posterboard or the like.

▶ As you tighten the locknut, putty will be forced out from under the basket's lip and from the underside of the basket beneath the sink. Remove the excess putty from both areas.

Making the Water and Drain Hookups

Connect the faucet supply tubes to the shutoff valves by first inserting the cut end into the fitting and tightening the nut onto the threads (Photo 10). The supply tubes go only about 1/4 inch into the compression fitting. They must be straight in the fitting or they'll leak. The brass compression washer, or ferrule, provides a leak-free fitting when it's pulled up tight.

▶ Test-fit the pieces of the drain assembly—the tailpieces, drain lines, and P-trap—cutting pieces as necessary to make a good fit. All these connections are secured with plastic slip nuts and beveled plastic slip washers. Use a miter box and hacksaw when cutting PVC pipe to ensure straight, clean cuts.

▶ Now assemble the tailpieces, drain lines, and tee. Then connect the tailpieces to the drain baskets (Photo 11).

▶ Tighten the waste arm to the drain stub coming out of the wall (Photo 12).

▶ Connect the P-trap to the waste arm and drain tailpiece. Note that the longer section of the P-trap slides up onto the tailpiece about 1-1/2 inches to fit into the waste arm (Photo 13).

Checking for Leaks

After connecting all the fittings, turn the water supply back on. If you've installed new shutoff valves, turn the water on at the water main first and then open the valves at the sink.

▶ First, inspect the water supply line fittings for leaks. Tighten a leaky fitting slightly with an adjustable wrench if necessary. If it still leaks, shut off the water and reassemble the connection. Don't reuse compression fittings, though; the ferrule is designed to be crimped only once.

▶ If the water lines are okay, let the water run into the sink and down the drain. Tighten any drain slip nut connections that leak. If a leak continues, make sure the slip washer is in place.

▶ Once the drain lines and supply lines are leak-free, put the sink basket stoppers in place and fill each bowl about two-thirds full. Then release the water in each bowl, one right after the other. This sudden surge of water is the best way to make a final test of the baskets and drain lines for leaks.

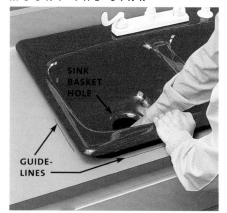

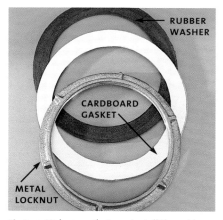

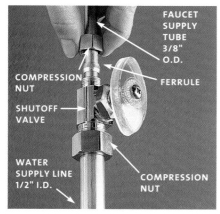

Photo 7. Set the sink in place by holding it through the sink basket holes. Use the penciled lines on the countertop to make sure the sink is properly positioned.

Photo 8. Install the sink baskets after the adhesive has set up. Use a spud wrench like the one shown here to tighten the metal locknut firmly, but not overtight.

Photo 9. Make sure that you install the rubber washer first, then the cardboard gasket, and finally the metal locknut exactly in that order.

Photo 10. Connect the faucet supply tube to the shutoff valve and secure it with the compression nut. The brass compression washer, or ferrule, ensures a leak-free connection.

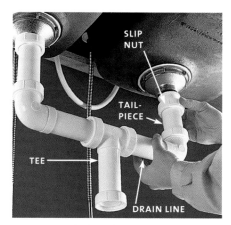

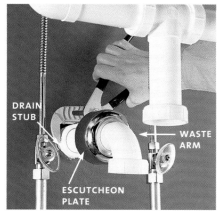

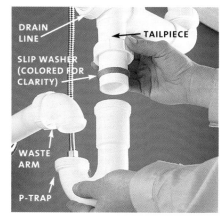

Photo 11. Attach the tailpieces to the sink baskets and connect the rest of the drain lines and tee. Dry-fit the pipe sections to make sure they're the proper lengths.

Photo 12. Tighten the waste arm onto the drain opening that extends out from the wall. The metal cover, or escutcheon plate, hides the hole in the wall.

Photo 13. Connect the P-trap to the drain line and waste arm. Slide the longer section of the trap 1-1/2 in. onto the tailpiece. Secure the joints with plastic slip washers and slip nuts.

Filter Your Drinking Water

Does your tap water hint of a swamp or a swimming pool? Is it cloudy or full of floating particles? Are you worried that it may be laced with lead? An undersink or whole-house water filter will provide purer water that is much less expensive than bottled water, faucet-mounted filters or countertop filters.

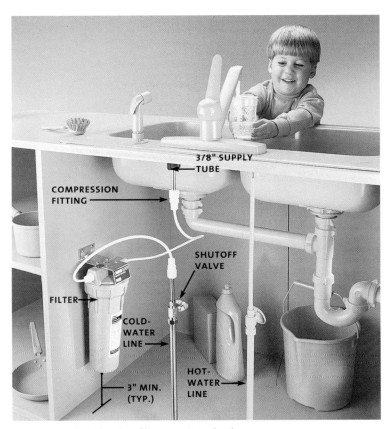

Photo 1. An activated-carbon filter mounts under the sink to remove tastes and odors such as chlorine. It filters cold water and attaches in minutes with compression fittings.

Sizing Up the Project

Installing an undersink water filter takes only basic skills. It requires cutting into the cold-water supply line beneath the kitchen sink and running new lines through a filter to the tap. The fittings and new tubing are included in most water filter kits.

A whole-house filter involves more work but again requires only basic plumbing skills. A centralized filter is mounted in the water main that supplies water to the entire house.

The project on these pages shows three common installations, but there are many variations, installed similarly. If you have water problems other than those described here, consult a water treatment professional (look under "Water Purification" in the Yellow Pages).

Three Problems, Three Filters

Three specific problems are fairly easy to identify and treat, each with its own type of filter:
- Bad taste or odor
- Lead
- Floating particles

For bad taste or odor and for floating particles there's no need for a water test—you know if you have a problem. For lead, however, you must have the water tested before you buy a filter. Every house is different: even if a neighbor has lead in his or her water and most of the city has lead problems, you still might not. Don't let yourself be stampeded into buying a filter you don't need.

Filter for Taste and Odor

This type of filter is a plastic cylinder that mounts under the kitchen sink and holds a replaceable activated-carbon filter. It removes odors and unpleasant tastes, including those given off by chlorine, from the cold-water line and reduces the amount of pesticide residues in water.

The filter unit usually includes all the necessary supplies. Replacement filter cartridges generally are inexpensive and last from several months to a year, depending on the amount of use and the water quality.

Here is how to install this type of filter:
- Screw the mounting bracket for the filter housing to the side of the cabinet so that the cartridge has 3 to 4 inches of clearance beneath it (Photo 1, left). This space is necessary to let you unscrew the filter housing and change cartridges. Use a torpedo level to make sure the bracket is level; a filter that is not level can hamper correct water flow in the cartridge.
- Turn off the water at the shutoff valve below the sink or at the shutoff for the whole house on the main water line.
- Cut out a length of the cold-water supply tube—the exact amount is usually specified by the manufacturer—with a tubing cutter or hacksaw, then file the ends of the tubes to remove any burrs.
- Screw on the compression-type plastic fittings and plastic hose supplied with the filter.
- Before screwing the fittings into the filter housing, wrap the threads three or four times with Teflon plumbing tape (Photo 2).

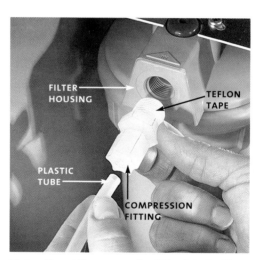

Photo 2. Thread the compression fitting into the filter housing, wrapping the threads with Teflon tape. Insert the tube and tighten the fitting gently with a wrench.

Tools You Need

Adjustable wrench

File

Hacksaw or tubing cutter

Pipe-joint compound

Teflon tape

Torpedo level

Materials

Filter kit, including fittings

Jumper wire and 2 pipe clamps (as needed)

Remove Lead

Lead in drinking water is a serious health hazard. Just like lead-laced paint chips, water with lead can produce permanent neurological damage, especially in children. Those most at risk are pregnant women, infants drinking formula made with tap water, children under the age of six, and adults who are exposed to lead on the job.

Testing for Lead

If you're concerned about lead, first call the water department. They can recommend independent laboratories for testing the water and tell you if the water service line from the street to the house is made of lead. Some municipalities also will loan money to replace a lead service line—the main source of lead in household water—at a yearly cost that should be less than the cost of filters.

After calling the water department, have the water tested. Use either an independent lab approved by the Environmental Protection Agency or a mail-order kit. Because there is more lead in water that has been standing in the pipes for hours than in running water, the lab will request both "first draw" water that has stood in pipes overnight and "fully flushed" water that has been run for several minutes.

Finally, determine if the lead level is too high. The federal Safe Drinking Water Act recommends you take action to reduce lead if the first-draw water has more than 15 parts per

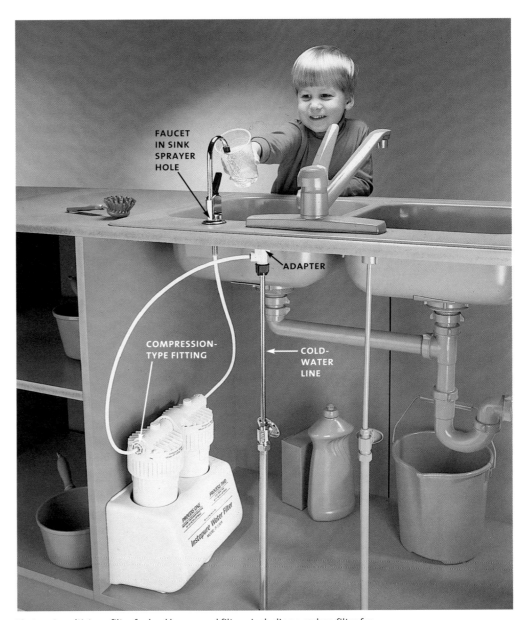

Photo 3. A multistage filter for lead has several filters, including a carbon filter for taste and odor. It connects like the one-stage unit, except the filtered water comes out of a separate faucet on the sink or counter.

billion (ppb) of lead. You can reduce your lead intake substantially if you follow these steps:
▶ Use only cold water. Hot water dissolves more lead from pipes. Cook with cold water, and heat up cold tap water to make infant formula.
▶ Let the water run before you use it. Don't consume water that has been standing in the pipes for more than 6 hours. Let it run until it's as cold as it gets, then fifteen seconds more.
▶ Install a filter specifically rated to remove lead. Such a filter can take out 85 percent or more of the lead from the water.

Installing a Multistage Filter for Lead

This type of filter is similar to an activated-carbon filter except that it has two or three separate cartridge holders (Photo 3, left). One of the filters is actually a carbon filter, so tastes and odors—as well as lead—are removed. The only other difference is that multistage filters typically use a separate faucet (supplied with the filter) that mounts on the sink or countertop. This makes the filters last longer and provides better filtration, because the flow is slower. The extra filtered-water faucet can replace a sprayer on the sink, or you can drill a hole in the countertop and mount the faucet there.

Depending on the model, filter cartridges will treat from 500 to several thousand gallons between changes. (One thousand gallons per year is a typical amount of drinking water for a family of four.) You can install a multistage lead filter using the techniques just described for the single-stage filter.

Install a Whole-House Filter

If your water contains flakes of rust or sand or is cloudy, a whole-house filter will help alleviate these problems and keep the particles out of your hot-water heater and other appliances. Inside the screw-on filter housing is a spun polyethylene filter that traps scale, cloudiness, and rust particles in water. You can also install a two-stage unit that includes an activated-carbon filter for improving the taste and odor of your water. These filters do nothing about dissolved iron in the water, which commonly results in rust stains in the toilet. For this you need a water softener or a specialized iron-removal filter. Consult a water treatment professional.

Install your whole-house filter as follows.
▶ Turn off the water at the main valve before cutting into the pipe, unless you have a shutoff valve at the sink.
▶ Cut out the amount of pipe recommended by the manufacturer downstream from the main water line's shutoff.
▶ Install the filter (Photo 4). Make sure it is perfectly vertical in the main water line and that you leave enough room below the filter unit to change filters. The filter housing usually has threaded openings. For copper pipe, attach two fittings that have appropriate-size male threads on one end and either a compression fitting or a soldered connection on the other. Be careful when threading metal pipe or fittings into the plastic threads of the filter unit, because it's easy to cross-thread them. For steel pipes, use a special union, available from a plumbing supply store, on one side of the filter.

▶ It's best to buy a unit with a built-in shutoff valve, but if the filter doesn't have such a valve, install one downstream from the filter. (See pages 130–131 for information on how to add a shutoff valve.) Use a full-flow valve. If the house has copper pipe, install a brass nipple between the valve and the filter.
▶ Look for wires clamped to the cold-water line or around the water meter. If any electrical wires are grounded to the pipes—and they probably are—you must place a jumper wire around the filter unit to maintain electrical continuity (Photo 4). Use two pipe clamps and No. 6 wire for up to 160-amp service, No. 4 wire for up to 220-amp service.

Caution

The filters shown here are not intended to remove harmful bacteria. They must be used on water that has been treated to be microbiologically safe.

Photo 4. A whole-house sediment filter is installed on the main water line, after the shutoff valve. The jumper wire must be added to maintain electrical continuity if the electrical system is grounded through the main water inlet.

Simplify Plumbing with a Shutoff Valve

A shutoff valve for a sink is like an emergency brake for a car—you don't need that extra safety very often, but when you need it you really need it.

Sizing Up the Project

If you have had some experience replacing faucets or solving other routine plumbing problems, you should feel comfortable about adding a shutoff valve where it's needed at a sink, toilet, or faucet.

Add a Shutoff Valve

Next time you have to replace a faucet or undertake some other plumbing repair, follow these steps to install an easily accessible shutoff valve while you're at it.

Out with the Old

▷ Remove the old supply elbows and tubes. In doing so, beware of the chain reactions that can occur when working with older plumbing. Some pipes will do their job until you start tampering with them, at which point they disintegrate. This is especially troublesome if the pipe that breaks is inside a wall or is an integral part of the faucet. Use a "hold back" pipe wrench to protect pipes farther down the line from turning and stress (Photo 1).

You may find copper, rather than threaded, pipe protruding through the wall. If so, cut the pipe with a tubing cutter, leaving it as long as possible for ease of working later.

In with the New

▷ Apply Teflon joint tape (Photo 2) or pipe joint compound to the male pipe threads to lubricate and, to a lesser degree, seal the joint.
▷ Insert the new shutoff valve (Photo 3). If you are connecting to copper pipe, use a compression fitting. Make sure that the valve outlet is facing upward.
▷ Connect the supply tube to the faucet nipple. Use flexible supply tubes (Photo 4), because they're easier to work with than rigid tubes.
▷ Connect the supply tube to the valve outlet (Photo 5). Then turn the water back on and check for leaks.

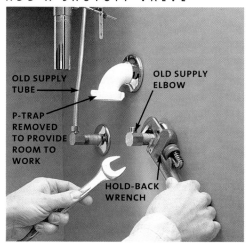

Photo 1. Remove the old supply elbows and tubes. Use a "hold back" pipe wrench to prevent the pipe from turning, and possibly breaking, inside the wall. Cut a copper pipe with a tubing cutter.

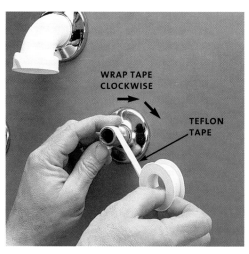

Photo 2. Apply Teflon joint tape (wrap clockwise) to lubricate and help seal the joint. Wrap the tape three or four turns around the male threads to ensure making a good seal.

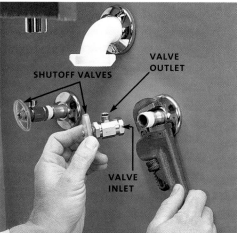
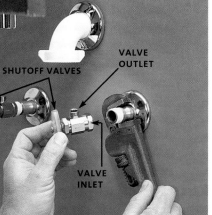

Photo 3. Install the new valve. Make sure to add the valve with its outlet facing upward. When connecting to existing copper pipe, use a shutoff valve with a compression fitting.

Tools You Need

Basin wrench

Open-end wrench

Pipe-joint compound

Pipe wrench

Teflon tape

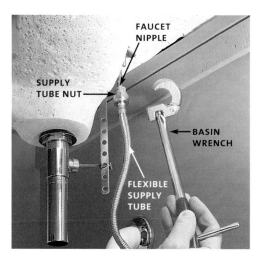

Photo 4. Connect the supply tube to the faucet nipple. Apply pipe-joint compound to the nipple. Use a basin wrench on hard-to-reach nuts. Immobilize the nipple with an open-end wrench.

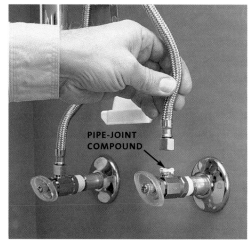

Photo 5. Connect the supply tube to the valve outlet. Again, use pipe-joint compound. Turn down the nut finger-tight, then make another half turn. Turn the water main back on and check for leaks.

Add an Outdoor Faucet

Rather than dragging a hose around the house from back to front or side to side, why not move the outside water supply closer to where you need it, simply by installing an additional outdoor faucet?

Sizing Up the Project

This project requires intermediate plumbing skills, most importantly the ability to solder copper pipe. You will begin by mounting a freezeproof sill cock outside the house. Using this type of faucet avoids having to shut off the outside water supply in the winter. The shutoff mechanism is located at the end of the copper water tube well inside the thermal envelope of the house, not inside the faucet itself. An anti-siphon device to prevent contaminated water from flowing back into the drinkable water supply is required by many plumbing codes.

Once the sill cock is attached, you must tap into an existing cold-water line inside the house to supply the new faucet. Because no two houses are the same, the exact route the new plumbing takes will vary, meaning that many types of plumbing fittings—ells, tees, couplings, and unions—might be needed.

Copper materials must be joined by soldering their connections, a process called sweating the pipes. Use only lead-free solder. Plastic pipes are joined using solvents and cements formulated for CPVC (chlorinated polyvinyl chloride). Where the pipe connects to the faucet, a plastic-to-copper compression fitting is needed. If the house has galvanized steel pipe, use a special adapter to make the transition from steel to CPVC or copper, and then finish the job with that material.

Before You Begin

The success of this project and the ease with which it is carried out depend significantly on where you place the new outdoor faucet and how you route the supply line to it.

Determining the Location

You won't always be able to put a new sill cock where you'd like. Obstacles, both outside and inside the house, must be considered. Look for penetration points where objects such as electrical service cables, telephone lines, or air-conditioning pipes already enter the house. By locating these spots and installing the new sill cock near one of them you more than likely will find the least amount of resistance in drilling through the house's siding and its foundation.

Planning the Interior Pipe Route

Once you have decided on an exterior location for the sill cock, move inside the house and examine that spot there. If you find, for example, that the pipe will enter a finished basement ceiling, choose a different location. Also check out the material you must cut or drill through. If, for instance, you would have to penetrate a concrete wall, try to find an easier installation spot.

Whenever possible, run the new line through the wood rim joist, a board that rests edge-down on the wooden sill that covers the concrete blocks of the foundation. The wooden joist is the easiest of the materials to drill through and usually doesn't require buying or renting special tools or accessories.

The new supply line has an inside diameter (i.d.) of 3/4 inch, which requires tying into the 3/4-inch main water line. Never connect to a smaller-diameter water line or there won't be enough water pressure in the new run. As a result, you may need to install a number of lengths of pipe to reach a 3/4-inch service line.

If it's impossible to gain access to the main water line, you can install a sill cock with a 1/2-inch i.d., if local plumbing codes permit this.

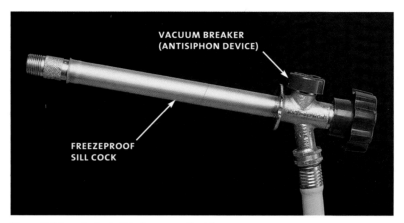

VACUUM BREAKER (ANTISIPHON DEVICE)

FREEZEPROOF SILL COCK

The antisiphon device in this freezeproof outdoor faucet prevents outside water from contaminating your house's water supply.

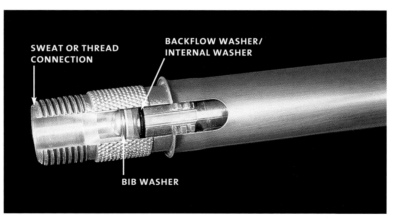

SWEAT OR THREAD CONNECTION

BACKFLOW WASHER/ INTERNAL WASHER

BIB WASHER

The shutoff mechanism shown in this cutaway view is located inside the house, assuring that this sill cock will be usable even in the dead of winter.

Tools You Need

Drill and 7/8-in. spade bit for wood siding

Hammer drill for concrete walls (rented)

Pipe reamer or file

Propane torch

Tape measure

Tubing cutter or hacksaw

Materials

Copper pipe (3/4" i.d.)

Emery cloth

Lead-free solder

90- and 45-degree angle copper elbows and unions, as needed

Pipe hangers

Soldering flux

Install the New Line

Start outside the house and work back to the cold-water line. This ensures that the installation point on the house's exterior will not fall on a siding joint or other undesirable spot. (To determine which is the cold-water pipe, turn on a couple of hot-water taps inside the house. After a few minutes, feel both water pipes to see which is cooler.)

Adding the Sill Cock

The sill cock must be installed at a slight downward angle so that the water drains out after it has been turned off.

▶ If the house has wood siding, drill through the siding and rim joist with a 7/8-inch spade bit. If you are drilling through concrete, use a hammer drill and masonry bit, available to rent.

▶ Set the sill cock in the hole and position the angled siding wedge, usually included with the unit, between the sill cock and the siding (Photo 1). Secure the sill cock to the house with the recommended fasteners, which are usually brass or galvanized wood screws.

▶ Open the sill cock fully by turning the handle counterclockwise. This prevents the faucet's internal rubber washers from burning and relieves the pressure from expanding hot air when the pipes are soldered.

Measuring and Assembling the Piping

No two installations will be identical, since obstacles and installation points will vary from house to house. Follow these basic steps and adjust them as needed. Sketch a map if necessary to help you plan the pipe's path and to buy the correct fittings and lengths of pipe.

▶ Once the sill cock is in place, measure the distance from the inside end of the sill cock to the cold-water line. Add an additional 3/4 inch for the soldered connection into the sill cock. Cut the necessary lengths of vertical and horizontal pieces with a pipe cutter.

▶ Clean the ends of the pipe and the insides of elbows and any other connecting fittings with emery cloth. Remove burrs in the cut ends with a pipe reamer or file.

▶ Apply flux to the insides of the fittings, the inside connecting area of the sill cock, and the cleaned pipe ends (Photo 2).

▶ Assemble the piping and fittings (Photo 3).

▶ If you must make a long run of pipe, support it every 6 to 10 feet with pipe hangers fastened to joists or some other supporting material. Don't cut into the cold-water supply pipe yet.

Tapping the Water Supply

The new copper pipe must be installed at a 90-degree angle to the cold-water supply pipe, which calls for careful measuring and marking.

▶ Measure from the inside edge of the nearest floor joist to the center of the diameter in the last length of new pipe. (In this case, it's the end of the sill cock itself.) Then mark this distance from the inside of the same floor joist on the cold-water pipe.

▶ Center the copper tee on this mark, then measure about 1/2 inch in from each end of the tee to accommodate the amount of pipe that is seated inside the fitting. Mark these spots on the cold-water pipe (Photo 4).

▶ Turn off the water at the water main. Before cutting into the main line, open the cold-water tap at the lowest point in the plumbing system,

for example a basement sink or laundry tub. This will drain as much water as possible from the cold-water line.

▶ Cut out the designated section of pipe (about 1-1/2 inches) between the two marks (Photo 5). Keep a bucket and rags handy to catch the drips.

▶ Dry the pipe before cleaning its ends with emery cloth and applying flux (see tip at left). The drier you can keep the pipe, the better the soldered joint will be. Clean and apply flux inside all ends of the tee.

▶ Finally, install the tee between the cold-water pipe sections and connect the short vertical pipe into the tee (Photo 6).

▶ Check again that the faucet outside is angled downward before soldering the joints.

Soldering the Joints

If you must solder near wood joists or other flammable material, use a flameproof cloth or piece of sheet metal to protect them from the torch flame. Wear heavy-duty gloves.

▶ Heat a fitting with a propane torch for about 30 seconds. Never touch the torch flame to the solder itself. Touch the tip of the solder to the edge of the fitting and allow capillary action to draw it into the gap between the pipe and the fitting (Photo 7). Bubbling or dripping solder means the joint is overheated.

If you are out of practice soldering, rehearse on pieces of scrap pipe and spare fittings to get a feel for how long to heat the fittings and how the melted solder is drawn into the joint.

▶ Continue to solder all the joints, using only lead-free solder.

▶ After all the joints are sealed, turn the water back on and check for leaks.

Drying Pipe for Soldering

Before soldering the tee to the supply line, stuff a small ball of white bread into each end of the cut pipe. It absorbs any residual water in the pipe and is flushed out when the water is turned back on.

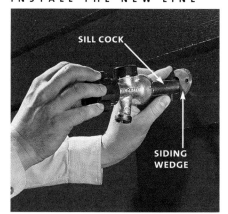

Photo 1. Install the outdoor faucet, or sill cock. Place the angled siding wedge between the sill cock and the siding. This wedge helps maintain a downward pitch for draining.

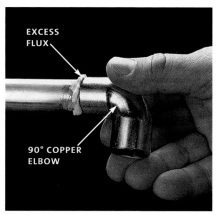

Photo 2. Clean the pipe ends and the insides of the fittings and sill cock with emery cloth. Then apply a liberal amount of flux to the ends of the pipe and the insides of the fittings.

Photo 3. Connect the fittings to all the sections of the new pipe. Dry-fit all the pieces to make sure that the new sections of pipe are the correct length.

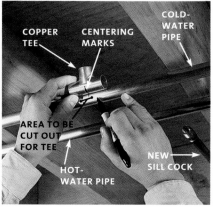

Photo 4. Align the center of the copper tee with the centering mark on the cold-water pipe. Measure 1/2 in. in from each end of the tee and mark these spots on the cold-water pipe.

Photo 5. Cut out the short section of pipe (about 1-1/2 in.) with a tubing cutter. Dry the pipe ends thoroughly. Clean the cut pipe ends with emery cloth and apply flux.

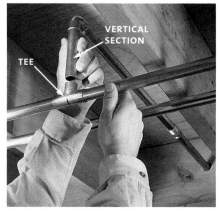

Photo 6. Install the tee between two ends of the cold-water pipes. Assemble the remaining section of pipe, making sure the faucet is angled downward.

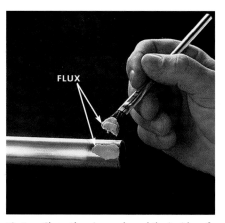

Photo 7. Sweat all the joints with lead-free solder. Make sure the sill cock is fully open, so pressure doesn't build up and the internal rubber washers don't burn.

protect against the elements

Power Wash Your House

Power washing is a one-day job that can do wonders for your home's siding.

138

Smart Suggestions for Exterior Painting

Follow these steps to achieve top-notch results.

140

Cure Wet Basements

Believe it or not, rain doesn't have to mean living with a sopping wet basement.

162

Smart Suggestions for Energy Efficient Insulation

Get the most out of your insulation with these basic steps.

166

**Renew Weathered
Exterior Wood**
Make your decks, fences, and siding look great again.

Pour and Form Concrete
Replace your buckled, cracked walkway with smooth new concrete.

Stucco-Over Concrete Block
This is a fun way to protect your foundation and add a touch of style in an unexpected place.

Hang Vinyl Gutters
If your gutters are leaking and sagging, replace them with durable vinyl gutters.

Vent Your Roof the Right Way
An unvented roof causes water leaks and roof damage. The solution is simple and inexpensive.

Defeat Ice Dams
Prevent winter's damage to your home's roof, walls, and ceilings. Defend yourself against ice dams.

Refurbish Your Windows
You can improve your windows—without replacing them—in one of three economical ways.

Power Wash Your House

In addition to general cleaning, power washing is a good way to prepare a house's surface for repainting. A thorough power washing removes not only dirt, mildew, and moss but also peeling, flaking, and chalking paint.

Sizing Up the Project

Power washing aluminum, steel, vinyl, or wood siding removes grit that acts like sandpaper when it's agitated by wind and rain, grinding away at paint. Thus, if you wash your house annually you may need to repaint less often.

Power washers are available for rent, usually by the day, from tool rental stores and some paint specialty stores. Make sure someone demonstrates how the equipment works and answers all your questions before you leave the store with the washer.

You can easily power wash even a very large house in a single day.

Successful Power Washing

You don't need a lot of skill to power wash a house, but there are some factors that make the job easier, safer, and more gratifying.

Choosing the Right Equipment

Power washers are rated by the pressure of their spray, measured in pounds per square inch (psi). For the average house, a rating from 1,200 to 2,500 psi, compared to about 60 psi for a garden hose, is sufficient. Units rated less than

1,200 psi won't do the job as effectively, and washers rated above 2,500 psi could cause damage if not handled skillfully.

You don't necessarily have to use a cleaning agent in a power washer—a clear-water power washing will usually do very well. However, if the siding suffers from chalking, oxidation, moss, or mildew, use a general-purpose cleaner, available at the rental site (Photo 1).

The nozzle's design and the width of its spray pattern are also important considerations. The three recommended sizes for power washing a house are 15-, 25-, and 40-degree nozzles, with the 15- and 25-degree nozzles being the ones that achieve the best results (Photo 2).

Handling the Equipment

You'll be working with a lot of water pressure, but with a little practice you should be able to control the wand. However, be prepared for more of a battle if you use a telescoping spray wand to reach higher floors (Photo 3). The wand kicks back 3–4 feet every time you depress the handle. You probably will tire from fighting the water pressure even without the telescoping wand. When you begin to flag, take a break.

Playing It Safe

▷ Do not let children operate a power washer.

▷ Never put your hands or fingers near the tip of the wand when it's operating or aim it at another person or an animal—the water will penetrate the skin and cause severe injury.

▷ Always wear eye protection when operating a power washer.

▷ Work with extreme caution when spraying near overhead electrical lines. Keep the wand at least 10 feet from power lines. If necessary, clean the area around power lines by hand, using a wood-handled scrub brush with synthetic bristles.

Keys to Success

Here are some do's and don'ts for power washing your house most effectively.

▷ Make sure all the windows are closed tightly.

▷ Cover the exterior electrical outlets and light fixtures with polyethylene film and duct tape.

▷ Place drop cloths over plants and shrubs. Move lawn furniture and other portable items away from the house.

▷ Watch the weather. If it's too windy, don't wash, to avoid nuisance overspray.

▷ Wash from the bottom up, but rinse from the top down (Photo 4). Otherwise, the detergent will run down on unwashed areas and leave streaks there.

▷ Keep the nozzle 10 to 12 inches from the surface, at approximately a 45-degree angle.

▷ Don't spray directly at windows—the water pressure can break them.

▷ Don't spray up under the laps of horizontal siding, which can lift them. Keep the angle of the wand downward.

▷ Don't spray directly into open eaves, crawl spaces, or gable-end vents.

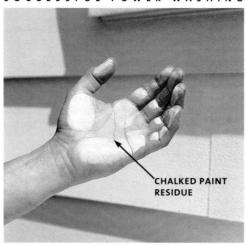

Photo 1. Chalking is a problem on many painted surfaces. Power washing is a quick way to remove chalking so a new coat of paint will adhere well.

CHALKED PAINT RESIDUE

15° NOZZLE PATTERN

Photo 2. Wash from the bottom up, to prevent dirt and the cleaning agent from running down onto the unwashed surface and leaving streaks.

TELESCOPING WAND

Photo 3. A telescoping wand makes it easier to reach upper stories, but it's harder to control the longer wand, so take more frequent breaks.

Photo 4. Rinse from the top down, to wash away the cleaning agent and dirt thoroughly and avoid leaving streaks on the clean surface.

Tools You Need

Drop cloths

Duct tape, polyethylene film

Eye protection

Wood-handled brush with synthetic bristles (as needed)

1,200–2,500 psi power washer (rented)

General-purpose cleaner

While You're at It

As long as you've rented the power washer for the day, use it to clean sidewalks, driveways, steps, trash cans, and even your car, truck, or RV.

Smart Suggestions for Exterior Painting

It's easy to think up reasons for not painting your house, but the only way to make your house look its best and to prolong the life of its exterior is to keep it painted.

If the surface is prepared correctly the job will look good for a long time. For the best results, follow these steps to prepare for painting and to deal with the most common problems that arise.

Clean the Surface

A power washer is the best way to clean off dirt and peeling or flaking paint (see "Power Wash Your House," pages 138–139). You may find after a power washing that your house needed only a bath, not repainting. Don't power wash a stucco house; it can destroy the stucco in seconds. If your house has wood siding, keep the wand 12 inches away to prevent gouging (Photo 1).

Scrape Off Loose Paint

Power washing won't remove all loose paint; some will still need to be scraped with a long-handled, heavy-duty scraper (Photo 2).

Scrape down to bare wood whenever possible, working with the grain. Once you have scraped away all the loose paint, sand or feather the edge between the scraped area and bare wood.

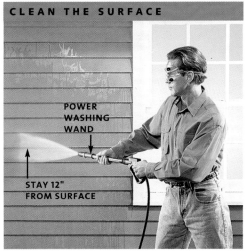

CLEAN THE SURFACE

POWER WASHING WAND

STAY 12" FROM SURFACE

Photo 1. Power wash your house to remove grit and flaking paint. Rent a unit with the right pressure.

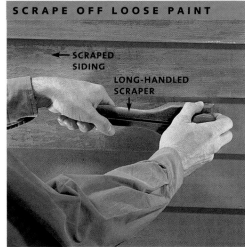

SCRAPE OFF LOOSE PAINT

SCRAPED SIDING

LONG-HANDLED SCRAPER

Photo 2. Scrape loose and flaking paint to bare wood. What's left is bonded to the surface, so paint over it.

Fill in Nicks and Gouges

Even with careful scraping and sanding, the siding will still show spots where the bare wood has been marred and the surface is lower than that of the old paint. Fill these surface imperfections before painting, with a surface-repair material like an exterior-grade spackling compound (Photo 3). A 4- to 6-inch broad knife will work well to ensure a smooth application. After the filler dries, in 30 to 60 minutes, sand it smooth with 100-grit sandpaper.

Caulk Joints and Gaps

To prevent water penetration and drafty rooms, and to ensure a good-looking paint job, caulk all joints where the siding meets the windows, door trim, and other openings (Photo 4). Even the smallest gap lets heat escape, which means dollars wasted on energy bills.

Remove all the old caulk and recaulk each joint with a high-quality paintable acrylic latex or silicone acrylic caulk. Don't forget to caulk around outdoor electrical boxes, outside water faucets, exterior lights, and under door thresholds and windowsills.

Reputty Window Glass

If your house's windows are more than twenty years old, the glass panes are likely sealed with glazing compound or putty. Before painting this type of window, make sure the glazing compound is in good shape.

Remove the old putty with a scraping tool specially designed for the nooks and recesses of window trim (Photo 5). Scrape down to the bare wood of the window sash, then use an artist's brush and an oil-base primer to seal the bare wood. After the primer dries, apply a new bead of glazing compound. Use a putty knife to bevel the putty so that water will flow off easily. Follow the directions on the compound's container for drying times.

Lead Paint

If your house was built before 1972, some of the original paint may contain lead. When scraping or sanding such paint, wear a face mask designed to filter out lead particles, wear old clothes that you can discard, and gather paint chips with a drop-cloth for disposal.

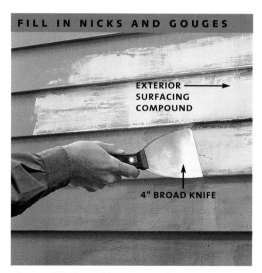

Photo 3. Fill holes and low spots with an exterior-grade surfacing compound. Allow the compound to dry according to the manufacturer's instructions, then sand it smooth with 100-grit sandpaper.

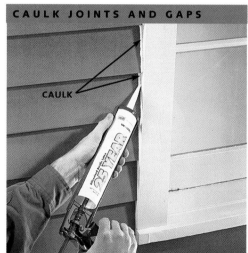

Photo 4. Caulk the joints between the siding and the window and door trim. Use a paintable acrylic latex or silicone acrylic caulk. Also caulk under the door thresholds and windowsills.

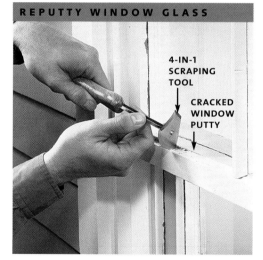

Photo 5. Scrape away cracked glazing compound, then reputty the windows. Prime bare wood on the window sash before applying a new bead of glazing compound. Then paint the window.

Prime All Bare Wood

Never apply paint to bare wood, which must be sealed with a primer so the new paint will adhere properly (Photo 6). Prime all new wood, any wood that was scraped and sanded, and all areas filled with surfacing compound. When in doubt, prime.

Primer is usually white, but your paint dealer can usually tint it that so it's close to the color of the top coat. Tinted primer assures more even color coverage of your final coat (Photo 7).

Use Top-Quality Tools

You can find any number of time-saving devices designed to make painting faster and easier. While they all work to some extent, the best way to prepare for and paint your house is still to use top-quality basic tools (Photo 8).

Brushes

You can paint an entire house using only two sizes of brush: a 2-1/2 inch angled brush for window sashes and small trim, and a 4-inch brush for wide trim and siding. Use nylon or other synthetic-bristle brushes for water-base latex paint. Do not use natural bristles with latex, because they absorb water, swell, and result in a sloppy job. Natural bristles are best used with oil- and alkyd-base paints, which won't wash out of synthetic bristles.

Buy high-quality brushes. Cheap ones only make the job harder, because they don't apply the paint evenly and don't last as long as good brushes.

Rollers

A paint roller works well for exterior painting. After applying the paint, go back and "back brush" it out before it dries. This process will eliminate the rough, textured effect that can result when painting with a roller.

A good-quality roller applies paint in a consistently thick coat and saves constantly dipping the brush so you can work faster, even though you must back-brush.

Paints

Check the label on the paint can for the product description or a list of ingredients. It should show you the percentages of the various additives, fillers, carriers, and resins. Look for a resin content of 20 to 25 percent; the higher the better, for durability.

Don't be taken in by low-priced paint. It may cost less initially, but your house will need repainting sooner than if you had used a premium-quality paint.

PRIME ALL BARE WOOD

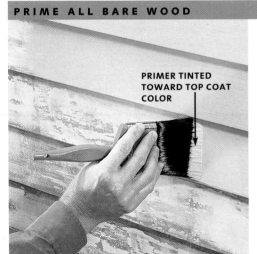

PRIMER TINTED TOWARD TOP COAT COLOR

Photo 6. Prime all bare wood and any scraped or sanded areas. A new top coat of paint won't adhere properly to unprimed wood.

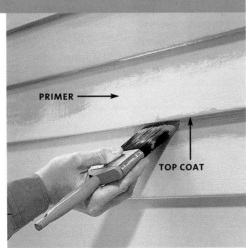

PRIMER →

TOP COAT

Photo 7. Have your paint dealer tint the primer to a color that's as close as possible to the top coat's color. This will ensure better coverage of the top coat.

USE TOP-QUALITY TOOLS

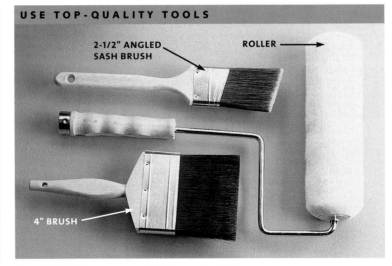

2-1/2" ANGLED SASH BRUSH

ROLLER →

4" BRUSH →

Photo 8. With these you can paint the whole exterior of your house: a 2-1/2 in. sash brush, a 4-in. siding brush, and a good-quality roller.

Common Paint Problems

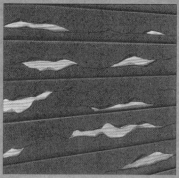
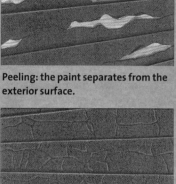

Peeling: the paint separates from the exterior surface.

Cracking: the paint breaks into small squares or rectangles.

Blistering: small pockets of vapor form beneath the paint film.

Peeling
Cause: Moisture penetrating from inside the house or bad surface preparation of the siding during a previous painting.

Solution: For moisture from within, locate the source and eliminate it. In a bathroom, install an exhaust fan to draw the moisture out of the house. In areas of less serious moisture problems, install vents in the siding to allow moisture to escape.

Cracking
Cause: Hardening of multiple layers of glossy, oil-based paint. Because the paint can no longer expand and contract with changes in the weather, it eventually cracks. An advanced stage of cracking, called alligatoring, occurs when the painted surface looks like an alligator's hide.

Solution: Remove the old paint, fill low spots, then prime and repaint. This repair takes lots of time and is hard work. Consider using a heat gun to soften the paint before scraping it.

Blistering
Cause: Most often caused by painting in direct sunlight or over hard, glossy surfaces. Blisters also result when water that is trapped behind the paint vaporizes and bubbles when exposed to intense heat from the sun.

Solution: Break open a blister. If bare wood shows, moisture is the problem. If a solid layer of paint is below the blister, the bubble is caused by heat. Either way, scrape, sand, and prime the blistered areas, then repaint the surface.

Mildew: a living fungus eats protein and nutrients found in the paint.

Nailhead staining: droplet-shaped rust marks form below the nailheads.

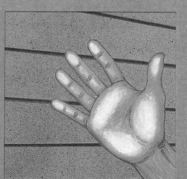

Chalking: on siding, a white powder that can easily be rubbed off.

Mildew
Cause: A combination of moisture and shade.

Solution: Prevent the surface from becoming too moist. The remedy may include trimming shrubs and bushes away from the house for better air circulation. To remove mildew, scrub the area with a solution of 1 quart household bleach in 3 quarts of water. Rinse with clean water. Cover your skin and wear eye protection when using this solution, and protect the nearby plants.

Nailhead Staining
Cause: Moisture in the wood, and improper patching with putty and primer when first painted.

Solution: Replace the nails with good-quality, galvanized nails. For nails that can't be removed, sand the rusted nailhead until bright metal shows, then spot-prime it or apply a rust-neutralizing agent to convert the rust to a harmless substance and seal the metal. Apply an exterior-grade filler or caulk, sand the siding smooth, and then paint.

Chalking
Cause: Poor-quality paint or waiting too long between paintings. Chalking occurs most often with light-colored paints.

Solution: Power wash the surface with trisodium phosphate (TSP) if your community allows it or an all-purpose cleaner otherwise, and then scrub. Thoroughly rinse the surface. Once it's dry, usually within a few days, reprime and repaint.

Renew Weathered Exterior Wood

Unfinished exterior wood will often naturally darken for the first year or two, then lighten again to a silvery gray. But because of the house's eaves, landscaping, and orientation, outdoor wood rarely receives uniform exposure to the elements, resulting in a blotchy look. The techniques here describe how to clean or brighten exterior wood in its natural state.

Sizing Up the Project

Renewing weathered wood is an inexact science. Considerations such as the type of wood, the climate, and the location of the wood must all be factored into the diagnosis and cure. The methods given here are for renewing wood, not removing paint. You can use the same products to clean wood with a worn coat of semitransparent stain (more than four years old) or water-repellent preservative (more than two years old), but the results won't be nearly as dramatic.

No one product or process is a cure-all, so always experiment in a small, out-of-the-way area first, following the manufacturer's instructions. If you like the natural color that returns after the cleaning process, apply a clear water-repellent preservative to protect against excess moisture and cracking, then let nature run its course. As long as you prevent mildew and keep dirt off, the wood will remain silvery gray.

If you plan to apply a semitransparent stain, remove the dirt and mildew with a household bleach, as described below. If you want to keep a natural wood look, you must apply and maintain some type of finish, or continue to renew the wood with a cleaner every year or two. Decks and porches, tortured by dirt, water,

baking sun, and foot traffic, require more cleanings and finish applications than siding, fences, and outdoor furniture.

Making decks, fences, and siding look great again requires just a few cleaning solutions and such basic tools as this stiff-bristled brush, garden hose, garden sprayer, and optional power washer.

144

Diagnose the Problem

Look for one or all of the following four causes of wood discoloration, and perform the tests for them in the order listed. Knowing the cause of the problem lets you select the correct cure.

▶ Dirt and grime cling to wood, especially if it's rough or textured. Scrub the wood with a stiff broom dunked in water and laundry detergent, then rinse. If it comes clean, this is all you need to do—but more than likely you will have additional problems.

▶ Mildew thrives on wood that has been subjected to high humidity, constant shade, or poor air circulation. Mildew may be black, gray, red, green, or brown. It is ugly, but it doesn't affect the structure of the wood the way a wood-rotting fungus does. To test for mildew, dab straight household liquid bleach on an inconspicuous section of wood (Photo 1). Let it stand for 30 seconds, then rinse. If it removes the discoloration, the problem is caused at least in part by mildew.

▶ Weathering from rain, sunlight, and other elements breaks down surface fibers and draws chemicals within the wood (called extractives) to the surface. Wood affected this way turns light tan to black and may change color dramatically where the eaves no longer extend to provide protection. Test for weathering with a solution of water and oxalic acid, which is sometimes marketed as wood bleach. Mix 1 ounce of oxalic acid crystals with a quart of water, then dab it onto the wood (Photo 2). Wait 5 minutes, then scrub it with a stiff-bristled, nonmetallic brush and rinse it off. If this brings the wood back close to its natural color, weathering is the culprit.

▶ Iron stains are most often caused by ungalvanized nails, wire brushes, and steel wool. Finishes can also be contaminated with iron residue from items such as a metal bucket or sprayer. Look for iron stains with the oxalic acid test just described.

Notice from these tests that the discolorations found in our wood are only skin deep—less than 1/16 inch thick. That's why cleaners and brighteners work so well—you need only penetrate this thin layer.

Choose a Solution

Any of the problems described can be remedied—or at least improved—with one of two widely available cleaning agents.

▶ Bleach-based products (or those containing sodium hypochlorite, as discussed below) are the easiest to apply, since they require little or no scrubbing. But even as they remove mildew stains, they can remove the natural color of the wood too. They tend also to raise the grain of the wood and can be corrosive to nails and screws, even galvanized ones, unless you thoroughly rinse them.

▶ Acid-based products such as oxalic acid leave wood with a more natural look, but they are more difficult to apply, they require scrubbing, and they don't always permanently kill mildew, which you must do if you're going to apply any type of finish. They are often in a powdered form and they require care in handling.

DIAGNOSE THE PROBLEM

Photo 1. Test for mildew by brushing liquid household bleach on a small section of the discolored area, then rinsing with a garden hose after 30 seconds.

Photo 2. Test for weathering by applying a water and oxalic acid solution, waiting 5 minutes, then scrubbing with a stiff nonmetallic brush and rinsing.

Bleach Away Mildew

If your tests showed that the wood is discolored primarily from mildew, clean it with either a homemade or store-bought bleach solution. Commercial products often contain sodium hypochlorite (liquid household bleach) or some other sodium compound. Check the label to see if it claims the product will kill mildew. (All wood brighteners and cleaners remove mildew; only those containing bleaches kill it.)

You can create a home brew by mixing 1 gallon of household bleach (the label should say 5 percent sodium hypochlorite) with 2 or 3 gallons of warm water and 1 cup of an ammonia-free cleaning detergent (but first see the important precautions on the next page). Decrease the amount of water to create a stronger solution.

▶ Spray on the solution with a pump garden sprayer, working from bottom to top for siding and fences (Photo 3). Wait 15 minutes, then spray it off with the highest pressure stream of water you can muster from your garden hose, rinsing from top to bottom. Scrub only if the instructions tell you to do so (Photo 4). Scrubbing with some bleach-based products actually makes the wood look worse.

▶ Rinse the wood surface with a full-force stream from your garden hose (Photo 5). Again, work from top to bottom.

▶ When you are finished, thoroughly rinse the garden sprayer with fresh water, because if you don't, bleach will destroy the gaskets.

BLEACH AWAY MILDEW

Photo 3. Apply cleaner or brightener using a pump-style garden sprayer. Clean from bottom to top, thoroughly wetting wood surfaces.

Photo 4. Scrub the wood surface with a stiff-bristled, nonmetallic brush. Not all cleaners require scrubbing, so be sure to read the instructions.

Photo 5. Rinse the surface using a forceful stream of water from a garden hose. Carefully rinsing with a pressure washer can brighten the wood even more.

Treat Stains

If your tests showed that the discoloration is caused mostly by weathering, or if the wood has iron stains, use a store-bought product containing oxalic acid, or mix your own. Create your own cleanser by dissolving 4 ounces of oxalic acid in a gallon of warm water.

▶ Apply it from bottom to top with a roller or sprayer, let it stand for 15 minutes, then scrub the surface with a stiff, nonmetallic brush and rinse it with a garden hose, from top to bottom.

▶ To prevent the black streaks caused by rusting nailheads from recurring, sink the nails 1/4 inch with a nail set and fill the holes with a wood-colored exterior caulk (Photo 6).

Finally, if your tests showed multiple problems—mildew, extractive staining, and iron stains—go through the two steps just mentioned, using the bleach product first, followed by the oxalic acid. Never mix the two products. Another option is to use an oxalic acid product, scrub vigorously, then rinse with a pressure washer. This method will usually eliminate most, but not all, of the mildew and discoloration. Follow the directions for power washing on pages 138-139.

TREAT STAINS

WOOD-TONE CAULK

Photo 6. Prevent staining from bleeding nails by setting the nails 1/4 in. below the surface, then filling the holes with a matching-colored caulk.

SAFETY

Chemical Considerations

As you deal with tools and chemicals, keep these precautions in mind:

▶ When using store-bought products, their directions take precedence over those described here. Some require wetting the wood first or applying the product on a cool surface. There are many variations in these products and their instructions, but their labels' directions are generally clear.

▶ Never mix commercial products with one another or with household cleaning products unless instructed to on the label. Bleach and ammonia together create a poisonous substance nearly as lethal as mustard gas.

▶ Always wear rubber gloves and goggles.

▶ Wear old clothes. Bleach will ruin colored clothes.

▶ Protect plants, shrubs, and grass. First, saturate their branches and leaves with water, then cover them with plastic. When finished applying and rinsing the cleaner, remove the plastic and rinse the plants and the surrounding area again with fresh water to dilute the solutions.

▶ Never use a wire brush or steel wool for scrubbing, or a metal pail or metal garden sprayer to apply a solution. Metal residue can create iron spots.

▶ Never use a paint sprayer for applying cleaners or brighteners.

▶ Be careful around power lines. Extension ladders, water, and electricity can make dangerous, even deadly, companions.

Preserve the Wood

Once you have finished the cleansing process, there are four basic categories of finishes you can use to keep your wood looking natural. Each has its tradeoffs.

▶ Semitransparent stains allow the texture and, to varying degrees, the grain of the wood to show through (Photo 7). Two coats of oil-base penetrating stain can last up to five or six years on rough-sawn or weathered wood and somewhat less on smooth wood. Be sure to apply the second coat before the first is fully dry. Latex-base stains, which are easier to apply and less likely to show lap marks, are also available but aren't as durable, since they don't penetrate the surface as deeply as oil-base stains.

Many companies offer semitransparent stains in cedar and redwood tones that mimic the original color of the wood. The final appearance is a blend of the stain and the natural color of the wood over which it's applied.

▶ Solid stains are basically thinned-down paints. They hide all the grain and most of the texture of wood. Never use them on decks, because they're a maintenance headache.

▶ Translucent, multicoat finishes let the wood show through yet have sufficient body and pigment to offer protection (Photo 8). The best of these, which are flexible enough to stand up to the elements and require several coats, can be very expensive. Check their labels to make sure they're meant for exterior use and contain

ultraviolet (UV) blockers to inhibit weathering and create a more uniform look.

Don't use marine or urethane varnishes outside; they rapidly become brittle and peel.

▶ Water-repellent finishes and water-repellent preservatives don't form a protective film but do help prevent water staining and checking (small cracks), and hold mildew at bay (Photo 9). Some repellents, both clear and tinted, contain UV blockers. Those labeled "preservative" offer better protection than plain repellents.

For best results, apply two coats of a water-repellent preservative after the brightened, cleaned wood is thoroughly dry. Follow up with additional coats every year or two on decks and every three or four years on siding and fences.

PRESERVE THE WOOD

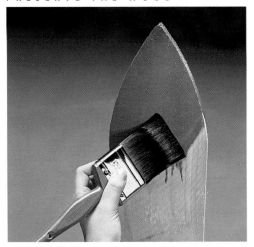

Photo 7. Semitransparent stains (this one is tinted a cedar color) offer protection for up to six years, but they let only some of the wood grain show through.

Photo 8. Translucent, multicoat finishes allow the natural richness of the wood to show through, but they are expensive and time consuming to apply.

Photo 9. Water repellents, sealants, and preservatives prevent water stains, checking, and mildew growth, but they must be applied frequently.

Pour and Form Concrete

If you are tired of tripping over chunks of chipping concrete or picking pieces of it out of the lawn before cutting the grass, you can repair that stretch of broken walkway and learn some very useful concrete-handling skills in the process.

Sizing Up the Project

This project requires some heavy lifting and a strong back. If you are replacing a broken walkway or a section of driveway or patio, you will have to wield a heavy sledgehammer to break up and remove the damaged section. And mixing new concrete in a wheelbarrow is hard on the back and arms. Massaging the newly poured concrete into shape also involves a lot of bending and working on all fours.

If you've never poured concrete before, start small. A short section of walkway like the 3x6-foot run shown in this project is manageable for a first-time DIYer. A small pad, whether it's for an air conditioner, trash cans, or a garden bench, is another good project to start with.

A short section of walkway like this 3 x 6-foot strip is a good way to acquaint yourself with the tools, materials, and techniques for working with concrete.

Protection While Demolishing and Pouring Concrete

Swinging a sledgehammer to break up old concrete sends chunks flying everywhere. Protect your house and yourself with the following measures.

Protect Your House and Grounds
▶ Stand scrap sections of plywood or drywall against walls and windows if you are working near the house.
▶ Cover favorite plants.
▶ Spread tarps or plastic sheeting over nearby grass to keep concrete chunks out of your mower later.

Protect Yourself
Concrete is quite caustic, and flying chips can do serious injury. Wear the appropriate clothing:
▶ Heavy gloves
▶ Long pants
▶ Long-sleeved shirt
▶ Work boots
▶ Dust mask when you are pouring dry mix

Rub clear silicone sealant onto the palms of your work gloves and let it cure overnight. You'll keep a firmer grip on the sledgehammer and other tools.

Proper eye protection is extremely important during concrete demolition. Everyday glasses can cause great injury if shards from a broken lens fly into an eye. Instead of regular glasses, wear goggles like those shown in the photos on the facing page, which fit closely all around and have side air vents.

Another good option is to wear a face shield, but don't rely solely on it. Wear goggles or safety glasses, available in your prescription if needed, under a face shield to guard against debris flying up.

To keep a face shield clean and scratch-free, cover the front with plastic wrap during use, then just peel that off and replace it next time.

Finally, keep curious children and "sidewalk demolition supervisors" at a safe distance unless they too are appropriately dressed.

Before You Begin
Proper preparation is the key to success for this project. Have all your tools and materials on site before starting. You can go solo on a job this size, but having a helper who can mix concrete and clean tools while you work the concrete will make the project go faster.

Timing the Job
Watch the weather. Ideal conditions for working concrete are 50 to 70 degrees F, with no rain forecast. Hot, dry weather will speed the hardening of the concrete, so under those conditions you'll have to work faster. Don't attempt this project if freezing is forecast. Watch out for rain, too. Keep a roll of thick polyethylene plastic on hand just in case.

Buying Materials
One 60-pound bag of concrete mix yields enough concrete to cover 1-1/2 square feet of walkway to a depth of 4 inches. The walkway shown here required 12 bags. Buy concrete mix that has gravel and sand already mixed, in such common brand names as Sakrete and Quikrete. Don't buy portland cement, mason mix, or mason sand, which don't have the necessary gravel and sand for this project. For more information on estimating and ordering concrete, see the box on page 153. If still in doubt, ask a knowledgeable salesperson at the dealer's.

Demolish the Old Slab

First get rid of the old concrete, after reviewing the facing page for how to protect yourself and your house. Then proceed as follows.

▶ Break up the damaged sections with a sledgehammer. Start at an open edge and work inward (Photo 1). As you near the good sections of walkway, slow down. Older sidewalks often crack all the way through at the control joint, as they're supposed to, and usually separate cleanly. But newer walkways may still be solid all the way through.

▶ With a masonry blade in a circular saw, deepen the control joint to at least 1-1/2 inches in three or four successively deeper passes (Photo 2). Then carefully whack off the remaining concrete.

Smooth the Soil

Tree roots are often the culprit behind or below cracked, crumbling concrete. If tree roots have broken up the slab, you can chop off the offending root a foot or so past the walkway, then coat its ends with a root preservative, available at most large nurseries. However, if you chop through large roots thicker than an arm, you can kill the tree. Oaks are especially vulnerable. Consult a tree expert before hacking away. If you love the tree and the root has to stay, you may have to reroute the walkway.

▶ Removal is hard, heavy work, so move the debris as few times as possible. Wheelbarrow it directly to its final resting spot or trash bin.

▶ After removing all the broken-up concrete, clean out and flatten the area. Tamp the area with the end of a scrap 4x4 (Photo 3). Fill low spots with sand, then sweep off the exposed ends of the good concrete sections.

Tools You Need

Circular saw
Drill
Edging tool
Finishing trowel
4-ft. level
Grooving tool
Hammer
Hoe or shovel
Paintbrush
Polyethylene plastic roll
Push broom
Sledgehammer
Wheelbarrow
Wood or magnesium hand float

Materials

Concrete mix
2x4 screed boards
1x3 stakes
Motor oil

DEMOLISH THE OLD SLAB

Photo 1. Break up the damaged section with a 16-lb. sledgehammer. Start at an open side, then work carefully toward good sections. Wear protective gear.

Photo 2. Cut and deepen the control joint to create a clean break between the old and new concrete sections. Use a masonry blade in a circular saw.

SMOOTH THE SOIL

Photo 3. Remove loose dirt and roots, flatten the area, then compact it with the end of a scrap 4x4. Fill any low spots with sand or gravel.

Construct the Forms

Use 2x4's to build the forms that will hold the concrete in shape as it cures. Make sure they are straight and without warps, bows, or twists. Any deformation in the forms translates into a malformed shape in the finished concrete.

▶ Lay down 2x4 forms, leveling them with a carpenter's 4-foot level so that the tops of the boards are level with the existing walkway sections. Extend the 2x4's past the good sections at least 6 inches.

▶ Hammer in foot-long 1x3 stakes at the ends of the 2x4's and every 2 feet in between (Photo 4). Secure these stakes to the forms with double-headed nails or drywall screws, making sure the tips don't extend inside the forms. And don't let the stakes protrude above the forms or they'll be in the way when you level the concrete. Bank dirt along the outside of the form for rigidity.

▶ Paint motor oil on the inside edges of the forms so they'll separate easily from the new concrete (Photo 5). If the soil is extremely dry, dampen it lightly so it won't absorb water from the concrete when you pour it.

Pour the Concrete

From the time you start mixing until the concrete is hard enough to broom-finish, you have about 3 to 5 hours of working time. The temperature and humidity will affect curing time slightly one way or the other.

Concrete shrinks very little as it hardens. The water doesn't evaporate but takes part in a chemical reaction with the cement, gravel, and sand mix.

If the ratio of water to dry material is off, or if the ingredients are not properly mixed, the finished product will be flawed even though it may look perfectly good at first. Fine cracks can admit water, which will crack the concrete as it freezes. Poorly mixed dry ingredients can also result in too much gravel ending up near the surface or pushed down too low in the wet mix, resulting in chipping, crumbling concrete at some future date.

CONSTRUCT THE FORMS

STAKES BELOW TOP OF FORMS

Photo 4. Secure the forms in place with 1x3 stakes every 2 ft. The stakes shouldn't protrude above the forms. Mound dirt along the outer edges for stability.

MOTOR OIL

Photo 5. Brush motor oil onto the insides of the forms so they will release easily from the cured concrete. Sweep the ends of the old walkway.

Once you are ready, mix the concrete.

▶ Set a bag of dry concrete mix in a wheelbarrow, slit the top with a utility knife, then dump. This can create quite a cloud, so be sure to wear a dust mask.

▶ Dry-mix the ingredients with a shovel or hoe. Add water, then mix thoroughly until all the ingredients are uniformly wet (Photo 6). Most mixes call for about 1 gallon of water per 60-pound bag. Make a small cone out of the mix. It should hold its shape. If it crumbles, add more water. If the cone won't hold its shape, add more dry concrete mix.

▶ Starting at one end, dump the concrete into the form. Use a screed board to level it off (Photo 7). Pack the corners and edges using a rake or shovel. Shuffle the screed board from side to side and up and down to level and compact the concrete.

▶ Continue until the form is completely full. Then go back and run the screed across it one more time. Fill in any remaining low spots with a few blobs of mix. Work the mixture until the surface is uniformly flat and level with the top of the forms.

POUR THE CONCRETE

Photo 6. Mix the concrete in a wheelbarrow with a hoe or shovel. First dry-mix the ingredients, then add water until the mix is firm but wet.

SCREED BOARD

Photo 7. Level the concrete even with the tops of the forms. Work the screed board in a side-to-side and up-and-down motion. Push concrete into the corners.

Finish the Surface

Patience and a deft touch with a trowel are important to smooth and finish the concrete.

Smoothing and Shaping

▶ Immediately after screeding, smooth the surface with a wood or magnesium hand float (Photo 8). Work in large arcs, holding the float at a slight angle so the leading edge doesn't dig into the concrete. The float pushes the gravel below the surface and further levels small dips. Don't overwork the concrete, because this will bring too much water and cement to the top, weakening the surface of the walkway. At this point just smooth out the ripples and ridges.

▶ While the concrete is still pliable— usually within the first hour—cut the concrete away from the forms to a depth of about 1 inch with a trowel, then edge the slab and cut the control joints. Push the edging tool in a series of short seesaw strokes (Photos 9 and 10). Edging the slab, as the name suggests, rounds and compacts the edges, making them easier on the feet and less susceptible to chipping.

▶ After completing an edge, go back and take one long, continuous swipe to smooth it out. Use the edging tool to round the new concrete where it meets the existing sections of walkway, too. Lightly wet the tool to help it slide along more easily.

▶ Cut control joints to match the spacing on the rest of the walkway. In the project here it was every 3 feet. Use the screed board as a straightedge to guide the grooving tool (Photos 11 and 12). Again work it in a series of short strokes. The gravel below the surface will want to block and misdirect the grooving tool, so be firm. Then go back over the cut with one long swipe.

▶ Use the float to remove the marks made by the edging and grooving tools. You may have to use the edging, grooving, and float tools a few times to make the surface flat and finish the edges just right.

▶ When all the surface water has disappeared and the concrete has set hard enough so it's difficult to indent with your fingers, use a finish trowel held at a slight angle to further smooth the concrete (Photo 13). Work in a series of arcs. A thick cream, or slurry, should rise to the surface to help fill small voids and grooves. Bear down hard. Go over the entire surface several times if the final surface is to be smooth. A single pass will suffice if you're adding a slip-resistant broom finish. If the concrete has become very hard, sprinkle a little water over the surface and work the trowel with both hands in a back-and-forth scrubbing motion.

▶ Match the surface texture to the texture of the existing sidewalk. To give it a broom finish, wait until the concrete has hardened sufficiently so a push broom with stiff bristles leaves crisp, stippled marks (Photo 14).

Curing the Concrete

Cover the area with plastic for two or three days to allow the concrete to cure, harden, and strengthen (Photo 15). Secure the edges of the plastic by laying boards over them. If vehicles will be driving over the new concrete, let it cure for at least a full week.

Remove the double-headed nails or drywall screws connecting the forms to the support stakes, then tap down on the forms with a hammer to release them from the concrete. Remove the forms, then fill in the spaces along the walkway with dirt and tamp it down.

Clean Up the Easy Way

Wash your tools with a hose and stiff brush as soon as you've finished with them. Wet concrete comes right off, but if it dries, you'll have to chip it away.

Photo 8. Even out the concrete surface with a wood or magnesium hand float to smooth the surface and push gravel farther down.

Photo 9. Use a hand edger like this to round off the edges of the new concrete slab and to give you a clean edge.

Photo 10. Round and compact the edges of the slab with an edging tool (left). Work in short, jabbing motions. Finish with a long pass.

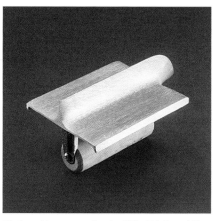

Photo 11. Use a grooving tool like this to cut the control joints. Guide it along the slab with a straight 2 x 4 screed board.

Photo 12. Cut control joints with a grooving tool (Photo 11) to about 1/4 the slab's depth. Space them the same distance as the joints in the rest of the walkway.

Photo 13. Smooth the surface with a flexible finishing trowel. Work in short arcs. A slurry of cement and water should rise to the surface to fill small gaps and grooves.

Photo 14. To create a slipproof surface, drag a push broom across the surface of the concrete. The broom should not push liquid, just leave slight ridges on the surface.

Photo 15. Cover the work area with plastic to allow the concrete to harden slowly. Keep it covered for three days for foot traffic, seven if vehicles will be driving over it.

Stucco-Over Concrete Block

You take special care to clean and paint your house's siding, but what can you do about its foundation of drab, gray concrete blocks? Now you can dress up your house's foundation with a nice finishing touch of colored stucco.

Sizing Up the Project

This project calls for no special skills, but working with heavy, wet stucco can quickly become tiring, and having someone to spell you occasionally might be worthwhile.

After applying a concrete bonding compound to help the stucco adhere to the bare concrete and then preparing the mixture, the stucco is applied to the concrete block foundation and smoothed out. The stucco can be tinted as it's mixed or you can paint it once it dries.

Stucco can be mixed by hand, but consider renting a 1/2-inch drill with a mixer attachment. It's faster than a hand mixer.

Before You Begin

This is not a damp-weather project—moist conditions almost double stucco's drying time. Nor is it one for a hot, sunny day—hot, sunny weather (above 80 degrees F) dries stucco too quickly, causing it to shrink and develop hairline cracks. If the stucco does develop small cracks, mix up a thin mixture of portland cement and water, called slurry, and brush the entire surface with it to moisten it and fill the cracks.

Mix the Materials

Place a drop cloth under the mixing bucket before starting to mix the stucco. Cement, sand, and water will inevitably splash out, and dried stucco is difficult to wash away. Cover the ground and any plants and shrubs around the foundation of the house.

Don't mix more stucco than you can use in about an hour. Once it starts to set, the goo becomes useless. Stir the mixture about every 10 minutes to slow the hardening process.

Mix the stucco as follows.

▶ In a 5-gallon bucket, combine about 8 pounds of portland cement and 8 pounds of sand with about 1/2 gallon of water. As a rule of thumb, 100 pounds of cement and 100 pounds of sand cover about 300 square feet of surface area.

▶ Stir the mixture until it has the consistency of heavy paste. If you are tinting the stucco, make sure you stir thoroughly so the colorant is evenly distributed. Add water or cement and sand as needed. If the stucco is too thin, it will dry too quickly and develop hairline cracks.

Apply the Stucco

Follow these steps for a polished-looking job.

▷ Scrape the foundation blocks with a wire brush to remove loose dirt or paint, then apply a liquid concrete bonding adhesive to the entire foundation (Photo 1). This adhesive continues to work even after it has dried.

▷ Scoop the stucco mixture from the bucket onto the cement trowel with a garden trowel instead of loading the cement trowel directly from the bucket (Photo 2).

▷ Trowel the stucco mixture onto the adhesive-coated blocks with the cement trowel (Photo 3). Apply a coat about 1/4 inch thick to cover the mortar joints between the blocks. Work in small areas of about 25 to 30 square feet.

▷ Smooth the entire surface with a rubber float, blending sections as you go (Photo 4). If you happen to pull out a portion of stucco with the float, just apply fresh stucco from the bucket, then use the rubber float to blend the patch.

▷ Once the stucco has dried completely—be sure to allow at least three days—you can paint it with latex house paint.

▷ Be creative. Experiment with swirls or other patterns in the stucco, as shown in Photo 4.

After-Care

When it comes time to clean your new stucco, first repair any cracks, then use a spray nozzle on a garden hose. Don't use a power sprayer, as it could cut right through the stucco.

Photo 1. Apply a liquid concrete bonding adhesive over the entire foundation before you start to apply the new stucco coating.

Photo 2. Use a garden trowel to scoop stucco from the bucket onto the cement trowel instead of loading it directly from the bucket.

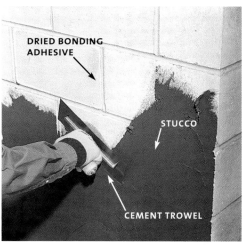

Photo 3. Trowel a 1/4-in. layer of stucco mixture onto the adhesive-coated concrete blocks, working in areas of approximately 25 to 30 sq. ft.

Photo 4. Smooth the surface with a rubber float, then work patterns into it if you like. Once it has dried, paint it with latex house paint.

Tools You Need

5-gal. bucket

Cement trowel

Garden trowel

Hand mixer or 1/2-in. drill with power-mixing attachment

Paint roller or paint-brush

Rubber float

Materials

Liquid concrete bonding adhesive

Mortar colorant (if desired)

Portland cement

Hang Vinyl Gutters

If your gutters are leaking and sagging and you're tired of trying to fix them, it's time to install a new system of vinyl gutters and downspouts. These gutters are literally a snap to put together and, best of all, once they are up they never need to be painted.

Sizing Up the Project

This project involves working on a ladder—an extension ladder, if your house has more than one floor—to attach gutter brackets to the fascia board running around the edge of the roof. It requires careful work and patience to achieve the correct slope so the gutters will drain properly, but you need no special DIY skills to install vinyl gutters. You will probably want a helper or two when it's time to attach the gutters to the house, because each section is about 10 feet long, and they can be awkward to put up by yourself.

Before You Begin

In case you are familiar only with older types of vinyl gutters, there are advantages to the systems now widely available that may persuade you to undertake the project.

Advantages of Vinyl

There are in fact many reasons why this is the perfect do-it-yourself project.

▶ The components are easy to work with.
▶ The sections are durable.
▶ These lengths don't leak at connections.
▶ They look like metal gutters, without the bulky connecting pieces in older vinyl systems.

Both the gutter and downspout sections are readily cut with a handsaw, but you might consider renting a power miter box to make the project go more quickly. One of these is much faster and makes a smoother cut edge than is possible with hand sawing.

The house shown here has a conventional soffit and fascia setup. If yours differs—for example, if the ends of the roof rafters are exposed—attach the gutters to the house with roof brackets. A 6-inch long Phillips screwdriver bit for your drill will span the distance from the front edge of the gutter to the fascia when installing the fittings and brackets.

Planning

Before buying your supplies, pick up a product brochure to help you figure out how much gutter and downspout material to purchase, along with which fittings and seals you need and how many of each to buy.

Here are some other things to keep in mind:

▶ Use one downspout for every 700 square feet of roof area.

▶ Try to have a downspout at each corner of the house, although this is not always possible.

▶ To avoid having water standing inside the gutters, slope them from the center of the roof's width to the drop outlet (the part that allows the water to drain into the downspout). One inch of slope per 20 feet of gutter length provides good drainage.

▶ Most roof shingles extend beyond the fascia board approximately 1/2 to 3/4 inch to prevent rainwater from running down between the fascia and the back edge of the gutter. However, if the edges of the roof shingles are flush with the fascia, install a metal drip edge (see the diagram on the next page). Slip this drip edge under the shingles, then lift the shingles enough to nail it directly to the roof sheathing, not through the shingles. If you are working in cold weather, be careful not to break the shingles.

▶ Make sure the downspout doesn't deposit water on sidewalks or around the house's foundation. Use a length adequate to carry the water away or add an extension at the bottom.

The new designs in vinyl gutters are not only easier to install than metal ones but have sleeker, better fittings than older vinyl systems.

Tools You Need

Carpenter's level

Chalk line

Handsaw

Tape measure

Variable-speed drill with 6-in. Phillips bit

Optional
Power miter box (rented)

Install the Gutters

Finding and marking the correct slope on the fascia is the first—and most important—step.

▷ For a gutter slope of 1 inch per 20 feet of length, make the first mark about 3/4 inch below the shingles, then make regular marks along the fascia for the correct slope. Snap a chalk line along these marks.

▷ Attach the drop outlet to the fascia so that the chalk line runs through the center of the screw holes in its mounting ears (Photo 1). Position the drop outlet far enough back, usually between 12 and 24 inches from the corner of the house, so you can secure the downspout bracket to the siding.

Connecting the Pieces

Slide the gutter mounting brackets onto the gutter. Use three brackets per gutter section or one every 24 to 30 inches (Photo 2). Attach four brackets if you live in a heavy snow area. Don't worry about the exact position of the brackets just yet; they slide easily for repositioning.

▷ Attach adhesive-backed gutter seals to each end of the gutter sections. Starting at the top edge of the back of the gutter, press the seal onto the gutter, following its contour (Photo 3). Don't overstretch the seal or it will leak.

▷ Snap the slip joint onto the end of the gutter section (Photo 4).

▷ Continue assembling lengths of gutter in this manner until an entire side of the house has been completed.

Hanging the Gutters

Having a helper or two is almost essential at this stage of the project.

▷ Position the gutter along the fascia with the open end resting in the drop outlet. Locate the gutter bracket that's farthest from the drop outlet and slide it back from the end of the gutter section about 24 inches.

▷ Line up the hole in the mounting bracket so that it is on the chalk line. Secure it to the fascia with a galvanized screw.

▷ Snap the end of the gutter into place in the drop outlet (Photo 5). Space the remaining gutter brackets evenly and attach them to the fascia with galvanized screws. Remember that the chalk line goes through the center of the hole in the mounting ear of each bracket.

Adding the Downspouts

▷ Hold one of the new vinyl elbows against the side of the house, then measure the distance between the end of that elbow and the one from the drop outlet (Photo 6). Add 3 inches to this measurement and cut a section of downspout to this length.

▷ Install this section between the elbows. Secure the lower elbow to the house with a downspout bracket.

▷ Finally, attach the downspout to the house at each elbow using a downspout bracket. Secure the brackets with the same type of screws used to attach the gutter brackets and the other fittings (Photo 7).

DIAGRAM

Drip Edge Installation Plan

If your roof shingles don't extend enough for water to drain into the gutter, slip a metal drip edge in place under the shingles and nail it to the sheathing, not through the shingles.

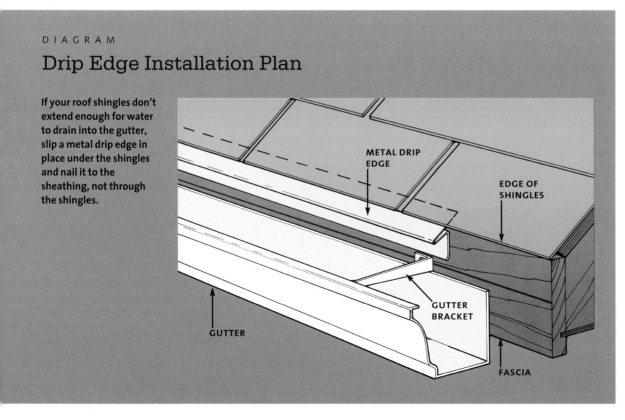

METAL DRIP EDGE

EDGE OF SHINGLES

GUTTER BRACKET

GUTTER

FASCIA

Photo 1. Attach the drop outlet to the fascia after you've snapped a chalk line on the fascia as a guide to the proper slope.

Photo 2. Slide the gutter brackets onto the gutter. Don't worry about the exact position of the brackets just yet; they slide easily.

Photo 3. Attach the adhesive-backed gutter seals to each end of the gutter sections. Don't overstretch the seal or it will leak.

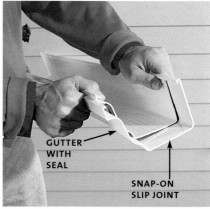

Photo 4. Snap the slip joint onto the end of the gutter section that is to be connected to the next section of gutter.

Photo 5. Snap the end of the gutter into the drop outlet. Space the other brackets evenly and secure them to the fascia.

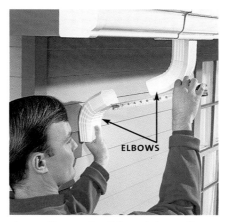

Photo 6. Measure the distance between the ends of the two elbows, add 3 in., and cut a section of downspout to this length.

Photo 7. Attach the downspout at each elbow. The lowest elbow needs a length of downspout adequate to carry the water safely away.

Cure Wet Basements

There aren't many house problems more upsetting than water in the basement, whether it's dribbling through your foundation, standing in puddles, or simply causing excess dampness. But a dry basement is possible, if you take the appropriate steps outlined here.

Sizing Up the Project

Sometimes a leaky basement is easy to fix and you can make the repair fairly inexpensively yourself, as when new or repaired gutters will solve the problem. At other times the problem and the cure are complicated and you will need to call in a professional. This chapter will help you assess the situation and decide whether you can handle it, on your own or with help.

Choose the Correct Repair

Drying out a wet basement can be one of the trickiest repairs to make in a house, because first you need to find how and why the water is getting in. The cause isn't always obvious.

Because the wall material determines the type of repair, begin by looking at whether the basement walls are made from concrete block or poured concrete, the latter type of repair being more complicated.

Waterproofing paint and hydraulic cement are simpler solutions not discussed here; this chapter focuses on water problems that require more complex remedies.

▶ The first repair shown, installing gutters and sloping the yard away from the foundation, can be made to a house with either type of basement wall material.
▶ The second repair, installing interior drain tile, is possible only with houses having block walls.
▶ The third repair, adding exterior drain tile, is the only option for houses with poured concrete walls, although it can be used with block walls.

Gutters and Grading

If your house has block walls and the top third of the wall is wet after a heavy rain, directing water away from the foundation will usually solve the problem. Water that pools on the ground near the foundation and soaks into the soil can seep into the basement.

Start by examining the edge of the roof and the landscaping around the foundation. If the house doesn't have gutters, downspouts, and downspout extensions to direct the water away from the house, the rain that runs off the roof has nowhere to go but straight into the ground next to the foundation. Couple that with a grade sloping toward the foundation and you're bound to have water problems sooner or later.

▶ Begin by installing gutters, downspouts, and extensions (see the previous chapter, "Hang Vinyl Gutters," pages 158-161) to carry water away from the house and prevent it from soaking into the ground near the foundation (see the diagram at right).

▶ Next, check the grade around the foundation. The downward slope should be at least 6 inches for every 10 feet away from the house. If the slope is less than that, or the slope is toward the house (below, right), correct it. A layer of water-impervious soil, such as clay, covered with topsoil and sod is the best way to shed excess water.

▶ Once you've made these changes, wait for the next heavy rain to see if they solve the problem. If not, consider making one of the more complex, and expensive, repairs described on the following pages.

Gutters and Grading

Good Drainage
Gutters, downspouts, and extensions carry runoff away from the foundation. The earth slopes away from the house so that it has at least a 6 in. drop for every 10 ft. away from the foundation.

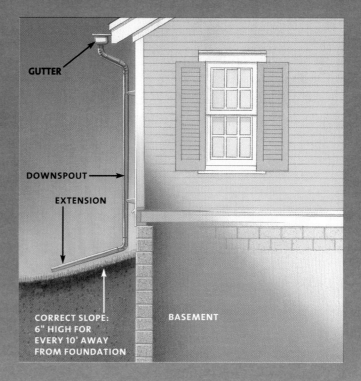

GUTTER

DOWNSPOUT →

EXTENSION

CORRECT SLOPE: 6" HIGH FOR EVERY 10' AWAY FROM FOUNDATION

BASEMENT

Bad Drainage
Here the lack of an extension to carry runoff away, or even a splash block to disperse water locally, leaves it pooling against the foundation because of a slope toward the house.

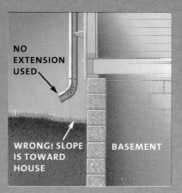

NO EXTENSION USED

WRONG! SLOPE IS TOWARD HOUSE

BASEMENT

Interior Drain Tile

If your home has a
concrete block founda-
tion, you can channel the
water into a central pump
and discharge it outside
with this system of inte-
rior drain tile.

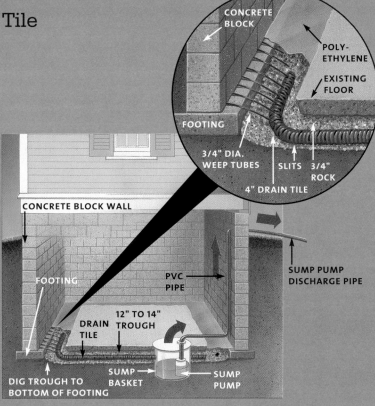

Interior Water Dam

This alternative to the
interior drain tile system
catches water at the base
of the wall, carries it to a
pump, and discharges it
outside.

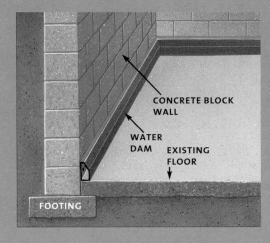

Interior Drain Tile

This repair works only in basements whose
walls are concrete block. This technique draws
the water in through the blocks, channels it to
a central location, then pumps it outside (see
the diagram at left). The water is directed
through short lengths of 3/4-inch diameter
plastic tubing called weep tubes inserted into
holes drilled into the cavities of each bottom-
row concrete block, including the cavity where
the ends of two blocks are mortared together
as well as the corner cavities.

The weep tubes drain onto a 4-inch diameter flexible plastic drain pipe with slits, which
channels the water into a large plastic sump
basket. Drain tile is sold in 50- or 100-foot rolls.
A sump pump in the sump basket pumps the
water up and out of the basement through
PVC plastic pipe.

This discharge pipe must extend far enough
out from the foundation so that the pumped
water drains away from the house and doesn't
find its way back into the basement.

This repair is the best way to eliminate a
water problem, because it brings the water in
at the wall's lowest point, where the block
rests on the footing. It can be done by a homeowner but is very labor intensive, so you are
probably better off hiring a professional.
Here's a quick overview of the steps involved if
you want to take it on yourself.

▶ With a jackhammer (using hand tools alone
is out of the question), break up and remove a
12- to 14-inch wide section of concrete floor at
the wall. Demolishing and hauling out old
concrete and dirt is slow, backbreaking work,
especially if you have to carry it up steps.

▶ Dig a trough around the basement's perimeter in the broken-up area, all the way to the
bottom of the footing (see Detail at left).

▶ Spread a 2- to 3-inch layer of 3/4 inch rock evenly in the trough.

▶ Drill 3/4-inch diameter holes in every cavity of each block using a hammer drill, available from most tool rental stores. Concrete blocks have either two or three empty cavities inside them. Determine which type of block you're dealing with by drilling a hole in the center of one block along the bottom row. If you hit an obstruction, you've found the center core of a two-cavity block; if you drill through easily, you've entered the empty center cavity of a three-hole block.

▶ Flush out these 3/4-inch holes with a garden hose so the water you invite into and through the block flows freely into the weep tubes, which are inserted now into the drilled holes.

▶ Lay 4-inch drain tile on the layer of gravel. Install the weep tubes into the block's holes.

▶ Next, spread a layer of 3/4-inch diameter rock over the drain tile.

▶ Finally, put down a layer of polyethylene film to cover the rock and weep tubes, then fill with concrete to finish the floor.

Calling in a basement waterproofing company will cost at least double what you have to spend to do this job yourself, but the pros will also have the job done in two to three days, and most professional installations come with a guarantee. Either way, interior drain tile is best for houses with concrete block walls.

An alternative to interior drain tile is the interior water dam system (see the diagram at left). This type of system, less efficient than the interior drain tile, catches water at the base of the wall on the basement floor, not below it at the footing. An enclosed channel then carries the water to a sump basket, from which it's pumped outside by a sump pump.

Exterior Drainage System

If your basement walls are poured concrete, this is your only repair option. It's also the cure of choice if the walls are concrete block and you don't want to tear up the basement. In either case, it's a job best left to pros. With this repair, you prevent the water from getting to the foundation in the first place, by using fill gravel around the foundation and footings, filter cloth, exterior insulation, backfill, topsoil, and, finally, the correct slope (see the diagram below).

This repair is expensive because of the heavy equipment needed to dig up the soil around the foundation all the way down to the house footings, which are often 8 feet below grade. Once everything is excavated, you need to spread a layer of 3/4-inch rock and install 4-inch drain tile

pipe. Onto the foundation install a rigid insulation board, polyethylene sheeting, and apply a protective coating of stucco or concrete over the insulation board. Then fill the area with a granular, water-porous backfill so the water that does get through the layer of properly sloped sod and impervious topsoil filters directly down to the drain tile.

Be prepared for much of your yard to be torn up by digging equipment. There's just no neat, simple way to dig around a foundation without causing a great deal of damage to your lawn and landscaping.

A professional contractor can complete even a repair this complex in less than a week. If you want to do the job yourself after someone digs everything out, plan on taking at least a month.

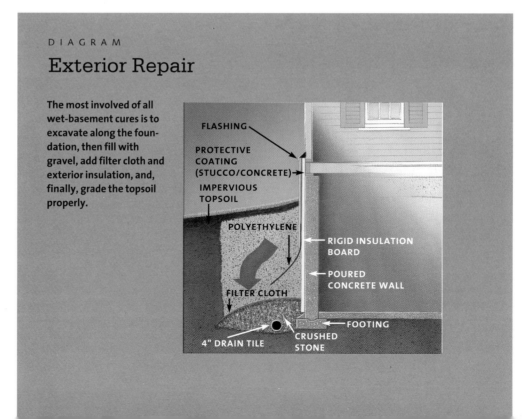

DIAGRAM

Exterior Repair

The most involved of all wet-basement cures is to excavate along the foundation, then fill with gravel, add filter cloth and exterior insulation, and, finally, grade the topsoil properly.

FLASHING

PROTECTIVE COATING (STUCCO/CONCRETE)

IMPERVIOUS TOPSOIL

POLYETHYLENE

FILTER CLOTH

RIGID INSULATION BOARD

POURED CONCRETE WALL

FOOTING

4" DRAIN TILE

CRUSHED STONE

Smart Suggestions for Energy-Efficient Insulation

Insulating attics, walls, and floors goes a long way to helping you save money on utility bills, but small gaps in your house's thermal envelope must be plugged to make the most of your insulation. These eight steps can increase your home's energy efficiency.

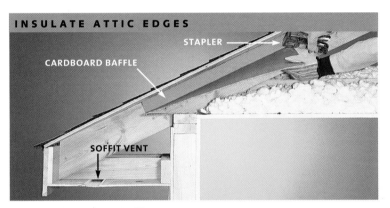

INSULATE ATTIC EDGES

STAPLER

CARDBOARD BAFFLE

SOFFIT VENT

Photo 1. Staple cardboard baffles to attic rafters to prevent the wind from blowing around insulation.

Insulate Attic Edges

Cardboard baffles stapled to attic rafters prevent wind from blowing through the insulation at the ceiling's edges and maintain an open channel for attic ventilation from the soffit vents (Photo 1). These baffles are available at home centers in sizes to fit between 16- and 24-inch centered joists. After stapling the baffles in place, push insulation into the void below, being careful not to compress the baffles upward (Photos 2 and 3). Wear heavy gloves when working with insulation.

Photo 2. Push insulation into the void below the new baffles. Be careful not to compress the baffles upward.

Photo 3. The finished job should look like this: fiberglass firmly in the ceiling edge and loose foam in behind it.

Seal Light Fixtures

Seal around electrical boxes and plug the holes in the boxes themselves with insulating urethane foam (Photo 4). Avoid boxing over recessed lights and covering them with insulation, which is a fire hazard (Photo 5). Whenever possible, don't use lights recessed into attics. If you have them, leave their tops open to allow heat to escape.

SEAL LIGHT FIXTURES

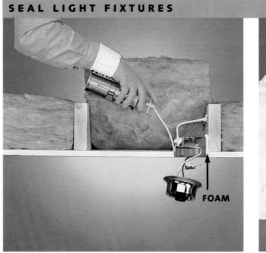

FOAM

DON'T DO THIS

Photo 4. Use insulating urethane foam to seal around electrical boxes.

Photo 5. Boxing in recessed lights with insulation is a fire hazard. At least leave the tops open.

Close Off Soffits

Cap any open soffits, such as the one over kitchen cabinets shown here, by covering them with drywall. Then caulk all the edges to seal leaks (Photo 6).

Seal the Plumbing Stack

Construct an airtight tent for your plumbing stack with plastic and caulk. Use wooden blocks and tape to hold the plastic in place, then caulk well for a lasting, airtight seal (Photo 7).

CLOSE OFF SOFFITS

ATTIC

DRYWALL

INTERIOR WALL

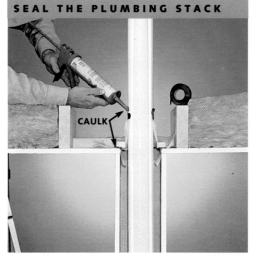

SEAL THE PLUMBING STACK

CAULK

Photo 6. Use drywall to cap open soffits like these over kitchen cabinets. Caulk all the edges.

Photo 7. Construct a permanent airtight seal around your plumbing stack with plastic sheeting.

Flash Around the Chimney

Do not fill the gap around your chimney with insulation. Instead, block the gap in the house framing around the chimney with metal flashing strips secured with 1-inch roofing nails to the frame. Seal the small remaining gaps with a high-temperature–resistant silicone caulk (Photos 8 and 9).

FLASH AROUND THE CHIMNEY

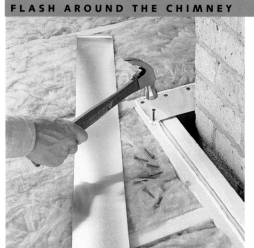

Photo 8. Nail and caulk metal flashing strips to joists around the chimney.

Photo 9. Instead of insulating the remaining gap, caulk the cracks with high-temperature silicone caulk.

Don't Compress Insulation

Properly laid insulation (Photo 10, right) fits without compressing and leaves no open spaces. Compressing the insulation (Photo 10, left) leaves gaps and constrictions that cut its insulating value in half. For easy trimming, compress a batt of insulation with a straight-edge and then cut it with a sharp utility knife (Photo 11).

DON'T COMPRESS INSULATION

IMPROPER   PROPER

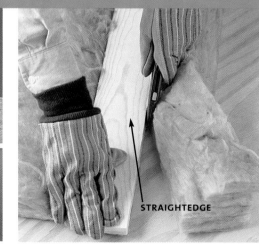

STRAIGHTEDGE

Photo 10. Lay insulation properly: flat, without compressing it (right), with no open spaces.

Photo 11. Cut insulation batts with a sharp utility knife after compressing it with a straightedge.

Stop Leaks at Rim Joists

Caulk and staple wax-coated cardboard to the floor, joists, and sill plate to block air leaks at the rim joists (Photo 12). Caulking creates an airtight seal and the waxed surface becomes a vapor barrier. The waxed cardboard found at produce stands or grocery stores to ship vegetables and fruits works well. Or you can buy waxed 16- or 24-inch baffles of the sort used to insulate your attic's edges.

Seal Wall Openings

Air flows readily up through interior walls and escapes into the attic. Apply caulk or urethane foam to close air leaks around gaps in the interior wall made by electrical or plumbing fixtures. Apply the material on both the exterior and interior walls. A gasket helps seal switches and receptacles (Photo 13).

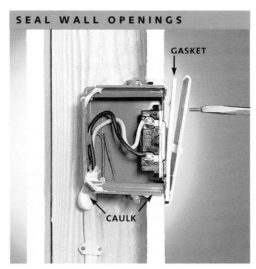

Photo 13. Caulk or use urethane foam to close air leaks around plumbing, electrical, and other points where the walls are penetrated.

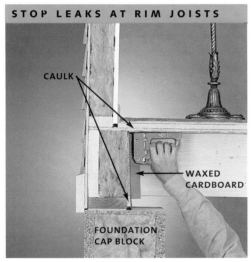

Photo 12. Block air leaks by stapling and caulking wax-coated cardboard to the joints around the floor rim joists.

Check for Backdrafting

When you insulate, remodel, or tighten up the air flow through your house, it's a good idea to check your oil, gas, and wood-burning devices for backdrafting, which is what occurs when there's insufficient air to create the proper updraft to vent exhaust fumes. To be sure your appliances are drawing properly, do the following test.

▶ Close up the house tightly as if it were winter, turn on all the exhaust fans (kitchen and range, bathroom, clothes dryer, and so on), and switch on the hot-water heater.

▶ Hold a fireplace match close to the vent hood to see if the vent is drawing properly (Photo A). If the smoke doesn't draw after 15 to 20 seconds, the device is probably backdrafting (Photo B) and dangerous fumes may be spilling out into your home. Have the system checked immediately by a licensed heating professional or the local utility.

▶ A carbon monoxide monitor is a good device to leave on duty to test for backdrafting when you're not present.

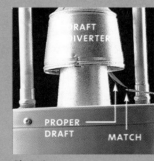

Photo A.

Photo B.

Vent Your Roof the Right Way

Proper ventilation will extend the life of your roof, cut down on your utility bills and prevent water damage from ice dams and dripping attics.

Sizing Up the Project

This project involves several steps, which require work in confined spaces and cutting holes in the roof to install vented louvers. It also calls for cutting holes in the soffits for vents.

Analyze Your Attic

Consider improving your attic ventilation if you have any of the following conditions.

▶ Soggy attic insulation, water-stained ceilings, or dripping water, which could well be moisture from ice damming or attic condensation (see An Unvented Roof, opposite).

▶ Curling shingles or other premature roof damage; unvented roofs can become so hot that they cook the shingles and void the manufacturer's warranty.

▶ New insulation for the attic floor; insulation changes the way the house "breathes."

▶ A house that overheats in the summer; excess attic heat may be turning the ceilings into gigantic radiators.

How Vents Work

Basically, vents allow an attic to breathe in a number of ways.

▶ Vents create a "cold roof" in the winter. You may think you want a warm roof in the cold winter, but this is not so. When heat from the house creeps into an unvented attic, it's trapped there to warm the roof boards and shingles. Snow on the roof then melts and runs down toward the edge of the roof. But when it hits an unheated eave it freezes, creating a dam of ice. This dam continues to grow higher until it forms a glacier that plows uphill and under your shingles. When the ice hits the warm part of your roof, it melts again and the water runs into your attic and home. (See the next chapter, "Defeat Ice Dams," pages 174–177, for more information.)

▶ Vents allow moisture to escape. Moisture in a house works its way through ceiling cracks, around vents and pipes, and into the attic. In the winter, if this moisture has no way to escape it condenses and freezes on the underside of the roof sheathing. Then, when the roof warms, the moisture drips into the attic, where it promotes rot, soaks the insulation, or seeps into the living space, causing further damage. For this reason, make sure bathroom fans and dryer vents exhaust outside, and not into the eave or attic area.

▶ Finally, vents create a cool roof in the summer. The temperature of an unvented attic can reach 150 degrees F or higher. This heat in turn transforms the ceiling into a huge radiator that pumps heat into the living space below. Placing vents high and low on the roof provides an escape path for this heat.

Vent Types and Placement

Both the venting capacity and the pattern of the airflow are important when determining where to locate vents. For good balance, half the ventilation must be positioned at the peak and half near the eaves. Having many small, evenly spaced vents rather than a few large ones creates a more uniform and effective "air washing" of the underside of the roof. Beyond that, venting is an inexact science, because a house's location and design greatly affect how air moves through its roof. (For more details, see "How Many Vents Do You Need?" on page 172.)

The project shown here employs box-type roof louvers and rectangular undereave vents, but there are others to choose from, including continuous ridge and soffit vents that run the entire length of the soffit and roof peak; turbine and power ventilators, which actively pull air out of the attic; and gable louvers, which are square or triangular openings in a gable-side wall.

In houses with vaulted ceilings or finished attics, each rafter space must be vented. Continuous ridge and soffit vents are the best way to vent these roofs, requiring 1-1/2 inches of air space between the roof sheathing and insulation for air movement.

On a house with no eaves, install roof louvers 3 feet up from the lower edge of the roof to serve as air inlets.

DIAGRAM

Venting Your Roof

A Vented Roof
A correctly vented roof keeps your roof cool both summer and winter, to avoid ice buildup at the eaves. In addition, the moisture accumulated in bathrooms, laundries, and kitchens is carried out before it can condense and drip in the attic.

An Unvented Roof
An unvented roof reverses the desirable flow of air and moisture: summer heat soaks back down from overheated attics into the living area, and winter freeze-thaw cycles leave ice dams that force melt-water under shingles and into the house.

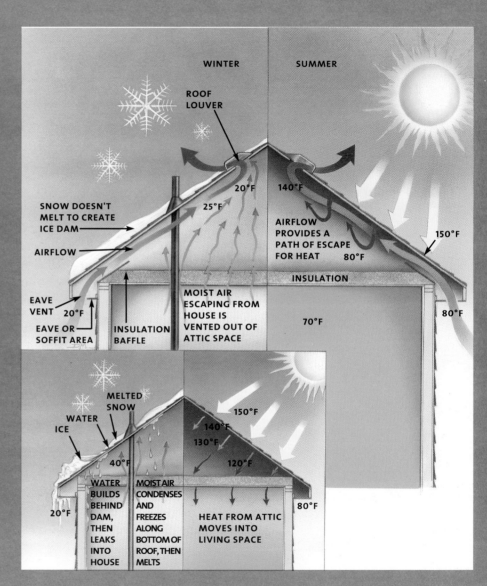

WINTER   SUMMER

ROOF LOUVER

SNOW DOESN'T MELT TO CREATE ICE DAM

AIRFLOW

20°F

25°F

140°F

AIRFLOW PROVIDES A PATH OF ESCAPE FOR HEAT

80°F

150°F

INSULATION

EAVE VENT   20°F

EAVE OR SOFFIT AREA

INSULATION BAFFLE

MOIST AIR ESCAPING FROM HOUSE IS VENTED OUT OF ATTIC SPACE

70°F

80°F

MELTED SNOW

WATER

ICE

150°F

140°F

130°F

120°F

40°F

WATER BUILDS BEHIND DAM, THEN LEAKS INTO HOUSE

MOIST AIR CONDENSES AND FREEZES ALONG BOTTOM OF ROOF, THEN MELTS

HEAT FROM ATTIC MOVES INTO LIVING SPACE

20°F

80°F

How Many Vents Do You Need?

Building codes require 1 square foot of net free venting area (NFVA) for every 150 square feet of ceiling below the roof. For houses with vapor barriers, the ratio is 1 square foot of NFVA for every 300 square feet of ceiling.

Net free venting area is the open area of a vent left after subtracting the thickness of the louvers or screens that run across it. Most vents have a label, stamp, or packaging that lists their NFVA. If not, calculate it by dividing the opening in the vent by these numbers:

- ▶ 1/8-in. screen: divide by 1.25
- ▶ 1/16-in. screen: divide by 2
- ▶ Louvers, 1/8-in. screen: divide by 2.25
- ▶ Louvers, 1/16-in. screen: divide by 3

Here are some typical examples.
To calculate the NFVA of a vent with an 8x9-in. (72 square in.) opening covered by 1/8-in. screen, divide 72 square in. by 1.25, for an NFVA of 58 in. or to determine the correct number of vents for a 24x40-ft. single-story house, calculate as follows:

- ▶ 24 ft. x 40 ft. = 960 square ft. of ceiling
- ▶ 960 square ft. ÷ 150 = 6.4 square ft. of NFVA (or 921 square in.)

Since half the venting must be at the ridge and half along the eaves, 3.2 square feet (or 460 square in.) is at the ridge.

The vents to be installed have an NFVA of 58 in., so 8 vents (460 ÷ 58 = 7.9) are needed at the ridge.

Follow the same procedure for determining the number of soffit vents.

Install Basic Vents

From inside the attic, look closely at the area where the roof meets the outside walls. In many cases you'll find short lengths of wood or insulation blocking off the eaves from the attic area.

▶ Open up the air path by knocking out or drilling holes through these blocks. Some blocking is structural, so consult a certified inspector if you are in doubt.

▶ Install insulation baffles between the rafters to keep the space open (Photo 1). Once you have established an open air path, install the roof louvers and soffit vents. By installing insulation baffles before the undereave vents, any insulation or blocking that falls onto the soffit can be removed while installing the undereave vents.

Roof Louver Considerations

Before you begin installing louvers, consider the following points.

▶ Locate roof louvers near the peak, but not so high that they interfere with the ridge of the roof. No part of a louver should rise higher than the roof peak of the house.

▶ Space the louvers evenly across one side of the roof. It doesn't matter which side. Most people position them away from the street for the sake of appearance. Otherwise one roof vent can become an air intake for a vent across the roof from it.

Mounting Roof Louvers

▶ Drive a locator nail up from the attic to identify open space between the rafters.

▶ With a circular saw, cut holes through the roof sheathing equal in size to the opening in the roof louver (Photo 2). The manufacturer will provide dimensions in the louver package.

▶ Cut and remove shingles so the top of the roof louver can slide under the two uppermost courses of shingles (Photo 3). A hooked shingle blade simplifies cutting.

▶ Pull nails that could interfere when sliding the louver under the two upper courses of shingles (Photo 4). Then apply roofing cement around the perimeter of the hole.

▶ Slide the roof louver under the top two courses of shingles and over the bottom two courses (Photo 5). Carefully lift old, fragile shingles. Nail the louver in place.

▶ Apply roofing cement to seal out wind-blown rain (Photo 6). Add dabs of caulk over exposed nailheads. Do not, however, apply caulk along the bottom edge of the louver.

Installing Soffit Vents

Put undereave vents near the outer edge of the soffit. Vents are available in 4-, 6-, and 8-inch widths. Use screws, because hammering can jar the fragile soffit.

▶ Cut holes in the soffit for the undereave vents (Photo 7). Drill starter holes, then use a jigsaw to cut through the plywood soffit.

▶ Secure the undereave vents to the soffit using self-tapping screws and a drill with a Phillips bit (Photo 8).

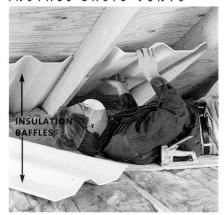

Photo 1. Install insulation baffles to provide an unobstructed airway between the eave and the attic area. Remove airflow-blocking pieces.

Photo 2. Drive a locator nail up from the attic to find the rafter opening, then saw through the roof sheathing for the roof louver holes.

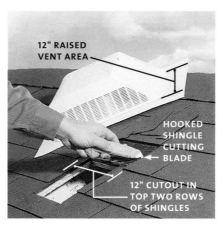

Photo 3. Cut and remove shingles so the top of the roof louver can slide under the two upper-most courses of shingles.

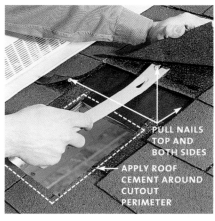

Photo 4. Pull nails under the two upper courses of shingles that could obstruct the louver. Then apply roofing tar around the hole's edge.

Photo 5. Carefully slide the roof louver under the top two courses of shingles and over the bottom two courses. Nail the louver in place.

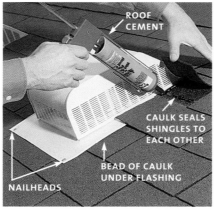

Photo 6. Apply roofing cement to seal the edges of the vent. Add dabs of caulk over the exposed nailheads.

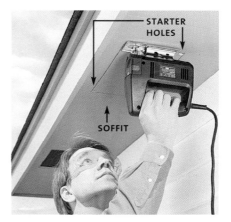

Photo 7. Drill starter holes through the plywood, then cut holes in the soffit for the undereave vents.

Photo 8. Secure the undereave vents with self-tapping screws. Using a power drill with a Phillips bit will make this overhead job easier.

Defeat Ice Dams

Ice dams can build up in winter and bring major repair bills in spring. The only way to handle them is to defeat them before they start. A few simple steps will ensure victory in this battle.

Anatomy of an Ice Dam
Poor ventilation and inadequate insulation combine to melt the snow blanket. Then pooled meltwater backs up under the shingles or roofing paper and damages walls and ceilings below, as well as rafters, sheathing, fascias, and soffits.

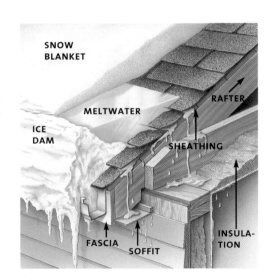

Sizing Up the Project

The best way to prevent ice buildup on your roof is to avoid warm air buildup in your attic. There are several ways to keep the roof cold in winter, all of which fall into two categories: improving the insulation so that less heat enters the attic, and upgrading the ventilation so that warm air escapes the attic quickly. These and other alternatives are explored here.

Know the Enemy

Ice dams that form on the roof, usually at the eaves, actually start in the attic, where inadequate insulation and poor ventilation first conspire to warm the surface of the roof (see "Anatomy of an Ice Dam," left). Heat escaping from inside the house rises through the attic and gathers under the roof. Because the warmest air rises farthest, the attic inside and the roof outside become warmest near the roof's peak but stay cooler down toward the eaves. If the upper part of the roof becomes warm enough, the snow blanket melts and trickles down the slope (see "A Warm Roof," opposite). As the meltwater reaches the lower, colder parts of the roof, it eventually freezes into a sheet of ice. Then, gradually, an ice dam

grows as more meltwater continues to flow. If this wall of ice becomes unusually large—and dams can grow to more than 2 feet tall—the weight alone can be a strain on the eaves. But most of the time it's the pool of water that backs up behind the dam that is the real villain.

Shingles, whether they are made of asphalt, wood, slate, or tile, repel water just fine—as long as it's flowing down the roof. The problem with ice dams is that they create reservoirs of standing water that can seep upward between the shingles to enter the attic and leak into the living space. The results are not only water damage to the house's interior but also wrecked shingles; rotted roof sheathing, rafters, fascia, and soffits; and compacted insulation.

Detecting Dams

Ice dams and the problems they bring aren't always obvious. They can hide under snow and do their dirty work invisibly before finally revealing themselves as water stains spread across the ceiling. Houses built before the mid-1970s, when attic insulation and ventilation improved markedly, are more likely to be ice-dam victims. The only way to know for sure whether you have an ice dam problem is to inspect the eaves during the winter. But a little detective work before the first snowfall can give you a pretty clear picture of the situation.

▶ First, try to recall what the roof looked like over the past few winters. Was it sometimes bare around the peak but snow covered toward the eaves, with big icicles hanging off? If so, it was probably harboring ice dams.

▶ Next, check for damaged shingles near the eaves, dribble stains running down exterior walls, other stains, rot, rusty nailheads, or blistering paint on soffits and fascias. Look for damage in the attic, too. Matted insulation and areas darkened by water stains or rot are indicative of a leaking roof and possible ice dams.

Defeating Dams

The first line of defense against ice dams is to keep the attic cool by insulating properly (see the diagrams, right). Improving your insulation may simply mean adding insulation or closing up the gaps after insulating (see "Smart Suggestions for Energy-Efficient Insulation," pages 166–169).

Whatever you do, be careful. Adding insulation to a poorly ventilated attic can lead to condensation on the underside of the roof. Improperly installed insulation can block the airflow above the soffit vents.

A Warm Roof

Warm air heats the roof and melts the blanket of snow. When meltwater reaches the cold eaves, an ice dam forms, causing water to pool behind it.

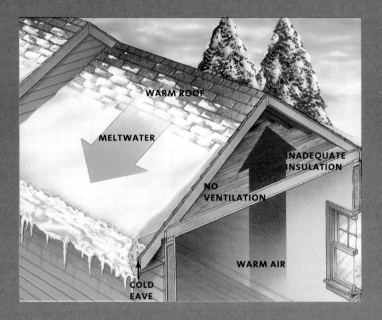

WARM ROOF

MELTWATER

INADEQUATE INSULATION

NO VENTILATION

WARM AIR

COLD EAVE

A Cold Roof

Adequate insulation cuts down on heat entering the attic, while proper ventilation allows the heat that does enter to escape quickly.

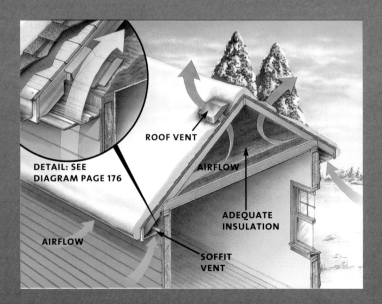

ROOF VENT

AIRFLOW

DETAIL: SEE DIAGRAM PAGE 176

ADEQUATE INSULATION

AIRFLOW

SOFFIT VENT

Other Alternatives

Insulation and ventilation, which eliminate the cause of ice dams, are by far the best weapons in this war. But there are some situations, particularly in houses with cathedral ceilings, where adding insulation or ventilation is difficult if not impossible.

Cathedral ceilings present their own problems because the ceiling is attached directly to the underside of the roof rafters. The few inches remaining between the roof and ceiling allow little space for insulation and airflow.

A surefire, but tedious, solution is to pull the snow off the roof with a roof rake, which is simply a metal blade attached to a long pole, before it begins to melt. If you do rake the roof, you must go all the way up to the peak. Raking only the lower areas may not do much good, because when the snow near the peak melts, the runoff will form ice dams just as if you hadn't raked at all.

Be careful using a metal roof rake. Contacting a power line with a metal rake can lead to a serious shock, and accidentally hooking a phone or cable line can interrupt either your own or someone else's service.

Electric Heating Cables

One way to deal with otherwise unbeatable ice dams is electric heating cables (see the Electric Heating Cable alternative, right). As long as they're not prohibited by your local building code, you'll find them at home centers. But be prepared to pay the extra electric bill from having to leave them plugged in as long as there's snow on the roof. Note also that unless the weather is extremely cold, heating cables will keep ice from building up around the cables themselves, but it is still possible for dams to form above them. Be certain to stay away from power lines.

If You Need a New Roof

A new roof isn't the solution to an ice-dam problem, but if you plan to lay down new shingles anyway, you have an opportunity to cut the chances of ice-dam damage. Rubberized asphalt flashing, also called an ice and water shield, is a sheet of tough, rubbery material that goes on critical parts of the roof sheathing before the shingles are applied (see the Ice and Water Barrier alternative, right). Available in various lengths and widths, it's designed to prevent any of the water that has seeped under the shingles from getting any farther. It's the last line of defense against ice dams when all other efforts have failed.

DIAGRAM

Ensuring Proper Airflow

Insulation stuffed between the roof sheathing and the top plate of the wall can block the airflow. Inserting Styrofoam or cardboard baffles can prevent this blockage.

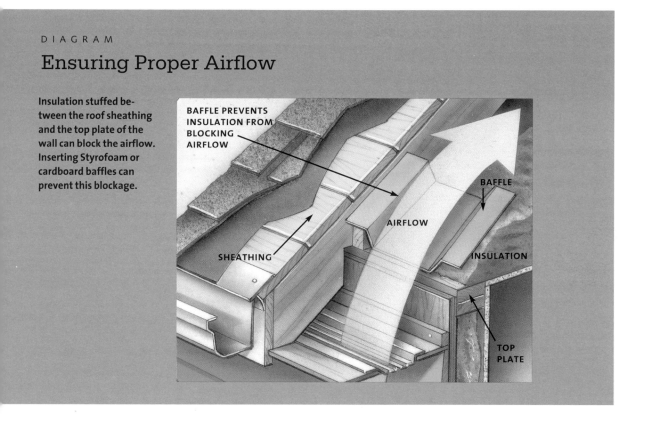

BAFFLE PREVENTS INSULATION FROM BLOCKING AIRFLOW

BAFFLE

AIRFLOW

SHEATHING

INSULATION

TOP PLATE

Electric Heating Cable

Heating cables should run through gutters and downspouts as well as across eaves.

HEATING CABLES

Ice and Water Barrier

An ice and water shield must extend at least 12 in. inside exterior walls.

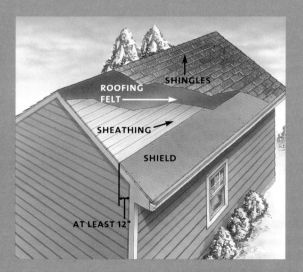

ROOFING FELT →

SHINGLES

SHEATHING ➚

SHIELD

AT LEAST 12"

A Last Warning

Ice dams don't play fair. They may make a surprise attack on your roof even after you've faithfully worked to prevent them—and when they do, you have to react fast. Using an ax, hatchet, or ice pick, chip grooves in the dam every 3 feet or so to let the water drain away harmlessly. But do this very gently, so as not to break the cold, brittle shingles. And if you have a tile roof, don't do this at all. You can hire a roofing contractor to steam the dam away. It's easier on your shingles, but can be hard on your wallet.

Finally, never use salt to melt ice on the roof. It can damage the shingles, gutters, and wood.

Refurbish Your Windows

Windows can warm a room with sunshine or cool it with fresh air. But they can also leak, let in noise, ice up, and expose furniture to the sun's damaging rays. Now you can refurbish your windows and overcome their drawbacks economically without replacing them.

Sizing Up the Project

There are three simple, inexpensive projects and products you can choose from that can solve most window problems. Best of all, they can raise your comfort level and lower your utility bills at the same time.

All three of the techniques shown here—combination storm windows (below, left), interior insulating windows (below, center), and window-tinting films (below, right)—can be done gradually, as you find the time and money.

Improving vs. Replacing

A new double-pane window is not only expensive, but to install one you must meddle with both the interior and exterior of your house. Also, you need to find windows to match the style of the house. In contrast, the tinting of windows can cost only a few dollars each. Even the most expensive improvement shown here—building and installing an interior insulating window—takes much less time and money than installing entirely new units.

Combination Storm Windows

Interior Insulating Windows

Window-Tinting Films

These upgrades will improve the efficiency of any window, regardless of age. The tinting films called low-E (for emissivity, for their ability to reflect the sun's infrared rays without affecting the visible rays) can rival or even exceed the qualities of factory-tinted low-E windows. An older single-pane window fitted with a snug interior insulating window can actually be more energy efficient than a new double-pane window. If a window is literally falling apart at the seams, replacement is the only course of action. Otherwise, consider one or more of these projects.

Even the most involved changes shown in these projects take no more than an hour or two per window and achieve attractive, energy-saving results.

OPTIONS

Combination Storm Window Features

Weatherstripping
Resilient pile weatherstripping on window inserts and frames provides the tightest seal against the elements and cuts down rattling.

Construction
Solid corners provide weathertightness and longevity. The triple-track construction shown on the "best" and "better" units allows the windows and screen inserts to be positioned anywhere within the frame.

Tilt-in Cleaning
Many combination storm windows now have glass inserts that tilt inward so that their panes can be cleaned on both sides from inside the house.

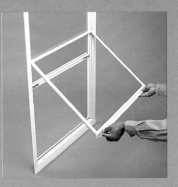

Combination Storm Windows
A combination storm window performs three basic functions: It acts as a first line of defense against strong winds; it creates an insulated dead-air space between itself and the existing window; and it is easily adjustable so it can be opened for ventilation.

Advantages
These windows put an end to the seasonal ladder climbing, window switching, and storm storing involved with storm windows with heavy wooden frames. The new combination storm windows include both glass and screening, with adjustable panels that ride along tracks, allowing them to be raised, lowered, or moved aside from the inside.

Combination storm windows work only on single- or double-hung windows (the type shown here), and horizontal slide-by windows. Because of the way they are mounted, they cannot be used on casement windows, which swing open on hinges like a door, usually with a crank mechanism located in the lower portion of the window. And combination storms come in only a limited number of finishes, usually brown, white, or plain aluminum.

Installation
First measure the window with a tape (Photo 1). Then place a framing square in each corner of the window frame. If it's extremely out of square, order your combination storm window about 1/4 inch larger in each direction, then trim and fit the fastening flange with tinsnips before installation. Don't twist the storm window to try and make it fit an out-of-square primary window, because it won't operate properly.

▶ When you are drilling holes for the mounting screws, keep them at the outermost edge of the framework (Photo 2). Most primary windows have a surface less than 1/2 inch wide for these screws to hit.

▶ Apply a bead of caulk along the top and sides of the window (Photo 3). Then seat the window firmly in it (Photo 4). Leave the weep hole area open to drain (Photo 5).

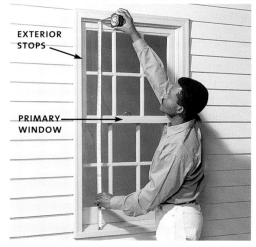

Photo 1. Measure the existing window at the outermost edges of the exterior stops. Give the manufacturer these measurements, allowing 1/4 in. extra all around for out-of-square windows.

Photo 2. Predrill holes along the fastening flange edges of the combination storm window frame. Space the holes 2 in. from each corner and then every 12 in. along each of the sides.

Photo 3. Apply a bead of caulk along the top and side exterior stops. Silicone caulk bonds well to both wood and aluminum while still managing to maintain its flexibility.

Photo 4. Position the storm window in the opening. Lift the window as high as possible, and then lower the expansion sill to close the gap at the bottom. Finally, install the screws.

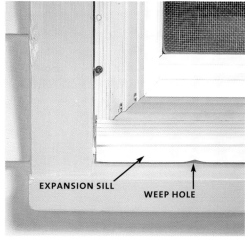

Photo 5. Make certain that moisture can pass freely through the weep holes at the bottom of the window frame. This is necessary to reduce the risk of wood rot.

Interior Insulating Windows

This window's name tells only part of its story. It does indeed insulate by creating a dead-air space between the existing primary window and itself. But it also excels at reducing air infiltration and noise, lowering condensation, increasing safety, and adding comfort.

Advantages

▸ Because insulating windows adhere to the primary window with magnets, Velcro, or some other weathertight system, they reduce air infiltration by up to 92 percent. This means that your expensively heated or air-conditioned air stays inside and unwanted outside air stays out.

▸ Adding an extra pane of glazing lowers noise levels in the house by up to 90 percent.

Insulating windows work so well that government agencies now use them to soundproof houses under the flight paths of jets.

▸ By creating a buffer zone between the house's interior and the outside elements, insulating windows eliminate or at least greatly reduce window condensation.

▸ These windows' acrylic plastic panes offer a shatter-resistant buffer between the house's occupants and the glass of the primary window.

▸ Any time you reduce drafts, lower noise levels, and eliminate condensation, you achieve a general increase in comfort levels. Insulating windows also block out dirt, pollen, and bugs.

These windows are the only type of add-on window that will work on casement, awning, or other tilting or swinging windows. One draw-back, however, is that to operate the primary window part or all of the insulating window must be removed or raised.

Insulating windows can't be seen from outside the house and are relatively unobtrusive inside it. They're often used in historical renovations to preserve the character of a room. Most can be primed and painted.

Installation

▸ Secure new wood parting stops to the top and sides of the window with finish nails set and filled with wood putty. Locate the stops far enough out so the hardware of the old window doesn't hit the new interior window (Photo 6).

▸ Clean the surfaces of the parting stops that you just installed, then apply the steel strapping that comes with the new interior window (Photo 7).

▸ Cut the new acrylic window to size, leaving whatever extra expansion and contraction space the manufacturer suggests, usually 1/16 inch (Photo 8).

▸ Trim the magnetic edging to length cleanly with ratchet-type pruning shears that don't crimp the material (Photo 9).

▸ Seat the magnetic edging strips on the top and side edges of the acrylic firmly with a rubber mallet (Photo 10).

▸ Rest the foam sill cushion on the bottom windowsill and place the new interior window in position (Photos 11 and 12).

You now have a second window inside your original, sealed as tight as a refrigerator door.

Interior Insulating Windows

One type of interior insulating window is glazed with acrylic plastic. The panels mount to the primary window with self-adhesive Velcro fasteners. Such windows are made to measure at the factory.

Another make offers an operable interior insulating window with glass panes. Mount these factory-made units by removing the existing interior trim and installing the new unit in its place. These windows can be ordered with a blind sandwiched between the primary and interior windows. The angle of the blinds can be adjusted by a rod, as shown.

WOOD PARTING STOPS

Photo 6. Nail new wood parting stops to the top and sides of the window far enough out so that the old window hardware won't hit the new interior window.

BACKING REMOVED FROM DOUBLE-FACED TAPE

STEEL STRAPPING

Photo 7. Apply steel strapping to the new wood parting stops. Thoroughly clean all surfaces to make sure that the double-faced tape will stick to them firmly.

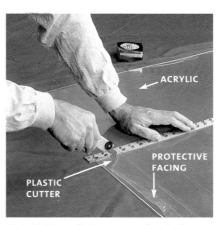

ACRYLIC

PROTECTIVE FACING

PLASTIC CUTTER

Photo 8. Cut acrylic to size according to the manufacturer's instructions. With all systems, you must leave room, usually 1/16 in., for acrylic to expand and contract.

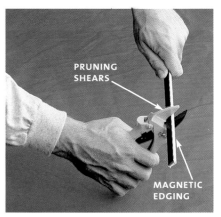

PRUNING SHEARS

MAGNETIC EDGING

Photo 9. Trim the magnetic edging to length with ratchet-type pruning shears, which will cut cleanly without crimping the U-shaped material as others would.

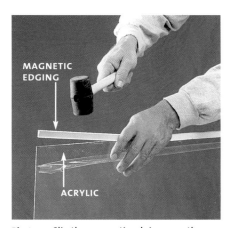

MAGNETIC EDGING

ACRYLIC

Photo 10. Slip the magnetic edging over the top and side edges of the acrylic, seating it firmly. Attach the bottom extrusion.

FOAM SILL CUSHION

Photo 11. Position the new interior window, making certain the foam cushion is resting on the bottom windowsill.

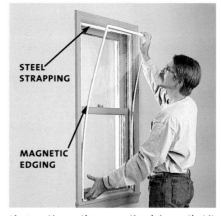

STEEL STRAPPING

MAGNETIC EDGING

Photo 12. Line up the magnetic edging so that it seals tightly to the steel strapping all the way around the window.

Window-Tinting Films

Early tinting films, developed in the 1970s, provided one—and only one—benefit: they blocked heat in the summer. But they had big drawbacks: they were short-lived, had a shiny appearance, and often needed to be applied to the vulnerable exterior of a window.

Today's films are greatly improved. They offer greater energy savings and comfort during both summer and winter. They can be applied to the interior surface of either single- or thermopane windows, are lighter colored, and provide better visibility than earlier ones.

In sun-drenched areas of the South, tinting windows can save hundreds of dollars yearly on air-conditioning bills. And new low-E tinting films now offer heating season benefits to people in northern climates.

Types of Tints

Tinting films can be classified into one of three basic groups.

- Low-E films
- Nonreflective
- Reflective

The type of film you should select depends on where you live, how you want your windows to look, and what functions you want the film to perform (see box on facing page). The following are among the benefits of applying tinting film.

- By blocking the sun's visible light rays, tints reduce the temperature gain in a house. This is a real advantage in warm southern climates, but it can be a negative factor in colder regions when the tints reduce the amount of solar heat.
- By screening ultraviolet rays, tints greatly reduce the fading effects of the sun on furniture, carpets, and drapes.
- The 50 to 60 percent reduction in incoming light that is typical of film reduces glare and eyestrain without producing a dark or cavernous feel to the house's interior. As a comparison, standard sunglasses reduce incoming light by 85 percent, and the tinted upper portion of an auto windshield reduces the incoming light by 70 to 75 percent. Many people find it more comfortable to work in a room with tinted windows.
- Reflective films offer the most daytime privacy, but in turn they create a silvery image in the interior at night.
- If a window breaks, tinting film holds the pieces of the window together, preventing sharp shards from exploding into a room.
- All films radiate heat back into the house to a certain extent, but low-E films help to substantially lower winter heating bills by reducing heat loss through windows.

DIAGRAM
The Three Basic Types of Window-Tinting Films

Low-E Films
These films block almost as much summer heat as reflective films and then, in winter, reradiate at least 50 percent of the heat back into the house. They offer fade protection, a natural appearance, and scratch resistance. They are compatible with most residential or commercial windows. These films are expensive, but they have a life expectancy of more than ten years.

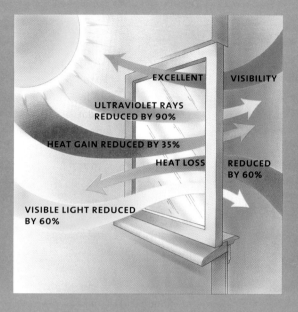

EXCELLENT VISIBILITY
ULTRAVIOLET RAYS REDUCED BY 90%
HEAT GAIN REDUCED BY 35%
HEAT LOSS REDUCED BY 60%
VISIBLE LIGHT REDUCED BY 60%

Reflective Films
These films, available in silver and tinted finishes, excel at blocking heat gain. They also offer the greatest degree of daytime privacy, although some people dislike their shiny look. They are the least expensive of all films, although in the smoke and bronze colors they cost more.

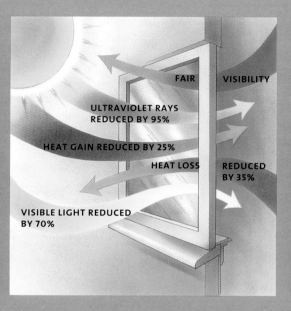

FAIR VISIBILITY
ULTRAVIOLET RAYS REDUCED BY 95%
HEAT GAIN REDUCED BY 25%
HEAT LOSS REDUCED BY 35%
VISIBLE LIGHT REDUCED BY 70%

Nonreflective Films
Designed primarily for automobile windows, these films are also used in residential applications. As the name implies, they don't reflect heat as well as other films, but they do an excellent job blocking glare and ultraviolet light. The adhesive on these films is more tenacious, so handle the film carefully once its backing is removed.

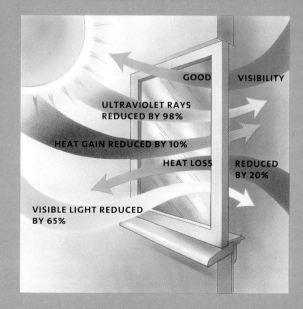

GOOD VISIBILITY
ULTRAVIOLET RAYS REDUCED BY 98%
HEAT GAIN REDUCED BY 10%
HEAT LOSS REDUCED BY 20%
VISIBLE LIGHT REDUCED BY 65%

Installation

In its degree of difficulty, installing window-tinting film falls somewhere between hanging wallpaper and applying adhesive-backed shelving paper. The most important installation guideline is simply to follow the manufacturer's instructions. Each type of film has its own particular application procedures, especially in regard to double-pane windows. But for any installation, keep in mind these points concerning tint film.

▷ There are two ways to apply films. The process shown in Photos 13–20 involves trimming the film after it has adhered to the window. This means performing two crucial tasks—squeegeeing (Photo 19) and trimming (Photo 20)—in a short period of time. The alternative is to adhere the film temporarily—with the backing still intact—to the window. Once it is cut to size, remove the film from the window and the backing from the film, then wet and reinstall the film. The second method is the easiest for novices working on large panes of glass such as patio doors.

▷ Most films should be applied when the outside temperatures are between 40 and 90 degrees F. Find a time to apply the film when the windows are out of direct sunlight.

▷ Make certain to leave a 1/16- to 1/8-inch gap around the edges (see Photo 20). This leeway provides a small escape slot for excess heat that might build up between double-pane windows.

▷ If you have windows with multiple small panes, make a template from rigid poster board and cut around that to mass-produce films.

▷ Don't be alarmed if tinting film clouds for a few weeks as it cures. This is normal and will eventually clear up.

▷ Tinting can be used in conjunction with glass combination storm and interior insulating windows. However, do not use tinting film on acrylic glazed windows.

WINDOW-TINTING FILMS: INSTALLATION

Photo 13. Clean the windows thoroughly, especially the corners and edges. Use a razor blade scraper then clean with a lint-free cloth.

Photo 14. Cut the film to size using a sharp utility knife and straightedge. Cut the film 1 in. longer and wider than the glass.

Photo 15. Spray the window surface with a wetting solution of 1 qt. water and 1/2 oz. clear liquid dishwashing soap.

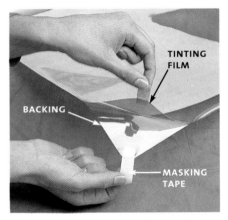

Photo 16. Separate the backing from the film using tape at the corners to help break the bond between the two surfaces.

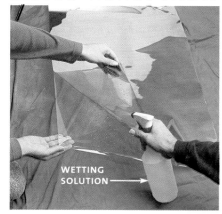

Photo 17. Remove the backing from the film while a helper wets the adhesive side of the film. Don't let the adhesive side touch itself, because it clings like flypaper.

Photo 18. Position the wet film on a wet window, taking care to avoid wrinkles and creases. The film must overlap onto the window sash on all sides.

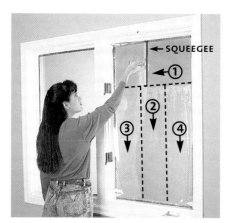

Photo 19. Squeegee the film after spraying the surface with the wetting solution used earlier. Start at the top with a single horizontal pass, followed by a series of vertical passes.

Photo 20. Trim off excess film to make a 1/16-in. gap around the edges. Rewet and resqueegee the film, adhering the edges firmly. To remove bubbles, respray and squeegee the bubbles out.

OPTIONS

Window Problems and Solutions

Each of the projects and products discussed in this chapter can cure multiple ills. Here's a quick list of window weaknesses and a summary of which improvement can help.

1. Air infiltration. Interior insulating windows and combination storm windows will both tighten up a house and help keep out dirt, pollen, and insects.

2. Heat loss. Interior insulating windows and storm windows create a dead-air space between themselves and the main window that acts as a form of insulation. Low-E tinting films cut heat loss, too.

3. Heat gain. All of the tinting films help reflect the sun's rays back outside.

4. Noise. Interior insulating windows, especially full-pane ones of acrylic, reduce noise by 90 percent. Combination storm windows help too, but less.

5. Condensation. Tight-fitting interior insulating windows eliminate even ice buildup.

6. Fading. Tinting films reduce fading by up to 95 percent.

7. Maintenance. Combination storms eliminate seasonal switchovers. And aluminum never needs painting.

8. Deterioration. Combination storm windows protect your windows from harsh elements.

Index

Sources

The following are some of the suppliers who sell specialized products that may not be available locally.

Cable Television Supplies
MCM Electronics
650 Congress Park Dr.
Centerville, OH 45459-4072
(800) 543-4330

Parts Express International
340 E. First St.
Dayton, OH 45402
(800) 338-0531; in Ohio (513) 222-0173

Ceiling Fan Support Brackets
Reiker Enterprises, Inc.
P.O. Box 939
Anniston, AL 36202
(205) 820-1520

Folding Stairways
American Stairways, Inc.
3807 Lamar Ave.
Memphis, TN 38118-3706
(901) 795-9200

Acknowledgments

Charles Avoles, Darwin Baack, Ron Chamberlain, John Emmons, Bill Faber, Bruce Folke, Al Hildenbrand, Duane Johnson, Bruce Kieffer, Mike Krivit, Phil Leisenheimer, Don Mannes, Susan Moore, Doug Oudekerk, Don Prestly, Dave Radtke, Art Rooze, Phil Rzeszutek, Rich Sill, Mike Smith, Dan Stoffel, Eugene Thompson, Mark Thompson, Bob Ungar, Alice Wagner, Gregg Weigand, Gary Wentz, Michaela Wentz, Gordy Wilkinson, John Williamson, Marcia Williston, Donna Wyttenbach, Butch Zang, Bill Zuehlke.

This book was produced by Roundtable Press, Inc.,
for the Reader's Digest Association
in cooperation with The Family Handyman magazine.

If you have any questions or comments, please feel free to write us at:

The Family Handyman
7900 International Drive
Suite 950
Minneapolis, MN 55425

More Top-Rated How-To Information From Reader's Digest® and The Family Handyman®

THE FAMILY HANDYMAN TOYS, GAMES, AND FURNITURE

Over 30 Woodworking Projects You Can Make for Children

Here is a collection of over 30 handcrafted wooden items that are beautiful and practical, and will be cherished for years. Tailored to please the littlest members of the family, these delightful homemade items are child safe; includes such projects as a push sled, a race car, a doll's cradle, and that perpetual favorite, the little red wagon.

192 pages
10 11/16 x 8 3/8
over 500 color photographs
ISBN #0-89577-790-8
$19.95

THE FAMILY HANDYMAN WEEKEND IMPROVEMENTS

Over 30 Do-It-Yourself Projects for the Home

Now all the how-to information homeowners need to complete short-term projects can be found in this one clear and comprehensive volume. From basic fix-ups to full-fledged facelifts, this book covers every room in the house and features great techniques for keeping the yard and the exterior of the house looking fit as well.

192 pages
10 11/16 x 8 3/8
over 500 color photographs
ISBN #0-89577-685-5
$19.95

THE FAMILY HANDYMAN UPDATING YOUR HOME

More than 30 Ways to Make Your Home Look and Work Better

A comprehensive collection of over 30 simple projects for getting both the inside and outside of a home into tip-top shape making it more livable, enjoyable, and valuable.

192 pages
10 11/16 x 8 3/8
over 400 color photographs
ISBN #0-89577-851-3
$19.95

THE FAMILY HANDYMAN DECKS, PATIOS, AND PORCHES

Plans, Projects, and Instructions for Expanding Your Outdoor Living Space

For homeowners who want to make the most of the great outdoors, here are a variety of projects for constructing a deck, porch or patio from the ground up as well as helpful hints for repairing existing structures.

192 pages
10 11/16 x 8 3/8
over 500 color photographs
ISBN #0-89577-852-1
$19.95

THE FAMILY HANDYMAN INTERIOR REMODELING

Projects That Will Bring New Life to Your Home

This comprehensive book presents the necessary know-how, innovative ideas, and smart suggestions for making over every room in the house. Those interested in a quick fix will discover how to paint or reface cabinets and replace countertops. For those looking for more exciting changes, there are instructions for enclosing a shower with fashionable glass blocks, and installing a whirlpool.

192 pages
10 11/16 x 8 3/8
over 500 color photographs
ISBN #0-89577-791-6
$19.95

THE FAMILY HANDYMAN WOODWORKING ROOM BY ROOM

Furniture, Cabinetry, Built-Ins and Other Projects for the Home

The easiest, most complete guide of over 20 different projects, ranging from straightforward items beginners can easily master to more sophisticated pieces for experienced woodworkers looking for new challenges; includes such projects as a country pine bench, traditional bookcase and Victorian hall stand.

192 pages
10 11/16 x 8 3/8
over 500 color photographs
ISBN #0-89577-686-3
$19.95

THE FAMILY HANDYMAN OUTDOOR PROJECTS

Great Ways to Make the Most of Your Outdoor Living Space

The most popular outdoor projects targeted for all skill levels are found in this easy-to-use volume. There's something for everyone in this comprehensive how-to guide — from a relatively simple garden bench and a children's sandbox to more complex structures — a spectacular gazebo and romantic garden arbor and swing.

192 pages
10 11/16 x 8 3/8
over 500 color photographs
ISBN #0-89577-623-5
$19.95

THE FAMILY HANDYMAN EASY REPAIR

Over 100 Simple Solutions to the Most Common Household Problems

Designed to help save hundreds, even thousands, of dollars in costly repairs, here is that one book that should be in every household library. It offers simple, step-by-step, quick-and-easy solutions to the most common and costly household problems faced at home, from unclogging a sink to repairing broken shingles to fixing damaged electrical plugs.

192 pages
10 11/16 x 8 3/8
over 500 color photographs
ISBN #0-89577-624-3
$19.95

Measuring the Metric Way

Use these guides and tables to convert between English and metric measuring systems.

Fasteners

Nails are sold by penny size or penny weight (expressed by the letter d). Length is designated by the penny size. Some common lengths are:

2d	25 mm/1 in.
6d	51 mm/2 in.
10d	76 mm/3 in.
20d	102 mm/4 in.
40d	127 mm/5 in.
60d	152 mm/6 in.

Below are metric and imperial equivalents of some common **bolts:**

10 mm	³⁄₈ in.
12 mm	¹⁄₂ in.
16 mm	⁵⁄₈ in.
20 mm	³⁄₄ in.
25 mm	1 in.
50 mm	2 in.
65 mm	2¹⁄₂ in.
70 mm	2³⁄₄ in.

Calculating Concrete Requirements

Multiply length by width to get the slab area in square meters. Then read across, under whichever of three thicknesses you prefer, to see how many cubic meters of concrete you will need.

Area in Square Meters (m²) (length x width)	Thickness in Millimeters		
	100	130	150
	Volume in Cubic Meters (m³)		
5	0.50	0.65	0.75
10	1.00	1.30	1.50
20	2.00	2.60	3.00
30	3.00	3.90	4.50
40	4.00	5.20	6.00
50	5.00	6.50	7.50

If a greater volume of concrete is required, multiply by the appropriate number. To lay a 100-millimeter thick patio in an area 6 meters wide and 10 meters long, for example, estimate as follows: 6 meters x 10 meters = 60 meters square = area. Using the chart above, simply double the concrete quantity for a 30-meter square, 100-millimeter thick slab (2 x 3 m³ = 6 m³) or add the quantities for 10 m² and 50 m² (1 m³ + 5 m³ = 6 m³).